LEARNING TO LEAD, LEADING TO LEARN

Open Access Book Series

The **Center for Engaged Learning** (CEL) Open Access Book Series features concise, peer-reviewed books and edited collections for a multi-disciplinary, international, higher education audience interested in research-informed engaged learning practices. CEL is committed to making these publications freely available to a global audience.
Series editors, Jessie L. Moore and Peter Felten

Select Publications

The SoTL Guide: (Re)Orienting the Scholarship of Teaching and Learning
Nancy L. Chick, Peter Felten, and Katarina Mårtensson
doi.org/10.36284/celelon.oa10

Inclusive Pedaoggy in Practice: Perspectives from Equity-Minded College Educators
Edited by Amelia Koford, Corinne Castro, and Christopher Bollinger
doi.org/10.36284/celelon.oa9

Counterstory Pedagogy: Student Letters of Resilience, Healing, and Resistance
Edited by Adriana Aldana
doi.org/10.36284/celelon.oa8

Becoming a SoTL Scholar
Edited by Janice Miller-Young and Nancy Chick
doi.org/10.36284/celelon.oa6

Writing Beyond the University: Preparing Lifelong Learners for Lifewide Writing
Edited by Julia Bleakney, Jessie L. Moore, and Paula Rosinski
doi.org/10.36284/celelon.oa5

What Teaching Looks Like: Higher Education through Photographs
Cassandra Volpe Horii and Martin Springborg
doi.org/10.36284/celelon.oa4

Learning to Lead, Leading to Learn

A Collaborative Syllabus for Higher Education Leadership

Edited by Linda Adler-Kassner and Chris W. Gallagher

Center for Engaged Learning at Elon University
Elon, North Carolina

Parlor Press
Anderson, South Carolina

Elon University Center for Engaged Learning
Elon, North Carolina
www.CenterForEngagedLearning.org

Series editors: Jessie L. Moore and Peter Felten
Copyeditor and designer: Sophie Grabiec

The current paperback edition is distributed and sold by Parlor Press with these ISBNs: ISBN (PBK) 978-1-64317-593-5 ISBN (PDF) 978-1-64317-594-2

Cataloging-in-Publication Data on File

TABLE OF CONTENTS

Acknowledgments

The editors would like to thank the inspiring leaders who contributed their labor, time, and wisdom to this collection; we are forever in their debt. We are also grateful to Jessie Moore and Peter Felten for their generous feedback, for shepherding this book through the publication process, and for ensuring that books like this one are open access.

PREFACE

The Learner, The Broker, and the Giver

Leadership Journey Through the Dark Side

Chng Huang Hoon, *Chua Thian Poh Community Leadership Centre, National University of Singapore*

> *"Learning to move past the abstraction, to think about people I sought to lead, their motivations, and the points of connection that we share—those are places where I was able to apply my knowledge to standing at the forefront of valuable institutional work, even where having no positional authority to demand that this work be done."*—Chris Blankenship, chap. 3, p. 78

> *"... if one wants to learn to lead, practicing giving is the place to start."*—Jeffrey Grabill, chap. 5, p. 119

It is not every day that someone knocks on our door and gives us a generous offer—to benefit from the wisdom derived from other people's experiences in leadership. And so, when Linda Adler-Kassner and Chris Gallagher invited me to read their book manuscript and to provide a preface for it, in spite of my overflowing plate for the coming months, I just could not let this wonderful opportunity pass me by. I am so glad that I did not let this one go.

Learning to Lead, Leading to Learn: A Collaborative Syllabus for Higher Education Leadership is a gem of a book for at least three reasons:

1. This volume gathers a collection of stories from people who are learners first and leaders/brokers second; and in the process of

"accidentally" (for most) but intentionally leading, have learnt to lead. Now that this treasure trove of experiences is offered to us, we can benefit from this leadership playbook that I know will facilitate the leadership work of many first-time leaders or those who are like me, still learning how to lead in spite of decades in academic leadership.

2. Reading these stories has given learners like me much comfort because they tell me that someone out there is facing or has undergone the kind of challenges I have been living with leading in my own institution. Significantly, these stories demonstrate that there is no one way to lead, and that context matters in defining how one leads.
3. Finally, this collection provides us with a ready-made community of scholar-leaders that signals to us that we are not alone, we belong, *and* we matter. Their experiences inform us that there are many ways to lead well but only one way to lead happily, and that is when we listen to those we lead with an open heart and mind, humbly learning and collaborating with them as collegial friends, advocating for them through the work that we have been appointed to do.

Unlike Chris Blankenship (and Elizabeth Wardle, another contributor who writes about non-positional leadership), in my two decades of service as an academic leader in my institution, I did enjoy the privilege of positional authority. I chose Blankenship's statement from chapter 3 as my opening quote because I share his view that it is crucial to "move past the abstraction, to think about people … their motivations, and the points of connection we share" in any leadership work one does. Or, as Jeffrey Grabill says in chapter 5, "All work begins and ends in relationships" (p. 110). My own leadership experience involves much brokering between those I lead and those I report to. My journey has been informed by doing the work on a daily basis and regular self-questioning, and by observing senior colleagues/role models in action. I have recognized that while institutional goals are important, people matter even more. While "why lead?" is a fundamental starting point, figuring out how we lead is in some ways even more essential. Colleagues' and students' welfare matter. And so, in doing change management in my university, I actively pay attention to the how. Because for me, the why is obvious—I give time and energy to enable other people's and institutional success. I am in full agreement that "respect is key in creating sustainable change" (Blankenship, chap. 3, p. 89) and "[h]ow we treat people matters" (Roen, chap. 9, p. 171) because quite frankly, collegial welfare and trust enable the work all leaders do.

I feel very grateful to the authors in this book who have reaffirmed and reminded me why I choose to devote time and attention to being an academic leader, and taught me about the joys and pitfalls of leadership. Their leadership narratives have also provided me with an opportunity to reflect on the liminal status of academics like me who have gone "to the dark side" (Isaacs, chap. 2, p. 60), reconciling one's scholarly career and the accidental path in academic leadership. Elsewhere, I have written about the challenges of doing work that matters (particularly on the personal plane) versus work that counts (i.e., institutionally rewarded; see Wu and Chng 2023). As academics, we are sometimes asked to choose between two seemingly unreconcilable career pathways. It is therefore both heartening and also empowering to read that many authors in this book have not only experienced this very same challenge of negotiating their identities as scholars-and-leaders, and that they have also, like me, concluded that the work is sufficiently meaningful in itself to persist down this path in spite of the rigid rules of the academy. Jonathan Alexander says it well: "Administrative work often rewards with immediate satisfaction or awareness of your impact (or conversely, your failure, to be sure). Such immediacy can be very satisfying" (chap. 14, p. 281). It is indeed satisfying, and I would go so far as saying, it can be a meaningful life of productive giving if one does work that can make a real difference in collegial and student welfare. As Adam Grant (2016) has said, "givers spend a lot of time trying to help other people and improve the team, and then, unfortunately, they suffer along the way" (n.p.). Like Grant, I believe our job is to help foster a culture where givers also get to succeed—the dark side is not inevitable if we collectively work to make this work count.

Quite separate from making leadership work count in academia, I would like to offer the view that negotiating between an academic career and a leadership pathway can also be reconciled through the idea of brokering that is frequently raised in this collection. Traversing boundaries is something all effective leaders know and do well. I argue in favor of the scholarly leader whose leadership is informed by scholarship (as many authors in this volume have testified in terms of deploying their expertise in rhetoric in their leadership work) and scholarly work being framed in leadership terms. It seems unfortunate to me that as scholars who are more than mindful of false dichotomies, many in the professoriate still view scholarship and leadership as separate domains. I think there is a need for us to bridge these two terrains for they are essential to our roles as scholar-teacher-leader in institutions of higher learning.

In addition to triggering the above useful reflections, I have learnt several excellent lessons from this collection, too many to numerate. I would however like to highlight the two that I most appreciate, both gifted to me by Heidi Estrem in her chapter on "Academic Leadership Beyond the Academy" (chap. 4, p. 95). Estrem's emphasis on process over outcome in transactional task-driven management practice (as opposed to transformational leadership culture) has my endorsement. Citing Annie Duke (2018), Estrem iterates that "What makes a decision great is not that it has a great outcome. A great decision is the result of a good process …" (p. 100). If leadership work is all about building trust and connections, and enabling collegial/institutional welfare, then a focus on process, on building consensus through dialogue and negotiation is truer to the spirit of an inclusive institutional culture. This brings me to the other lesson Estrem underscores in her chapter: When it comes to culture building and change management, "more conversation is better than less" (p. 103). Importantly, too, as Jonathan Alexander cautions in his contribution, "our desire to create engagement and dialogue cannot always be on our terms" (p. 295)—we need to listen, without prejudice or judgement to stakeholders' perspectives even as we work to drive the institution forward.

I cannot say enough how much I have enjoyed learning from the generous sharing by the authors whose experiences in leadership are captured in this important book. I wish to close this opening segment with a final point about stewardship, an issue close to my heart. For me, stewardship requires that we do not hold on to the privilege of (positional) leadership as some kind of personal lifelong project. Instead, all responsible leaders must in my view work towards obsoleting themselves. To this end, Jonathan Alexander's statement that "learning to lead is as much knowing when to step aside and let others take over as anything else" (p. 296) resonates for me. Leaders must have the grace and the humility to know when it is time to let go, step off, and allow succession planning to occur, for the sustainability of their organization.

References

Duke, Annie. 2018. *Thinking in Bets: Making Smarter Decisions When You Don't Have All the Facts*. Random House.

Grant, Adam. 2016. "Are You a Giver or a Taker?" TED. Accessed July 21, 2025. https://go.ted.com/eUdXU.

Wu, Siew Mei, and Huang Hoon Chng. 2023. "Our Journeys through the Scholarship of Leading: What Matters and What Counts?" In *Narratives of Academics' Personal Journeys in Contested Spaces*, edited by Namrata Rao, Anesa Hosein, and Ian M. Kinchin. Bloomsbury Publishing. http://dx.doi.org/10.5040/9781350196988.ch-011.

INTRODUCTION

Course Overview

Linda Adler-Kassner, *University of California, Santa Barbara*
Chris W. Gallagher, *Northeastern University*

Welcome! We're thrilled that you've chosen to be here and are excited to work with you. We know this is an unusual way to open, but we want to invite you to experience this book in an unusual way: as a kind of course, complete with syllabus, readings, and videos. Why? Because it's a collection about learning, but also a collection of resources that we hope you can use to intentionally facilitate your learning. To achieve this goal, we'd like you to be attentive to the learning experience you're having as you engage with this course, just as we've asked the contributors to highlight not just what they know and believe about leadership and institutional change, but also how they've learned these things.

There are many excellent books, articles, conferences, and other resources (online and offline) about higher education leadership. There are books about vision and strategy in leading academic change (Maimon 2018), how-to books (Mitchell and King 2018), case studies in leadership (Wall and BaileyShea 2011), and guides to leading (Ruben, De Lisi, and Gigliotti 2023; Buller 2014). There are books on leading amidst technological transformation (Carbonaro and Breen 2021; Miller and Ives 2020), books about "leading from the margins" (Hinton 2024), and books on leadership that "fosters liberatory systemic change" (Carducci, Harper, and Kezar 2024). There are many books for women leaders or aspiring leaders in higher education (Ambar, Christ, and Ozumba

2020; Hass 2021; Longman and Madsen 2014), particularly African American women, and leadership (Bower and Wolverton 2009; Burkinshaw 2015; Hills 2013; Katuna 2019; Longman and Masden 2014; Schnackenberg and Simard 2018). There are books advancing LGBTQ+ leadership (Crossman 2022), equitable leadership (Harrison and Hatfield 2017; Kezar and Posselt 2020), inclusive leadership (Stefani and Blessinger 2017), creative leadership (Peterson 2013), visionary leadership (Cowen 2018), transrelational leadership (Branson 2020), sustainable leadership (Haddock-Fraser, Rands, and Scoffham 2018), democratic leadership (Hall and Winn 2017), crisis leadership (Gigliotti 2019), antiracist leadership (Alcalde and Subramaniam 2023), shared leadership (Holcombe et al. 2021), and strategic leadership (Marshall 2019). Importantly, recent books have considered how to lead from and toward equity (Alcalde and Subramaniam 2023; Kezar and Posselt 2020). The USC Pullias Center for Higher Education and the USC Race and Equity Center both provide outstanding online resources for higher education leadership, as do organizations like the American Council for Education, the Association for American Colleges and Universities, and others.

While influenced by many of these resources, this book is different. The course concept is intended to highlight its distinctive approach—specifically, its focus on how people learn to lead in higher education. We have convened a set of distinguished senior leaders to reflect on and articulate their own learning processes, and we will invite you to do the same. You might think of them as guest lecturers or, even better, guest conversation partners—people here to facilitate your thinking by sharing theirs.

These leaders—about whom we'll have more to say shortly—are, to be sure, experts. Their thinking is grounded in learning theory and research and in their own experiences. They have developed what Kinchin, Cabot, and Hay (2008) describe as the "ability to navigate." Their actions are situated within complex understandings of their current situations, they apply ideas or theories from situations that may or may not seem "related" to those current situations from previous ones, and their understandings are manifested in relatable and interpretable actions (320; see also Kinchin 2016). In this course, you'll see how they've thought through this navigation. More importantly, you'll see how they've *learned* to think through it.

There are, then, two emphases here, and we urge you to keep them in mind as you read. One emphasis is on what: what leaders have learned. The second emphasis is on how: how leaders learned what they did, and how they learned to put that learning into practice. These emphases on what and how parallel the distinction between declarative knowledge ("knowing about things") and functioning knowledge ("knowledge that informs action, where performance is underpinned by understanding") (Biggs and Tang 1992, 80–81). Empirical and theoretical research on learning consistently emphasizes that effective learning occurs when learners are able to identify and situate their learning in specific contexts, and, within those contexts, use declarative knowledge to inform functioning knowledge. We've found the distinction between what and how to be important for the development of our own leadership practices, and we think that they can contribute to your thinking, as well.

You've probably gleaned already that the kind of thinking that we're asking you to do as you ~~read this book~~ engage with this course involves metacognitive reflection—what the learning theorist Donald Schön (who figures in Emily Isaacs' chapter) calls "reflection-in-action" (Schön 1983). This kind of thinking can be challenging—especially, perhaps surprisingly, for experts. In fact, learning theorists tell us that the more expert one becomes, the more the constituent elements of their expertise tend to become "tacit" and "commonsensical." Experts sometimes struggle to explain (or teach) what they know because "many experts forget what is easy and what is difficult" for learners who do not have their experience or perspectives (Bransford, Brown, and Cocking 2000, 44). This is called "the expert's blind spot" (Ambrose et al. 2010, 99), and it explains, in large part, why unstructured mentorship in complex environments is so often of limited value. On top of that, mentors (especially when they are busy professionals, like higher education leaders) often don't have time to uncover and explain what they know. That's why we think this book is so important: each of our contributors has generously taken the time to reflect on and articulate what they know and—importantly—how they came to acquire that knowledge and put it into practice. Because they are aware of learning theory and research, they can put themselves into a learner's mindset with the intention of providing not a catalog of "leadership successes," but a rich tapestry comprising the threads of what and how they've learned. This is very much the resource the two of us wish we'd had when we embarked on our leadership journeys, and we've learned a great deal from the chapters collected here even as experienced leaders ourselves. (We both have extensive experience with leadership at the program, college, and university levels.)

We imagine you've come to this course as either an aspiring or a practicing leader in higher education. Maybe you're thinking about leadership as the "dark side" of higher education—a phrase our contributors and Chng Huang Hoon explicitly discourage—and you're interested in what you can learn if you make this choice. Maybe you're transitioning from a traditional faculty role or program-level administration to institution-wide leadership and are interested in the learning journeys of others who have made this shift. Or maybe you've been in leadership roles for years and are looking for a rejuvenating conversation about learning and leading with brilliant, thoughtful colleagues.

Wherever you are in your career trajectory, and however you come to this course, you're in the right place. We only ask that you engage with it as a learner, by which we mean someone who has a wealth of prior knowledge and skills and a desire to build on and deepen that knowledge and those skills in the company of other learners. "Other learners" in this case could mean the contributors to this volume—after all, effective leaders never stop learning about leading, and we've asked contributors to approach their chapters as learners. "Other learners" could also include your colleagues in reading groups, workshops, seminars, and classrooms. Whether you're alone or with others as you engage this book, we hope you will use it.

Use it to do what? Good question.

Learning ~~Outcomes~~ Aims

We in education have become accustomed to talking about "outcomes." That's because the test-based accountability policy regime has taken firm hold at all levels of education in the US (Addison and McGee 2016; Branson 2022; Gallagher 2007; Sharer et al. 2016), the UK (Pearson 2021; Power 1997; Shore and Wright 1999, 2012; Shore and McLauchlan 2012), across OECD countries (Högberg and Lindgren 2021; see also the special issue of *Journal of Education Policy* on Testing Regimes, Accountabilities and Education Policy) and in parts of the Global South (Daghigh 2022). We are so focused on metrics and reporting that speaking in terms of outcomes (or outputs) has come to seem only natural.

But as senior leaders, the two of us have seen in our own administrative work over the past three decades that the language of "outcomes" often leads to rigidity and fixity of ends and a narrow focus on easily measurable results. This approach excludes what we think of as emergent learning, or what the American philosopher and educator John Dewey calls "collateral learning" (Dewey 1938, 29). To be sure, educators and students should have learning goals that shape the learning experience, but Dewey observes that fixed outcomes—especially those formulated before the learning experience even begins—tend to pull our attention away from the quality of the experience in real time. They are often imposed from outside, separated from the ongoing interactions of teachers and students, by policymakers or administrators remote from the immediate learning context (see Gallagher 2012).

We prefer to use different language, then, to describe what we hope you will take away from Learning to Lead: learning aims. Aims, too, can be divorced from and imposed on teachers and learners, as Dewey observes in *Democracy and Education* (1916). But to our ears, while outcome connotes what Dewey calls a "fixed end," aim makes us think of a goal we have in mind, or what Dewey called an "end-in-view." A fixed end is just what it sounds like: an immutable desired outcome, impervious to present circumstances. By contrast, ends-in-view are hoped-for aims that guide present action, but are also capable of being revised as situations and learners change. When we think about aims this way, they become what Dewey elsewhere calls "redirecting pivots in action" (1922, 225). You will read about many such pivots in the chapters ahead; it's worth considering how the authors' aims guided them in these moments.

The following, then, is a set of learning aims we propose as starting points for your thinking as you embark on this course.

Aim 1: Enhance your metacognitive awareness.

Metacognition is "thinking about thinking," and effective learners use it to reflect on, predict, monitor, and make decisions about what, how, where, and with whom they learn (Bransford, Brown, and Cocking 2000, 12). One goal of this course is to help you consider how you learn and who you are as a learner. This will begin with what you already think and know about leadership, which you likely have practiced, and no doubt have observed, across many contexts. We hope to help you identify and describe to and for yourself the ideas, theories, people, or practices that have informed your thinking about leadership and your experiences as a potential or practicing leader.

Aim 2: Define and refine your personal and professional principles.

Principles are statements of beliefs, ethics, ideals, values, identities that we hold to—that give meaning, purpose, and focus to our work and our lives. "Compassion above all." "A leader's most important job is to put people in positions where they can succeed." "Equity sometimes requires treating people differently." "Assume people are doing their best—unless they prove you wrong." These may sound like slogans, but for someone who takes them to heart, they may serve as North Stars. While principles are by definition consistent—they apply across different situations and hold over time—we invite you to treat them the same way we have urged you to treat aims: as ideas to think with. Here's Dewey, writing about the value for teachers of operating with principles in mind:

> Because the range of understanding is deepened and widened, [the teacher] can take into account remote consequences which were originally hidden from view and hence were ignored in his [*sic*] actions. Greater continuity is introduced; he does not isolate situations and deal with them in separation as he was compelled to do when ignorant of connecting principles. At the same time, his practical dealings become more flexible. Seeing more relations he sees more possibilities, more opportunities. He is emancipated from the need of following tradition and special precedents. His ability to judge being enriched, he has a wider range of alternatives to select from in dealing with individual situations. (Dewey 1929, 10)

Notice that this pragmatic conception of principles opens up rather than closes down possibilities; it suggests that principles can make us more flexible, rather than more rigid. At the same time, principles remind us of what we hold most dear and give us "guard rails" to help us determine when to say *yes*, when to say, *okay, but*, and when—crucially—to say *(oh hell) no*. One of the goals of this course is to help you reflect on and name your personal and professional principles and to use them to guide your learning and growth as a leader.

Aim 3: Explore and develop your leadership identity.

People hold principles and work from theories, but these are enacted through identities. There's an extensive literature on leadership identities. Many of the texts that we pointed to earlier focus, for instance, on how important it is for leaders holding traditionally underrepresented identities among leaders to be included in leadership. There are also books and resources for current or aspiring leaders holding those identities to learn to lead (e.g., Hass 2021; Chance 2022; Kuykendall, Smith, and Jackson 2022). You'll learn from our colleagues in this collection, too, how, and how much, identities matter, and how enacting their principles and theories can make a difference. Questions about how much one may, can, and/or should give or hold back are enmeshed with issues of race, class, sexuality, and gender identities. White, cisgender males, for instance, have dominated institutional leadership. Behavioral norms associated with these identities are seen as more "typical" and therefore tend to be considered to be "right," while deviations from them are read as deficiencies or defiance (we will see examples of this in some of the chapters). For any leader, though, making conscious choices about what identities to enact or withhold are central to the actions that we take. Thinking with the contributors will help you explore how you want to create or hone your own leadership identity, as well.

Aim 4: Contextualize your knowledge and adapt (or "transfer") what you've learned about leadership to new situations.

Throughout this course, we'll ask you to contextualize what you've learned about leadership—that is, to reflect on its "conditions of applicability" (Ambrose et al. 2010, 35). After all, different contexts will call for different knowledge and skills. That said, one characteristic long associated with expertise is the ability to identify how what you know and can do might be useful or applicable across situations. Dewey referred to this characteristic as "plasticity," or the ability to learn about and adapt to novel situations. Following Dewey, researchers have studied how learners adapt prior knowledge in new contexts—or struggle to do so—whether across university courses (Beaufort 2007; Moore and Bass 2017; Nowacek 2011; Yancey, Robertson, and Taczak 2014) or between academic and workplace contexts (Brent 2012; Dias 1999; Machura et al. 2024; Smith, Girdharry, and Gallagher 2021). Here, we've cited studies in our own field of Writing Studies, but researchers in many fields are building on the important theoretical work on learning transfer by education scholars such as Perkins and Salomon (1998), Beach (2003), Bronfenbrenner and Morris (2006), and Tuomi-Gröhn, Engeström, and Young (2003). Readings for this course will provide explicit illustrations of how contributors have adapted their knowledge and skills in new contexts and situations. We invite you to note these instances and to consider how to contextualize what you've learned so that you can activate it in the future.

Aim 5: Formulate your own learning aim(s).

As Dewey insisted (1897, 1916), and more recent work on "intentional learning" has confirmed (Bereiter and Scardamalia 1989; Sinatra and Pintrich 2003; Eodice, Geller, and Lerner 2016), learning is most meaningful and lasting when the learner's interests, motivations, and aims drive their inquiry. What interests bring you to this course? What drives your desire to learn about leading? What do you hope to learn from this course? We urge you to keep your aims and goals front-and-center as you engage with the mentor texts in this collection. As you decide what seems most relevant (and less so), keep a record of why: What makes one contributor's learning processes speak to you more than others? What do these interests imply about your identities as a leader, your theory of leadership, and/or your theory of change? You can use the Playbook accompanying this course to record your ideas and scaffold toward a new (or revised) set of ideas to propel your learning process.

Leadership and Institutional Change

These aims are designed to help you think deeply and creatively about *how* you define and enact your theory of leadership and institutional change. As longtime leaders ourselves, we've thought a great deal about our own theories. In this introduction, the beginning of the course, we've resisted the urge to account fully for these because we want you to build and refine your own theories as you work with the materials. But you will see our influences throughout, including for instance how our focus on identities and equity is informed by Black feminists such as bell hooks (1994), Audre Lorde (1984), and Kimberle Crenshaw (2017).

Perhaps you've noticed, as well, that we've already invoked John Dewey more than once. (Prepare yourself: there's more to come!) We are heavily influenced by Dewey's thinking, along with that of other so-called pragmatists, from William James (1904) and Charles Sanders Peirce (1878) in Dewey's day to more contemporary thinkers such as

Cornel West (1989), Hilary and Ruth Anna Putnam (2017), and Charlene Haddock Siegfried (1996), among others. Pragmatism is sometimes caricatured as settling for whatever you can get under a set of given circumstances, but it's actually a rich philosophical tradition. Again, we don't want to go on at great length about our theoretical commitments, but we do owe it to you to explain a bit about where we're coming from. So here are a few core pragmatic principles that have shaped our thinking about leadership and change, and thus about this course, starting with the one that influenced how we framed the previous section on aims:

- *Aims are best thought of as ends-in-view, not fixed termini of actions.* We've discussed the dangers of rigidity and fixity. We would add here that as leaders seeking institutional change, we return to this idea frequently to remind ourselves not to get overwhelmed or paralyzed when our ultimate goals seem far away. For instance, we want our institutions, and higher education in general, to be equitable and just. Some days, they seem anything but. Institutional change is frustratingly slow and uneven; sometimes it even moves in what we consider to be the wrong direction. If we think of equity and justice as "out there," somewhere in the future, waiting to be realized, we quickly become disillusioned and disheartened. We can even begin to think of them as a precondition for meaningful action in the present ("What's the point when the institution is so inequitable?") If we instead think of these aims as "in here," with us, guiding our everyday actions and interactions, we can take heart that we are doing what we can, where we can, in service of our aims.
- *The value of ideas, including theories, lies in what they do*. Pragmatists are experimentalists. That means they are constantly testing ideas in practice. But it also means practice gives rise to ideas. In fact, most good ideas begin with a moment of uncertainty or doubt arising from an experience that confronts us with something new, something our previous frameworks do not fully account for. As leaders seeking institutional change, we find here a reminder to

keep decision-making close to those who experience the impacts of those decisions on the ground. We've seen more than a few "exciting innovations" fail because they didn't address the actual needs and ambitions of students and faculty. And if they don't do that, they have little value, no matter how shiny and cool they might be in the abstract.

- *Contexts always matter*. As experimentalists, pragmatists know that what works under one set of conditions or with one population may fall flat in another. That's because our experiences are the result of our interactions with our environments. We both undergo/undertake experiences and *make sense of* experiences in and through our environments and those with whom we share them. This means people in different environments will have different experiences. But because experience results from the dynamic interplay of individuals, groups, and environments, no two people will have the same experience, even in the same environment. In fact, even the same individual will have different experiences in the same environment at different times. It's all very dizzying, but as leaders seeking institutional change, it comes down to this: Our job is to *shape environments* in which people are mostly likely to have productive, fulfilling, even joyful experiences. We use the word "likely" because we can't *make* people have certain experiences or guarantee that they will have them. That depends as much on them and their relationships with others in the environment as it does on us. But as leaders, we strive to build contexts that are responsive to everyone's needs and in which everyone can do their best work.

These are just a few of the pragmatic principles we take to heart; you will surely detect others as you work through this course. We invite you to put your own influences and ideas in conversation with ours. Even if you are new to considering academic leadership, you have theories about leadership and ideas about how change happens (or how you'd like it to happen). You might not have made them explicit (even to yourself) or considered them "theoretical," but we will help you excavate and articulate these ideas. We'll also guide you to explore how the theories in this collection intersect or diverge, both from each other and from your own evolving ideas. As with aims and principles, we encourage you to think of theories not as fixed termini, but as guiding vehicles: if you want to get anywhere, you're going to need these theories, but you also are going to need to adapt them in order to navigate the unfamiliar terrains you will encounter.

None of this important reflective work is easy, and it's time-consuming. But it's greatly enhanced, and accelerated, when you put yourself in conversation with other people who have thought deeply and carefully about leadership—especially when they can articulate, as our contributors can, both *what and how they've learned to lead.*

~~Readings~~ Mentor Texts

We generally refer to "mentor texts" as texts that students can read multiple times for different purposes. Readers of mentor texts pay careful attention, both because of what the texts say and how they say it.. Sometimes they are used as models for student writing, but that's not what we have in mind here. Rather, we want to invite you to read and engage with the chapters as if they were written by your mentors. And by mentors we don't mean people to model yourself after, but knowledgeable and experienced peers who are generously sharing hard-earned insights and with whom you are in conversation. You will doubtless find some chapters more resonant or helpful than others, but we believe they all repay careful attention and are worthy of engaging, perhaps more than once.

These new mentors of yours are an impressive bunch. They are senior leaders who hold or have held a variety of positions within higher education, from department chairs to retired university presidents, from institutional assessment leaders to leaders of online education for large higher education systems. Most are located in the United States. All have two things in common. First, they have been successful in what senior leader David Marshall calls "thinking *through* bureaucracy… understand[ing leadership] as an intellectual problem" and administration as "a mechanism through which thinking must take place"

(2007, 34). Thinking through bureaucracy means that these leaders have confronted the specific circumstances and values of their institutions along with forces, policies, guidelines, and regulations that impact what is possible. The contexts can be local (cities and communities), state, regional (accreditors), national (federal regulations), or international (the European Higher Education Area and the Bologna Process). Thinking through bureaucracy also means that our contributors have made conscious decisions about when, how, and *whether* to work within or reject regulations or guidelines. They reflect on these regulations or guidelines in the context of their values, determine whether they conflict with these values, as well as whether their institutions should comply with or challenge elements of the extra-institutional structures and forces. Identities play a role in thinking through bureaucracy, too—you'll see the importance of who they are and how they work through their discussions.

Second, these leaders share common disciplinary roots. They (and the two of us) have come up through the ranks of the field variously known as Composition and Rhetoric, Writing and Rhetoric, or Writing Studies. (For the sake of brevity, we will refer to this discipline as "Writing Studies.") This is a field of study, often but not always housed in English Departments, devoted to the study of how writing is taught, learned, and practiced in academic, professional, and public contexts.

If you're in another discipline, we want to reassure you—this book is for you, and it is focused on broad institutional leadership. We've gathered the contributors we have because we think that they have something to share with *everyone*, regardless of disciplinary background. That's because Writing Studies scholars who become administrators are incredibly effective leaders. Their effectiveness comes from their ability to act as what Etienne Wenger calls "brokers"—people who can "introduce elements of one practice into another," create meaningful connections, and contribute to synergizing new ways of thinking (2000, 235). This effectiveness is rooted in a fundamental reality: Writing is everybody's business. Writing teachers know this, because people tell us on a regular basis what the business of writing instruction should be. This happens as people tell us, for instance: What you should be doing. What students can't do. What's wrong with writing today. What's wrong with students today... on it goes. Effective Writing Studies scholars, then, learn systematically and strategically to: a) respectfully engage in genuine discussion with others about their ideas; b) bring what they know from their research field and learning research in general to these discussions; and c) create proactive strategies to enact forward-looking approaches to writing and learning that serve *everyone*—students, instructors, future employers.

The combined emphasis in Writing Studies on brokering, learning, and research leads people in the discipline to study and develop expertise in institutional leadership, often through work as writing program administrators, or WPAs. Their degree programs offer courses in writing program administration; they also often study formations of leadership as part of their academic work. In addition to institutional literacy, then, they also develop what is called "pedagogical content knowledge" (Shulman 1986, 1987), including the ability to listen to learners, to understand what matters to them, to make connections between learners in order to connect their interests, scaffolding knowledge-creation and feedback over time.

Importantly, they also leverage their pedagogical knowledge in their leadership practice (see, for instance, the Transparency in Learning and Teaching (TILT) Framework, Middendorf and Shopkow 2018; Bransford, Brown, and Cocking 2000; Ambrose et al. 2010). They are ideal teachers of leadership. Although they share a disciplinary background, their contributions are relevant for a multidisciplinary, international readership of leaders across all ranks, whether faculty, staff, or administrators.

We bring you these experienced academic leaders because we know that in virtually any endeavor, as learners move toward expertise, they benefit by engaging in dialogue with those who have significant experience in the thing they want to learn. This dialogue is all the more beneficial when mentors are willing to put their expertise, identities, and experience (both positive and negative) on the table. We invite you to do the same as you engage with the contributions. No matter your current level of expertise or institutional context, we hope you approach the texts in the spirit of shared inquiry into learning and leading.

While each contributor naturally has had their own unique leadership journey, we encourage you to read *across* these pieces. One feature you'll find across all of these chapters is that these leaders make conscious decisions about how to act as "bridges, brokers, [or] boundary spanners." A "bridge," in this context, is someone who brings outsiders in to coordinate conversation. A "broker" mediates communication between people in different communities (or communities of practice). A "boundary spanner" helps to facilitate the creation of shared meanings between those communities, potentially coming up with new meanings (Long, Cunningham, and Braithwaite 2013; see also Wenger-Trayner et al. [2015]'s concept of "knowledgeability"). You'll find, in and across the chapters, leaders making conscious decisions about how and/or whether to facilitate engagement and communication among individual networks and between multiple networks.

Another thing you'll notice is that all of the contributors describe learning to develop and/or enact leadership grounded in *theories of change*. In keeping with our grounding in the work of pragmatists, we refer to William James (summarizing Charles Sanders Peirce) to clarify this use of theory *as a belief that establishes "rules for action."* Theories of change help leaders consider "what conceivable effects of a practical kind" may transpire from different actions. "Theories," wrote James, "thus become instruments, not answers to enigmas, in which we can rest" (1904, np). You'll see theories that start with building and cultivating relationships (e.g., chapter 1, chapter 4); others that focus on collaborating to reframe understandings (of learning, of assessment) to create shared meanings and increase colleagues' investments and interests (e.g., chapter 10, chapter 3). You'll also see theories of change that focus on the leader themselves, especially as they develop new identities (e.g., chapter 7, chapter 8, chapter 14, and chapter 15).

Formulating your theories of change helps ground your practice, navigate the vicissitudes of an ever-evolving profession (and world!), and move ahead even in difficult times. And these are difficult times for all of us in higher education. We and our contributors worked on this book from 2023 through 2025, a period that includes the 2024 election in the United States and during which we've seen a shift toward autocracy across the globe (see Applebaum 2024). Summarizing the shockwaves that rippled through higher education in the US since the election would require its own book; between the time it was written and publication, it probably will have changed considerably in any event. Suffice to say, then, that the years ahead will be particularly trying ones for higher education.

In this context, we ask you to attend to the ways our contributors use their hard-won theories, principles, and perspectives as guides for and prods to action. The chapters show leaders encountering difficulty, experiencing personal frustration, encountering racism, sexism, institutional isomorphism, and wrestling with what it means to *be*—to be Black, to be queer, to be a woman or a leader without authority or a person who has made mistakes or taken missteps—amid these challenges. And importantly, they show how these leaders have learned to lean on their strengths—to employ metacognitive awareness, to act on principles, employ theories, work from identities—to achieve a kind of equanimity. By equanimity, we don't mean that they are always calm or emotionless; we mean that they are able to maintain a semblance of balance and perspective even amid their strong feelings about unfolding events and situations. Their actions are grounded—or regrounded, or even more firmly grounded—in their ideas about leadership and institutional and social change. The chapters model different ways to call on one's grounding beliefs and knowledge while simultaneously holding oneself open to new learning in changing environments. As you read the chapters, we ask you to reflect on ways in which *what you believe* and *how you think* about leadership shape *how you do* leadership, no matter the circumstances.

The mentor texts are organized into two parts, which invite different kinds of engagement and reflection from you.

Part 1: Learning from Experience

Again, it's easy to find resources on types of leadership or tools for assessing your leadership personality or leading in times of trouble, etc., but perhaps the core leadership competency—and the one that's hardest to learn or even find time for—is the ability *to continually and critically reflect on and learn from experience*. In these pieces, contributors demonstrate how they engage in reflective practice and explore what they learn from it. We invite you to read both for *how* they make meaning from their experiences and *what* insights about leadership emerge. Consider as well how you can build reflective practice into your own learning and leading journeys.

This section opens with an invitation from us (Linda and Chris) to consider, or perhaps reconsider, what it means—and what it looks like—to learn from *experience*. Turning again to John Dewey's work, we hope to prepare you to get the most out of the mentor texts in this part of the course.

You'll start by reading Elaine Maimon's description of how what she learned from experiences as a student of theater and feminism as a young scholar contributed to abilities she describes as critical for her much later role as a university president: careful listening and strategic speaking. Maimon provides examples of instances where she put what she learned into action in situations where smart, empathetic leadership was critical. Emily Isaacs picks up where Maimon leaves off, reflecting on the idea of transfer of knowledge—in this case, from experience as a classroom teacher to several administrative roles—in action. She focuses sharply on the role that reflection plays in both sets of those roles, and on how that practice can be so helpful when things don't go as planned.

Following Maimon's and Isaac's contributions, Jeff Grabill and Staci Perryman-Clark invite us to consider some key relational and dispositional complexities of leadership. Grabill takes up the disposition of "kindness," along with its attendant behavior, "giving," theorizing the latter both as a way of leading and a way of *learning* to lead. Perryman-Clark discusses her difficult journey as a Black feminist interim dean, describing manifestations of systemic inequity and interpersonal dynamics that she has encountered and the tension she experiences navigating institutional relationships and decision-making. She outlines critical recommendations based on what she has learned in leadership roles.

The next two authors, Chris Blankenship and Heidi Estrem, take up institutional and inter-institutional policy and politics from unusual positions: Blankenship in a "non-positional" leadership role within his institution and Estrem as an academic officer for a state board of higher education. Both authors show how they draw on their disciplinary training as well as their previous experiences as they learn how to navigate unfamiliar contexts and challenges.

Erin Lehman and Beth Brunk each focus on how they learned to develop new leadership abilities that they realized were not included in their "preferred" ways of operating or their prior experience. A self-proclaimed group project skeptic, Lehman realized when she took over as the leader of online learning for her statewide two-year college that she couldn't go it alone. She describes how she learned to lead as a collaborator. Brunk's contribution invites you into a moment where she began to wonder, after a leadership evaluation, if she was *too* centered on listening and supporting others' ideas, realizing that she needed to learn to be more assertive while supporting others. She describes how she learned to act on her core principles—harmony, collaboration, compassion, and integrity—as part of her growth as an "incomplete leader."

Duane Roen's contribution concludes the section on Learning from Experience—as it should, because his experiences are so extensive. He describes what and how he has learned, and continues to learn, from the entirety of his life, from working on a dairy farm in Wisconsin, to working in multiple leadership positions at Arizona State University, from undergoing cancer treatment to teaching workshops for members of the community.

Across these contributions, you'll see a great deal about *what* experiences your mentors have had that contribute to their leadership. Consistent with our emphasis on *how* people learn to lead ("functioning knowledge"), you'll read a great deal about how these experiences contributed to leaders' approaches, including and not limited to their ideas about how change occurs. If you read the book sequentially, we urge you to keep these experiences in mind as you move into part 2.

Part 2: Theorizing Practice, Practicing Theory

Whereas mentors in part 1 invited you to think with them about how they've learned from experience, those in part 2 underscore the dialectical relationship between theory and practice in their learning processes by explicitly applying, and often revising, core leadership theories and principles throughout their careers. In our introduction to this set of texts, we'll encourage you to pay close attention to the integral connections between these leaders' identities and the theoretical frameworks that shape their learning experiences. Taken together, these mentor texts draw on two key ideas. First, identities are central to learning, especially when learning is challenging (e.g., Ladson-Billings 2021; National Academies 2018; Yosso 2005). Second, theory isn't something that exists in a realm remote from experience. As Etienne Wenger once said, echoing James and other pragmatists, "theory is something that gives a name to something you already see" (Wenger, personal communication). We recognize that this is a particular definition of theory—in fact, we recognize that the term "theory" has different meanings in different disciplines. (For instance: in some disciplines, theories are primarily scientific, falsifiable hypotheses; in others, they are flexible frameworks or lenses.) For the purposes of this collection, as we've suggested, we are asking you to think of theories as "guiding vehicles" for action. In these chapters, you'll see interlocutors engaging in extended discussion of one or more key ideas—central theories or sets of theories—that have shaped their leadership journeys through their reading and studying, but just as importantly, through their lived experiences and their many identities.

The section opens with two chapters that home in on ways in which leaders both navigate and challenge borders and boundaries that define institutional life in the academy. Elizabeth Wardle applies concepts from boundary brokering among communities of practice, non-positional leadership, and feminist interpretations of sensemaking to describe how she has learned to lead transformational change efforts at two institutions.

Carmen Kynard turns to Fred Moten's (2003) concept of fugitive learning to discuss her rejection of formal leadership roles in favor of organizing to enact a consistent and fierce commitment to create spaces where she and students can push against the everyday "norms and logics" of systemically inequitable and racist universities (and societies).

Next, you'll find two leaders describing how important metaphors—"*comunidad*" for Candace de León-Zepeda, "code" for Jonikka Charlton—have helped the authors learn and enact leadership at their institutions. Both leaders write from the position of working in Hispanic Serving Institutions in the state of Texas, describing how theories and ideas they encountered in their formal educations and their lived experience contribute to their engagement with students, faculty, and staff. León-Zepeda discusses learning to enact principles of *comunidad* in ways small and large, from writing emails to faculty to advocating during extraordinarily difficult social and cultural moments. Reflecting on her experience as a parent and a senior administrator, Charlton describes how she has learned to go "back to code" in multiple roles and situations to translate, advocate, and keep students at the center.

Jonathan Alexander and Sheila Carter-Tod provide powerful final statements for this section because both consider how they wrestle with what they see as disjunctures between theoretical ideas and practical application to their lived experiences. Alexander grapples with notions of "leaderly success," discussing how he continues to learn what it means to "queer" administrative and leadership work as a queer person dedicated to question norms, trajectories, and notions of success outlined for leaders (and students) in postsecondary institutions. Carter-Tod examines the tension she has felt throughout her leadership career, dating back to college and graduate school, between her innate capacity and affinity for leadership and her reluctance to fully embrace the identity of "leader," owing largely to how few women of color she saw in higher education institutions. Carter-Tod's contribution underscores the institutional imperative to have diverse leaders in place, because *who* is leading changes what leadership can mean, opening up new avenues for folks who might otherwise "learn" from institutions that they are imposters, or not "leadership material."

As you consider these mentors and their texts, we invite you to reflect on what leaders have learned working within and against hierarchical and inequitable systems to promote diversity, inclusion, belonging, and justice. And of course, we ask you to reflect on your own identities and the structures and systems that shape your life and work.

We close the course with a "Final Class" that guides you to consolidate and condition what you've learned for future use. We encourage you to think of this course as only one experience in your ongoing learning and leading journey and to continue building your own leadership curriculum. More than ever, higher education needs leaders who learn—and learners who lead.

Okay, a few final pieces of housekeeping before we embark.

~~Grading~~ Self-Assessment

We know you'll be disappointed to hear this, but there will be no quizzes or tests. But that doesn't mean there won't be assessment; throughout, we'll ask you to engage in the most important kind of assessment: self-assessment. By "self-assessment," we mean gathering and analyzing information about your learning, monitoring your learning, making intentional decisions about your learning—in short, paying attention to how you build on prior knowledge and set yourself up for acquiring new knowledge. In each section, we will provide prompts that ask you to reflect on and revisit your learning aims. And again, in the "final class," we'll think together about how to consolidate and contextualize what you've learned for future use, and you'll create a learning action plan for your own future as a leader. You'll find additional materials to help with this in the Playbook that accompanies this book, too.

~~Policies~~ Invitations

1. Take this course alone or with others. (If you take it alone, tell others about it!)

2. Use the Playbook available on the companion website at any time (www.CenterForEngagedLearning.org/books/learning-to-lead/playbook); moving back and forth between the book and the materials is perfectly appropriate.
3. Read the contributions in any order you want, but we do encourage you to read our section introductions, which are designed to contextualize the readings and prepare you to engage them.
4. Even if you are a seasoned leader, approach the contributions in the same way we asked the contributors to write them: with a learner's mindset.
5. Add your own invitation here, either for keeping yourself accountable or for shaping a learning community with others (you could even expand this into a set of community agreements or commitments).

~~Additional Resources~~ Playbook

This course is intended to be a launch pad for your own thinking, and so we think it's important to provide materials that support you as you (re)construct ideas during and after you read and talk with others. We've designed the Playbook to be used side-by-side with the materials here. It includes reflective questions that you can use before or after your reading, videos in which contributors discuss their own experience learning to lead and leading to learn, and other materials that we think can help you make your own sense of what you're learning here.

Let's dive in!

References

Addison, Joanne, and Sharon James McGee. 2016. *Writing and School Reform: Writing Instruction in the Age of Common Core and Standardized Testing.* The WAC Clearinghouse; University Press of Colorado.

Alcalde, M. Cristina, and Mangala Subramaniam, eds. 2023. *Dismantling Institutional Whiteness: Emerging Forms of Leadership in Higher Education*. Purdue University Press.

Ambar, Carmen T., Carol T. Christ, and Michele Ozumba, eds. 2020. *Junctures in Women's Leadership: Higher Education*. Rutgers University Press.

Ambrose, Susan A., Michael W. Bridges, Michele DePietro, Marsha C. Lovett, and Marie K. Norman. 2010. *How Learning Works: Seven Research-Based Principles for Smart Teaching.* Jossey-Bass.

Applebaum, Anne. 2024. *Autocracy, Inc.: The Dictators Who Want to Run the World.* Penguin Random House.

Beach, King. 2003. "Consequential Transitions: A Developmental View of Knowledge Propagation through Social Organizations." In *Between School and Work: New Perspectives on Transfer and Boundary Crossing*, edited by Terttu Tuomi-Gröhn and Yrjö Engeström. Emerald Group Publishing.

Bereiter, Carl, and Marlene Scardamalia. 1989. "Intentional Learning as a Goal of Instruction." In *Knowing, Learning, and Instruction: Essays in Honor of Robert Glaser,* edited by Lauren Resnick. Lawrence Erlbaum Associates.

Beaufort, Anne. 2007. *College Writing and Beyond: A New Framework for University Writing Instruction*. Utah State University Press.

Biggs, John and Tang, Catherine. 1992. *Teaching for Quality Learning at University*. Routledge.

Bower, Beverly L., and Mimi Wolverton. 2009. *Answering the Call: African American Women in Higher Education Leadership*. Stylus Publishing.

Bransford, John D., Ann L. Brown, and Rodney R.Cocking, eds. 2000. *How People Learn: Brain, Mind, Experience, and School: Expanded Edition*. The National Academies Press. https://doi.org/10.17226/9853.

Branson, Christopher M. 2020. *Leadership in Higher Education from a Transrelational Perspective*. Bloomsbury Academic.

Branson, Tyler S. 2022. *Policy Regimes: College Writing and Public Education Policy in the United States*. Southern Illinois University Press.

Brent, Doug. 2012. "Crossing Boundaries: Co-Op Students Relearning to Write." *College Composition and Communication* 63 (4): 558–592. https://doi.org/10.58680/ccc201220299.

Bronfenbrenner, Urie, and Pamela A. Morris. 2006. "The Bioecological Model of Human Development." In *Handbook of Child Psychology,* edited by R. M. Lerner and W. Damon, vol. 1. Wiley.

Buller, Jeffrey. 2014. *Change Leadership in Higher Education.* Jossey-Bass.

Burkinshaw, Paula. 2015. *Higher Education, Leadership and Women Vice Chancellors: Fitting into Communities of Practice of Masculinities.* Palgrave Macmillan.

Carbonaro, Antonella, and Jennifer Moss Breen, eds. 2021. *Effective Leadership for Overcoming ICT Challenges in Higher Education: What Faculty, Staff, and Administrators Can Do to Thrive Amidst the Chaos.* Emerald Publishing Limited.

Carducci, Rozana, Jordan Harper, and Adrianna Kezar. 2024. *Higher Education Leadership: Challenging Tradition and Forging Possibilities.* Johns Hopkins University Press.

Chance, Nuchelle L. 2022. "Resilient Leadership: A Phenomenological Exploration into How Black Women in Higher Education Leadership Navigate Cultural Adversity." *The Journal of Humanistic Psychology* 62 (1): 44–78.

Cowen, Scott. 2018. *Winnebagos on Wednesdays: How Visionary Leadership Can Transform Higher Education.* Princeton University Press.

Crenshaw, Kimberle. 2017. *On Intersectionality: Essential Writings.* The New Press.

Crossman, Raymond E., ed. 2022. *LGBTQ Leadership in Higher Education.* Johns Hopkins University Press.

Daghigh, Ali Jalalian, ed. 2022. *Neoliberalization of English Language Policy in the Global South.* Springer.

Dewey, John. 1897. "My Pedagogic Creed." In *The Early Works of John Dewey, 1882–1898,* vol. 5 of *The Collected Works of John Dewey, 1882–1953*, 2nd release, 84–95. Electronic edition.

Dewey, John. 1916. *Democracy and Education.* In *The Middle Works of John Dewey, 1899–1924*, vol. 9 of *The Collected Works of John Dewey, 1882–1953*, 2nd release, 3–374. Electronic edition.

Dewey, John. 1922. "The Nature of Aims." In *Human Nature and Conduct: An Introduction to Social Psychology*, 223–237. Modern Library.

Dewey, John. 1929. "The Sources of a Science of Education." In *The Later Works of John Dewey, 1925–1953*, vol. 5 of *The Collected Works of John Dewey, 1882–1953*, 2nd release, 3–40. Electronic edition.

Dewey, John. 1938. *Experience and Education.* In *The Later Works of John Dewey, 1925–1953*, vol. 13 of The Collected Works of John Dewey, 1882–1953, 2nd release, 3–62. Electronic edition.

Dias, Patrick. 1999. *Worlds Apart Acting and Writing in Academic and Workplace Contexts.* Lawrence Erlbaum Associates.

Eodice, Michele, Anne Ellen Geller, and Neal Lerner. 2016. *The Meaningful Writing Project: Learning, Teaching and Writing in Higher Education.* University Press of Colorado.

Ferris, Sharmila Pixy, and Kathleen Waldron. 2021. *Higher Education Leadership: Pathways and Insights.* Emerald Publishing Limited.

Gallagher, Chris W. 2007. *Reclaiming Assessment: A Better Alternative to the Accountability Agenda.* Heinemann Publishing.

Gallagher, Chris W. 2012. "The Trouble with Outcomes: Pragmatic Inquiry and Educational Aims." *College English* 75 (1): 42–60. https://www.jstor.org/stable/24238306.

Gigliotti, Ralph A. 2019. *Crisis Leadership in Higher Education: Theory and Practice.* Rutgers University Press.

Haddock-Fraser, Janet, Peter Rands, and Stephen Scoffham. 2018. *Leadership for Sustainability in Higher Education.* Bloomsbury Academic.

Hall, Richard, and Joss Winn, eds. 2017. *Mass Intellectuality and Democratic Leadership in Higher Education.* Bloomsbury Academic.

Harrison, Laura M., and Monica Hatfield Price. 2017. *Interrupting Class Inequality in Higher Education: Leadership for an Equitable Future.* Routledge.

Hass, Marjorie. 2021. *A Leadership Guide for Women in Higher Education.* Johns Hopkins University Press.

Hills, Laura. 2013. *Lasting Female Educational Leadership: Leadership Legacies of Women Leaders.* Springer.

Hinton, Mary Dana. 2024. *Leading from the Margins: College Leadership from Unexpected Places.* Johns Hopkins University Press.

Högberg, Björn, and Joakim Lindgren. 2021. "Outcome-Based Accountability Regimes in OECD Countries: A Global Policy Model?" *Comparative*

Education 57 (3): 301–21. https://doi.org/10.1080/03050068.2020.1849614.

Holcombe, Elizabeth M., Adrianna J. Kezar, Susan L. Elrod, and Judith A. Ramaley , eds. 2021. *Shared Leadership in Higher Education: A Framework and Models for Responding to a Changing World.* 1st ed. Stylus.

hooks, bell. 1994. *Teaching To Transgress*. Routledge.

James, William. 1904. *Pragmatism: A New Name for Some Old Ways of Thinking*. Longman and Green.

Katuna, Barret. 2019. *Degendering Leadership in Higher Education.* Emerald Publishing Limited.

Kezar, Adrianna J., and Julie R. Posselt, eds. 2020. *Higher Education Administration for Social Justice and Equity: Critical Perspectives for Leadership.* Routledge.

Kinchin, Ian, Lyndon B. Cabot, and David B. Hay. 2008. "Visualizing Expertise: Towards an Authentic Pedagogy for Higher Education." *Teaching in Higher Education* 13 (3): 315–326. https://doi.org/10.1080/13562510802045345.

Kinchin, Ian. 2016. *Visualising Powerful Knowledge to Develop the Expert Student: A Knowledge Structures Perspective on Teaching and Learning at University*. Sense Publishers.

Kuykendall, John, Dimitra Jackson Smith, and Joy M. Jackson, eds. 2022. *The Future of Black Leadership in Higher Education: Firsthand Experiences and Global Impact.* IGI Global.

Ladson-Billings, Gloria. 2021. *Culturally Relevant Pedagogy: Asking a Different Question.* Teachers' College Press.

Long, Janet C., Cunningham, Frances C., and Braithwaite, Jeffrey. 2013. "Bridges, Brokers and Boundary Spanners in Collaborative Networks: A Systematic Review." *BMC Health Services Research* 13 (158): 1–13. https://doi.org/10.1186/1472-6963-13-158.

Longman, Karen, and Susan R. Madsen, eds. 2014. *Women and Leadership in Higher Education.* Information Age Publishing Inc.

Lorde, Audre. 1984. *Sister Outsider*. Penguin.

Machura, Ina Alexandra, Michael John DePalma, Michelle J. Eddy, and Tara Taczak. 2024. "Designing Writing Across the Professions (WAP) Programs at the Intersection of Work-Integrated Learning and Writing

Transfer Research." *Writing & Pedagogy* 15 (3): 285–308. https://doi.org/10.1558/wap.22417.

Maimon, Elaine P. 2018. *Leading Academic Change: Vision, Strategy, Transformation.* Routledge.

Marshall, David. 2007. "The Places of the Humanities: Thinking Through Bureaucracy." *Liberal Education* 93 (2): 34–39.

Marshall, Stephanie, ed. 2019. *Strategic Leadership of Change in Higher Education.* 2nd ed. Routledge.

Middendorf, Joan and Leah Shopkow. 2018. *Overcoming Student Learning Bottlenecks: Decode the Critical Thinking of Your Discipline.* Stylus.

Miller, Garry E., and Kathleen S. Ives, eds. 2020. *Leading the E-Learning Transformation of Higher Education: Leadership Strategies for the Next Generation.* 2nd ed. Taylor & Francis Group.

Mitchell, Brian Christopher, and W. Joseph King. 2018. *How to Run a College: A Practical Guide for Trustees, Faculty, Administrators, and Policymakers.* Johns Hopkins University Press.

Moore, Jessie L., and Randall Bass, eds. 2017. *Understanding Writing Transfer: Implications for Transformative Student Learning in Higher Education.* Routledge.

National Academies of Sciences, Engineering, and Medicine. 2018. *How People Learn II: Learners, Contexts, and Cultures.* National Academies Press. https://doi.org/10.17226/24783.

Nowacek, Rebecca S. 2011. *Agents of Integration: Understanding Transfer as a Rhetorical Act.* Southern Illinois University Press.

Pearson, William. 2021. "Policies on Minimum English Language Requirements in UK Higher Education, 1989–2021." *Journal of Further and Higher Education* 45 (9): 1240–52. https://doi.org/10.1080/0309877X.2021.1945556.

Peirce, Charles Sanders. 1878/1992. "How To Make Our Ideas Clear." In *The Essential Peirce*, vol.1, edited by Nathan Houser and Christian Kloesel, 124–141. Indiana University Press.

Perkins, David N. and Gavriel Salomon. 1988. "Teaching for Transfer." *Educational Leadership* 46 (1): 22–32.

Peterson, J. Fiona. 2013. *Creative Leadership Signposts in Higher Education—Turn Left at the Duck Pond!* SensePublishers.

Power, Michael. 1997. *Audit Society: Rituals of Verification.* Oxford University Press.

Putnam, Hillary and Ruth Anna. 2017. *Pragmatism as a Way of Life: The Lasting Legacy of William James and John Dewey.* Harvard University Press.

Ruben, Brent D., Richard De Lisi, and Ralph A. Gigliotti. 2023. *A Guide for Leaders in Higher Education: Concepts, Competencies, and Tools.* 2nd ed. Routledge.

Schnackenberg, Heidi L., and Denise A. Simard. 2018. *Challenges and Opportunities for Women in Higher Education Leadership.* IGI Global.

Schön, Donald A. 1984. *The Reflective Practitioner: How Professionals Think in Action.* Basic Books.

Sharer, Wendy, Tracy Ann Morse, Michelle F. Eble, and William P. Banks. 2016. *Reclaiming Accountability: Improving Writing Programs through Accreditation and Large-Scale Assessments.* University Press of Colorado.

Smith, Kevin G, Kristi Girdharry, and Chris W Gallagher. 2021. "Writing Transfer, Integration, and the Need for the Long View." *College Composition and Communication* 73 (1): 4–26. https://doi.org/10.58680/ccc202131585.

Shore, Cris, and Laura McLauchlan. 2012. "'Third Mission' Activities and Academic Entrepreneurs: Commercialization and the Remaking of the University." *Social Anthropology/Anthropologie Sociale* 20 (3): 267–286. https://doi.org/10.1111/j.1469-8676.2012.00207.x.

Shore, Cris, and Susan Wright. 1999. "Audit Culture and Anthropology: Neo-liberalism in British Higher Education." *The Journal of the Royal Anthropological Institute* 5(4): 557–75. https://doi.org/10.2307/2661148.

Shore, Cris, and Susan Wright.. 2000. "Coercive Accountability: The Rise of Audit Culture in Higher Education." In *Audit Cultures: Anthropological Studies in Accountability, Ethics and the Academy*, edited by Marilyn Strathern. Routledge.

Shulman, Lee S. 1986. "Those Who Understand: Knowledge Growth in Teaching." *Educational Researcher* 15, 4–14.

Shulman, Lee S. 1987. "Knowledge and Teaching: Foundations of the New Reform." *Harvard Educational Review* 57, 1–22.

Seigfried, Charlene Haddock. 1996. *Pragmatism and Feminism: Reweaving the Social Fabric.* University of Chicago Press.

Sinatra, Gail M. and Paul R. Pintrich, eds. 2003. *Intentional Conceptual Change.* Routledge.

Stefani, Lorraine, and Patrick Blessinger, eds. 2017. *Inclusive Leadership in Higher Education: International Perspectives and Approaches.* Routledge.

"Testing Regimes, Accountabilities and Education Policy." 2013. Special Issue, *Journal of Education Policy* 28 (5).

Tuomi-Gröhn, Terttu, Yrjö Engeström, and Michael Young. 2003. "From Transfer to Boundary-Crossing Between School and Work as a Tool for Developing Vocational Education: An Introduction." In *Between School and Work: New Perspectives on Transfer and Boundary-crossing*, edited by Terttu Tuomi-Gröhn and Yrjö Engeström. Emerald Group Publishing.

Wall, Andrew F., and Chelsea BaileyShea. 2011. *Case Studies in Higher Education Leadership and Management: An Instructional Tool.* Self-published.

Wenger, Etienne. 2000. "Communities of Practice and Social Learning Systems." *Organization* 7 (2): 225–*246.* https://doi.org/10.1177/135050840072002.

Wenger-Treyner, Etienne, Mark Fenton-O'Creevy, Steven Hutchinson, Chris Kubiak, and Beverly Wenger-Trayner. 2015. *Learning in Landscapes of Practice: Boundaries, Identity, and Knowledgeability in Practice-Based Learning.* Routledge.

West, Cornel. 1989. *The American Evasion of Philosophy: A Genealogy of Pragmatism.* University of Wisconsin Press.

Yancey, Kathleen Blake, Liane Robertson, and Tara Taczak. 2014. *Writing across Contexts: Transfer, Composition, and Sites of Writing.* Utah State University Press.

Yosso, Tara. 2005. "Whose Culture Has Capital?: A Critical Race Theory Discussion of Community Cultural Wealth." *Race and Ethnicity in Education* 8 (1): 69–91. https://doi.org/10.1080/1361332052000341006.

PART 1

Learning from Experience

As we noted in the Course Overview, aspiring, new, and practicing leaders can always turn to widely available resources on the theory and practice of academic leadership: books, guides, trainings, courses, workshops, webinars—you name it. These are needed resources, because most academic leaders—many of them coming from the ranks of faculty—were not professionally trained to lead. We would venture that most of us, most of the time, learn most of what we know about leadership "on the job." In other words, from *experience.*

This is both good news and bad news. Taking the bad first: as the common phrase "I learned it the hard way" suggests, learning from experience is often a matter of trial-and-error, trying things out and seeing what works and what doesn't. Some amount of any complex activity—writing, parenting, teaching, leading—necessarily involves this. Our institutions, indeed our society, is complex and ever-changing, as are the people who populate them, so we can't expect to foresee the consequences of everything we do. Sometimes, we simply have to take our knocks.

But there's also a lot of good news to go with the bad. First, humans are endlessly adaptive creatures who continually learn from experience. This is in large part how we achieve growth. And we already know how to learn from experience: we habitually reflect on what we do and what happens to us—we can hardly help it. That said, we can build our capacity to learn from experience. That's what this part of the book intends to help you do.

To that end, we begin with the recognition that although sometimes learning from experience is more or less instinctual or reflexive—the child touches a flame, for instance, learns that flame = hot = pain and adjusts their behavior accordingly—mostly it is not. In fact, even the child is doing a rudimentary, compressed version of what we do when we learn from experience: we turn *what happens—what we undergo and what we undertake—into an experience and then we take what we learn from that experience into future situations.*

John Dewey, often credited as the father of "experiential learning," helps us think about experience deliberately. For Dewey, experience is active ("trying") *and* passive ("undergoing") (1916, 139). It's the intentional connection between the activity and the consequence that constitutes *experience*—"[e]xperience as trying involves change, but change is meaningless transition unless it is consciously connected with the return wave of consequences which flow from it" (139). Learning from experience, then, involves *constructing* and *reconstructing* our experiences. As we face novel circumstances or new problems, we adapt, developing new conceptions of ourselves and our worlds. This doesn't just happen; we are not just passively letting events wash over us. (Even the young child doesn't merely shrug and reach back into the flame.) Instead, we are engaged in active meaning-making, seeking understanding. Dewey effectively turns the phrase "trial and error," which implies blind luck, into informed, disciplined inquiry into our experiences. This occurs as we situate our experiences within the context of aims: What difference(s) will *this* action take within the overall context of our activities? What is the relationship between this experience and our aims?

An experience is both a process and a product: it's what we do and what we make. Dewey also insisted that human experience is always embedded in culture, both in in its primary form—the immediate, holistic impression of what is happening—and in its secondary form, when (usually prodded by something unusual, unexpected, or problematic) we reflect further on and explore and assign meanings to what has happened. Experiences don't happen in a vacuum; rather, they are the name we give to our interactions with, and our perspectives and conceptions of, our environments and the people in them (see Dewey 1910, 1916, 1938).

An example might be helpful here. You're running a meeting. It's nearing the end of the hour, and there's some cross-talk—and then general fidgeting and face-making—around the table. The team is looking at you, the leader, for… something. Before you even register that someone has said something that bothered, maybe even offended, others, you are rewinding in your mind. Who said what? When did things get tense? Something's wrong, but you don't know what. Or—wait. Are you actually over time, and people are silently signaling to you to wrap up the meeting? Is it possible they were restless and unhappy before? If so, why? What is needed here is an inquiry into what is happening: you need to understand, name, and address *the kind of experience you and your team are having.*

Let's say it's the worst-case scenario: one of your team members *did* say something problematic *and* you're out of time. You only learn this later, after you hastily call an end to the meeting, when a couple team members visit your office to complain. So begins your process of inquiry into *what happened.* You listen carefully to the team members who have come forward. You talk to other team members, to the colleague who made the comment, and to trusted colleagues who were not in the room (to whom you say, *I had an experience in that meeting…*). You determine whether the event warrants reporting to an institutional authority or office. You consider the institutional and cultural power dynamics at play. (Was the offender speaking from a place of privilege, or from a marginalized position? Could cultural, and well as interpersonal, differences be relevant?) You reflect on your prior experiences and on the principles you hold dear as a leader. You think through the tension between *don't call out a team member in front of the team* and *protect the community the team has built.* You construct and reconstruct the experience, seeking understanding that is informed by gaining multiple perspectives. You use your evolved understanding to address the incident as appropriate, whether institutionally, privately with the individual, or—if you determine that the team would benefit from revisiting the experience together—in the next meeting. Crucially, you also reflect on and plan for how you might better handle a similar situation in the future.

It would be a mistake to call this "trial and error." You are not just trying things that may or may not work—*c'est la vie*! You're actively reflecting on and gathering information about what the experience means (to you and to your team), putting this in the context of your own principles (which are themselves developed in and through experience), identifying the relevant circumstances, considering how best to handle the situation, and thinking about how this experience how it can prepare you for future experiences. You are looking to make this what Dewey called an "educative experience," one that, ideally, prepares both you and your colleagues "for later experiences of a deeper and more expansive quality" (1938, 28). This is called growth, and it's the aim of all learning.

The chapters that follow all provide opportunities to observe various ways in which effective leaders in different contexts learn from experience—both in the moment and in retrospect. We want you to pay attention not just to *what* they learn through their experiences, but *how* they learn it—how they make meaning from what they undergo and undertake—and how they take their understandings into new situations.

To get you started, we invite you to notice:

- How your leader-mentors engage in rigorous self-reflection and learn from failure at least as much as from success. For example, while emphasizing that leaders must build on their strengths, Emily Isaacs (chapter 2) also narrates her "worst leadership experience" (no spoilers here) and turns "shame and regret" to ongoing "reflective practice" (Schön 1984). Erin Lehman (chapter 7) writes about a "humbling" experience of underestimating her team—which led her to "resituate [her] leadership approach."
- How they draw from various, sometimes unusual, sources to make sense of their experiences. While all of the contributors look to their disciplinary training and mentors in Writing Studies, they go well beyond them. For instance, Duane Roen (chapter 9) turns

to, among other people, historians, scholars, a university president, a sports commentator, and Bill Nye the Science Guy! Meanwhile, Chris Blankenship (chapter 3) reaches all the way back to ancient Greek rhetoric, putting it in conversation with contemporary work on conceptual metaphors.

- *How they continuously reflect on their core values.* For instance, Jeff Grabill adds "kindness" to his set of key leadership dispositions long after he started running leadership workshops. Beth Brunk interrogates the potential downsides of her core value of "listening," while also holding fast to it.
- *How they transfer and transform their learning from one context or role into another.* For example, Heidi Estrem describes how the values and practices she learned as a writing program administrator play out in her new role at the Idaho State Board of Education. Chris Blankenship (chapter 3) writes about how he had to rethink institutional power and authority as he moved from faculty to administrative roles.
- *How they inquire into leadership in the context of their cultural identities.* For example, Staci Perryman-Clark (chapter 6) takes seriously the question of whether she can bring her "authentic self" into institutional leadership positions. Elaine Maimon reflects on her leadership career through the lenses of a former theater student and as a feminist.
- *How they "think through bureaucracy" (Marshall 2007; see Course Overview).* For example, Elaine Maimon (chapter 1) reveals how she came to understand the "moves" she would need to make to break through to inattentive bureaucrats. Erin Lehman (chapter 7) shares how an institutional reorganization and a new role caused her to rethink her leadership identity and expand her leadership practices.

These are just some of the *hows* we notice as we read across the pieces. What do you notice?

References

Dewey, John. 1910. *How We Think. In The Middle Works of John Dewey, 1899–1924*, vol. 6 of *The Collected Works of John Dewey, 1882–1953*, 2nd release, 178–357. Electronic edition.

Dewey, John. 1916. *Democracy and Education.* In *The Middle Works of John Dewey, 1899–1924*, vol. 9 of *The Collected Works of John Dewey, 1882–1953*, 2nd release, 3–374. Electronic edition.

Dewey, John. 1938. *Experience and Education.* In *The Later Works of John Dewey, 1925–1953*, vol. 13 of *The Collected Works of John Dewey, 1882–1953*, 2nd release, 3–62. Electronic edition.

Marshall, David. 2007. "The Places of the Humanities: Thinking Through Bureaucracy." *Liberal Education* 93 (2): 34–39.

Schön, Donald A. 1984. *The Reflective Practitioner: How Professionals Think in Action.* Basic Books.

CHAPTER 1

A Case Study in Presidential Leadership in Perilous Times

Rhetoric, Theater Training, and Life Experience

Elaine Maimon, *Governors State University*

When I started my career as an English professor specializing in composition and rhetoric, I did not imagine that I would learn to address governing bodies on crucial matters of higher education funding. And yet, as a college president, this was one of the activities I engaged in regularly. And how I learned to do this came from my experience as a writing teacher, theater student, feminist, program leader, and an increasingly experienced adult.

My PhD was in American literature, so the composition and rhetoric specialization developed later from curiosity and necessity. My University of Pennsylvania PhD dissertation was entitled *The Biographical Myth of F. Scott Fitzgerald*. In a funny way that perhaps only I understand, my interest in composition and rhetoric is not unrelated to my work on Fitzgerald. I was fascinated with the author of what might be considered the most successful American novel, *The Great Gatsby,* in part because I had trouble believing that the same writer just a few years previously could write the drivel of *This Side of Paradise* and *The Beautiful and Damned* and then proceed to write a masterpiece. My movement from Fitzgerald's novice attempts at self-expression to his soaring prose illustrated the guiding principle of my career, "Only Connect," the epigraph to E. M. Forster's *Howard's End*. I've been known to challenge friends at social events to randomly name two unrelated items, and I will speedily find a connection.

That ability to make unusual and largely invisible connections is an unsung quality of leadership. Leaders must frequently identify common ground where others see only divisiveness and polarization.

Early in my career as a junior faculty member at Beaver College (now Arcadia University), I was assigned to teach many sections of composition, a course I had never myself taken, since the University of Pennsylvania exempted me from the requirement. But I was fascinated with the challenge of developing a meaningful course. I had spent the two and half previous years in a strange assistant professorship at elite, all-male (at that time) Haverford College. Not on a tenure track and, at twenty-five, one of only two full-time female professors, I was substituting for professors on leave and therefore teaching a wide variety of courses, including composition. I have many tales to tell about my experiences there—for another volume. I will say that I learned one important leadership principle from the bizarre Haverford experience. A sense of humor is essential. Sometimes you just have to throw your head back and laugh.

I also learned important points about composition teaching. Haverford is a highly selective liberal arts college. Every admitted student has a stellar academic record. And yet most students, perhaps because of their own internally high standards, struggled with writing. Writer's block was an epidemic. The good part was that even in the 1970s, Haverford taught composition in an enlightened way based on the British tutorial system. Students would meet with me in small groups to read and critique drafts of their essays. I brought this experience to my subsequent teaching at Beaver College.

In the 1970s, many of us were becoming self-taught experts. At a memorable meeting in New York City of the Modern Language Association (MLA) in 1975, Mina Shaughnessy, director of composition at the City University of New York (CUNY), where open admissions had been implemented, called on a ballroom full of English professors to "dive in" to the study and teaching of composition to students who had been named "basic writers" (1976). These were students deemed (by external agents) incapable of effective, mature expression—but

Shaughnessy believed that these students were smart, able, and capable and urged us, as composition teachers, to think about them in this way, too. Shaughnessy was my first comp/rhetoric teacher. Her scholarship pushed me and others to think about students and teaching composition in ways that defied both traditional perspectives on students, and traditional beliefs about the teaching of writing. It was my introduction to advocating for different ways of operating. We read international texts, too—for example, *How the French Boy Learns to Write* (Brown 1915) and James Britton's work (e.g., 1970, 1975). We read brave US-based scholars, Edward P.J. Corbett (e.g., 1969), James Kinneavy (e.g., 1971), Richard Lloyd-Jones (e.g., 1977), W. Ross Winterowd (e.g., 1968), Frank D'Angelo (e.g., 1973), and more, all of whom were defying conventional wisdom about valuing literary scholarship over their own ground-breaking work in the teaching of writing. We avidly attended the Conference on College Composition and Communication (CCCC) to listen and learn.

For me, these learning opportunities led to the realization that the teaching of writing was complex, while most of academe defined it simplistically as a matter of spelling and commas. As an assistant professor, who had just been assigned a full-time position, I decided nonetheless that the only way to succeed in teaching writing was to involve the whole campus. This process of learning from colleagues in various disciplines was an early leadership experience. With the help of senior colleagues from inside and outside my college and substantial grants from the National Endowment for the Humanities (NEH), writing across the curriculum (WAC) was born. In its essence, WAC involves shared responsibility for an expanded and sophisticated definition for teaching writing. In every area, writing—from lab reports to philosophical arguments—manifests the essence of the discipline. Students demonstrate their underlying understanding of everything from anthropology to zoology by writing effectively in the inherent genres. In some cases, the writing is discipline-specific, illustrating ways of thinking in the field. But WAC also invites writing-to-learn activities to generate and to test ideas.

Learning from Composition and Rhetoric Scholars in Beaver College's Writing Across the Curriculum Program

Beaver College's NEH grant for the WAC program provided funding for scholars in rhetoric and composition to work with a multidisciplinary group of Beaver College faculty members in January and July of each year from 1977–1980. In essence, these scholars influenced an eclectic group of Beaver College professors to reconceptualize writing. After these illuminating interactions, we always reserved a day for discussions around the question, "What does this mean for Beaver College?" This practice inspired a long-standing leadership principle: always explore what theories mean pragmatically and ask what we should do with them.

While I learned a great deal from all the visiting scholars, Richard Young's visit to Beaver College was particularly enlightening. He introduced us to Rogerian rhetoric, "a form of argumentative reasoning that aims to establish a middle ground between parties with opposing viewpoints or goals.... [T]he speaker seeks compromise, acknowledging positive aspects of each party's argument to arrive at a mutually beneficial solution to an issue" (OWL). I had read Young's coauthored book with Richard E. Young, Alton L. Becker, and Kenneth L. Pike, *Rhetoric: Discovery and Change* (1970). But the real impact of Rogerian rhetoric was from my direct interactions with Young when he visited Beaver College.

Distinctive among scholars in composition/rhetoric, Young placed a strong emphasis on listening. At first, this Rogerian requirement of listening acutely enough to impartially repeat others' positions was useful in the development of writing across the curriculum itself. As the director of the NEH program, I was untenured, totally lacking in institutional power. Listening to colleagues and then asking them for advice (rather than telling them what to do) became a highly effective tool in the transformation of the College into a model WAC institution. But what I learned became even more powerful as I became a higher education administrator.

From directing WAC, I moved on to increasingly responsible administrative positions, culminating in twenty-four years as the chief executive officer at three public universities: Arizona State University West, University of Alaska Anchorage, and Governors State University (GSU), a public regional university in the Chicago suburbs. I've often said that everything I know as a university president, I learned as a writing program administrator, especially directing the WAC program. Listening, connecting, and building consensus were key among the strategies I learned. Moving from listening and learning to framing and communicating a strategy was essential. I emphasized this forty years later when I wrote a book called *Leading Academic Change* (2017), where I wrote that "a vision without a strategy is a fantasy" (11).

But how to create and communicate the strategy? This is where my background, particularly my experience with Rogerian rhetoric learned during my years developing the WAC program, was so critical.

Learning to Testify Before the Legislature

Let's fast-forward thirty years from 1977 to 2007. As the president of Governors State University (GSU), at least once a year over a thirteen-year span (2007-2020), I defended my university's budget. Each year, the Illinois legislature through its education committees reviews the finances of its thirteen public university campuses. How did they spend the funds appropriated during the previous year? What were their accomplishments in enrollment and graduation rates? How did they plan to manage taxpayer funds in the coming year? Formal training for this essential task existed nowhere. But from the start, I felt better prepared than most university presidents because of my background in rhetoric, theater, and storytelling.

I knew that every spring I would travel to the state capitol in Springfield on two separate occasions to make my case before the Senate and House higher education budget committees. Although the Illinois Board of Higher Education presented an overall budget for public higher education, all campus presidents were required to justify their individual financial requests by reviewing previous expenditures and accomplishments as well as future projections.

As a newbie, I was happy for the opportunity to watch and listen as more experienced colleagues met the challenge. In that first round of testimony, nearly all of the presidents read the statements that would be submitted into the record. So that's what I did, too. When it was my turn, even though I made sure to make eye contact and to read with some animation, it became clear to me right away that verbatim reading was not a good strategy. Few legislators listened to the statements. Many actually left the room. Some never returned; others came back for the question period. It became perfectly clear that it was the question period that was important. The elected officials preferred to talk rather than to listen to canned speeches from university representatives. And talk they did.

The question period was often raucous and unpredictable, exemplifying regional conflicts, individual hobby horses, and sometimes a general distrust of higher education. I particularly recall one early exchange. It must have been in 2008 or 2009. One legislator asked me what I was doing to stop the incessant playing of video games on campus. I answered honestly that we did not have any video games on our campus. These were the days before the eternal presence of hand-held devices. Maybe because free-standing video game machines were ubiquitous at the time, the legislator was not satisfied and repeated the question at least four times with rising decibel levels. I responded each time, politely and patiently, with the same factual answer. We were not using state funds to provide video games to students. I must confess that in that instance, it was not Carl Rogers or Richard Young whispering in my ear. Instead, I drew on my theater training, allowing me to remain poised and even-tempered during the ridiculous interrogation. (Here's where a strong sense of humor is also helpful.)

I'm relieved to say that not all legislators displayed that degree of unreasonableness. In fact, a few took me aside afterward and were personally helpful with suggestions about crafting future testimony. One local representative, who was avidly rooting for our campus to receive improved funding, told me bluntly never to read my testimony verbatim—and I never did again. My written testimony was a packet of slides with visual and verbal elements—a set of soundbites with charts, graphs, and pictures. I referenced the bullet points without reading each one and reflected on what the legislators were viewing. "As you can see," I might say, "we were able to attract students who had temporarily dropped out by contacting them and ascertaining what was preventing their return. Often we could help with additional financial aid—or, sometimes, by waiving a fee for an unreturned library book."

Through the years I also learned to draw on fundamentals of my teaching experience. I followed simple adages like, "Show, don't tell." The slides would show visual evidence of students engaged, for example, in a voter registration drive—something dear to the heart of the legislators. When I did tell, it was in narrative mode and with what I hoped would be memorable lines. For example, I was always asked to name my university's competitors. Since this was an expected question, I could be prepared with the appropriate research. As it turned out, the vast majority of Governors State University's applicants who did not wind up attending GSU did not go to other universities, private colleges, or community colleges. They went nowhere. Higher education lost them. This was a powerful fact. We are not talking about "summer melt." We found that throughout the year, students would apply, earn admission, and then become discouraged, mainly because of perceived financial challenges, and decide that it was immediately important to work additional hours and earn a larger paycheck for their families. I was able to respond to the expected legislative question by saying, "Our biggest competitor is *nowhere.*"

I could then explain the steps we were taking to address the challenge of this insidious competitor, emphasizing frequent follow-up with applicants, especially about scholarships, financial aid, and work-study opportunities. I could also point out that this intensive pre-college advising required additional staff time. Bottom line, it cost money. In effect, the legislator's question about competition brought us to a legitimate reason to request additional resources. My colleague regional public university presidents asked their own research offices to check about nowhere as a competitor. Many found that nowhere was the destination of many of their own applicants. Together, we could make this issue more powerful. It was even picked up by the press. I learned from experience and from my general identity as a rhetorician that it's important to be prepped by research, but that's not enough. It's also crucial to tell a compelling story.

Let me make another point about working together with other universities. Over the years, the Illinois public university presidents developed a silent rule: Never bash another university, even when elected officials goad you to do so. And legislators often put us on the spot with questions tempting us to say how much better we were than a particular sister university, especially when one had been singled out in the media for special opprobrium. Most of us resisted the temptation, since it's always a terrible idea to circle the wagons and shoot in.

Another thing I learned over the years was to partner with a student leader for our testimony. Legislators always listened more intently and courteously to students. They would even adjust the time of a scheduled testimony to accommodate the student's academic or work obligations. They didn't care at all about the presidents' calendars and would sometimes unexpectedly postpone a hearing until the next day, necessitating an unanticipated overnight stay—and additional hotel costs charged to the state. Having a student with you provided some insurance that the student's time would be respected, even if your own was not.

Preparing the student leader for testimony was often the most enjoyable part of the experience. It was gratifying to help students tell their own stories in their own ways. The public forum with real stakes attached to their performance was an effective teaching tool. I recall one student leader powerfully testifying that he was one of those applicants who might have gone *nowhere*. Instead, he chose to go somewhere and now, as he looked forward to graduation, he had the intellectual mobility to go anywhere he chose.

Lessons Learned from Theater Experience and Feminism

Let me expand on the value of theater experience. During my childhood I took what were called elocution lessons from retired actress Mae Desmond. At five, I participated in a radio play of *The Five Little Peppers and How They Grew*. Throughout K-12, I participated in every theatrical experience available, culminating in my role as Gloria, the reporter, in my high school's production of *Damn Yankees*. In college at the University of Pennsylvania, I performed with Candace Bergen (we called her Cappy!) in Penn Players' production of Jean Giraudoux's *The Enchanted*. Here is what I learned from these formative experiences:

Teamwork with a wide range of participants

At my neighborhood high school, I was in what was called the block roster with courses reserved only for students with a record of high grades in academic subjects. My extracurricular theater experience allowed me to work with and form friendships with a wide range of students talented in diverse areas. A top inspirational memory of my teen years is the after-performance party at my West Philly house, where the music teacher played "You've Gotta Have Heart" on our piano and the *Damn Yankees* cast and directors joined in the singing.

Role-playing

It's a fact of life—and certainly of leadership—that everyone must learn to play multiple roles. While maintaining core values, we must learn to act on them in different ways in various situations. While being consistent in values and character, leaders must wear public masks to accomplish goals. In a sense, the university presidency is a role to be played. To do so effectively, it's important to separate one's emotional self from the task at hand. I recall many instances, when I had to respond professionally to people who were attacking me. That's role-playing—an ability learned from theater experience.

Empathy

As Thoreau wrote, "Could a greater miracle take place than for us to look through each other's eyes for an instant?" (1854, n.p.) People are locked in their own perspectives. It's extremely difficult to escape from this natural subjectivity. But when you enter from stage left as another character—someone entirely different from you —you must experience and project an understanding of "the other." All those years ago with Penn Players, I played the role of an elderly woman whose hearing disability required her to use what was called an "ear trumpet." Even though she was a comic character, I have always recalled what the world would be like if I couldn't hear very well. Empathy is essential to leadership. Some call it emotional intelligence—the ability to connect meaningfully with other perspectives. Theater training helps leaders to develop this difficult ability.

Listening and observing

My acting experience enhanced what I learned from Rogerian rhetoric. Actors must listen intently. In my role in *The Enchanted*, I had to strain through a disability to hear the other characters. But whatever parts actors play, they must listen intently to the dialogue. You can't just wait for your cue. You have to be fully in the scene whether you are speaking or silent. You also have to watch carefully every movement on the stage. Directors spend endless hours with what is called "blocking," the strategic design of every on-stage movement. Careful listening and observing are essential to leadership.

Readers might connect what I learned from theater and rhetoric to the foundations of feminist theory. In the 1970s, I was one of the organizers of the first NOW (National Organization for Women) chapters in my Philadelphian suburban neighborhood. Team spirit and empathy are foundational in feminism. These principles were reinforced by my active involvement in the movement.

Concluding Lessons

Overall, here's what I learned about presidential communication and leadership from rhetoricians, theater training, feminism, friendly legislators, teaching experience, and common sense:

- When communicating with internal or external audiences, become familiar enough with your message to speak with spontaneity. A list of bullet points will jog your memory. Reading verbatim from a script will ensure that faculty members, students, or legislators will stop listening.
- Be brief. During practice sessions, my legislative liaison would time my opening statement, always encouraging greater brevity. It's important to be brief when speaking to all audiences. I was proud that my Commencement remarks clocked in at under three minutes.
- Involve students in university communication whenever possible. For legislative testimony my mantra was, "Bring a student; teach a student. Even if the overall testimony does not go as well as you would like, your student partner will have an unforgettable, meaningful experience."
- In any dealing with the media—and sometimes with internal audiences as well—context can be your enemy. If you are quoted, it's not an adequate defense to say that your remarks were taken out of context. In fact, when you are not telling a story, you often have to talk in a series of clear, quotable soundbites, any one of which could wind up in the media or on the internal rumor mill. Even when you are talking to faculty members, who are themselves lecturers, don't lecture.
- Especially for external audiences, written communication should be a series of attractive, compelling PowerPoint slides, with short sound-bite length oral explanations. Whenever possible, incorporate visuals. Be aware of the specialized genres dictated by different situations.
- For both external and internal audiences, whenever possible, invite questions. Listen intently to the questioner. Use the Rogerian

strategy of repeating a version of the question as part of your response. But make the response brief and to the point.

- Stay calm and poised even under personal attack.
- In 2023–24, we witnessed painful Congressional testimony from university presidents. In their cases, it was not possible to use PowerPoint or visual communication. It's difficult to know how they prepared, but from my perspective I found myself thinking that they would have been better served by studying previous Congressional testimony (its own genre). A little video training might also have helped.

Leadership, exemplified by public testimony or by the myriad other responsibilities of a university presidency, depends on well-framed messages informed by careful listening. That applies to inspiring the Faculty Senate to expand courses for working adults, encouraging the faculty to work with community college colleagues for seamless student transfer, and the full range of communication challenges. It's not necessary to be a rhetoric/comp scholar to learn how to implement a vision through listening and interacting with others. What's essential is to be a life-long learner.

References

Britton, James. 1975. *The Development of Writing Abilities (11–18).* Macmillan.

Brown, Walter Rollo. 1915. *How the French Boy Learns to Write.* Harvard University Press.

Corbett, Edward PJ. 1969. "The Rhetoric of the Open Hand and the Rhetoric of the Closed Fist." *College Composition & Communication* 20 (5): 288–296. https://doi.org/10.2307/355032.

D'Angelo, Frank J. 1973. "Imitation and Style." *College Composition & Communication* 24 (3): 283–290. https://doi.org/10.2307/356855.

Kinneavy, James L. 1971. *A Theory of Discourse: The Aims of Discourse.* Norton.

Lloyd-Jones, Richard. 1977. "The Politics of Research into the Teaching of Composition." *College Composition & Communication* 28 (3): 218–222. https://doi.org/10.58680/ccc197716365.

Maimon, Elaine. 2017. *Leading Academic Change.* Stylus.

Online Writing Lab. n.d. "Rogerian Rhetoric." Accessed January 25, 2025.
https://owl.purdue.edu/owl/general_writing/academic_writing/historical_perspectives_on_argumentation/rogerian_argument.html.

Shaughnessy, Mina P. 1976. "Diving in: An Introduction to Basic Writing." *College Composition & Communication 27 (3): 234–239.* https://doi.org/10.58680/ccc197616563.

Thoreau, Henry David. 1854. *Walden; Or, Life in the Woods. Project Gutenberg. Accessed May 13, 2025.* https://www.gutenberg.org/files/205/205-h/205-h.htm.

Winterowd, W. Ross. 1968. *Rhetoric: A Synthesis.* Holt, Rinehart, and Winston.

Young, Richard E., Alton Becker, and Kenneth Pike. 1970. *Rhetoric: Discovery and Change.* Harcourt.

CHAPTER 2

Leading Like a Teacher

Emily Isaacs, *Montclair State University*

Most of the mistakes I've made as a leader were when I forgot, ignored, or rejected the lessons I learned on my journey from novice to accomplished teacher. I became an accomplished teacher by becoming a reflective practitioner: I learned how to uncover and lean into my strengths, assess and see my teaching practice from multiple points of view, and figure out how to use these views to critically reflect on my practice and implement changes that would make me more effective.

Becoming a reflective teacher wasn't easy. I had to learn strategies for viewing my teaching from different angles. Even harder, I had to develop the confidence and emotional maturity to take and grow from criticism I gleaned from students and from thinking deeply about the distance between my intentions and what I observed. I grew the ability to view my teaching with enough detachment to engage my analytic skills to see, reflect on, and revise my teaching strategies. Ultimately this is the same capacity that I have, over many years, nurtured in myself as a faculty leader, and which I strive to develop when I coach other leaders. My journey developing as a teacher was greatly facilitated by great mentors and excellent teachers—in that way I was lucky. But my journey to becoming a leader was mostly a solo one, with no investment or encouragement for leadership development, and few leaders who shared with me how they developed, and how they learned from mistakes especially. I write this to readers whom I imagine have not had consistent mentorship or professional development as leaders with the hope that sharing my journey and ideas about how we can take charge of our growth and development as leaders will be helpful, whether you have ever been a teacher or not. A cornerstone to it all is taking time to mine this "course" along with other sources for insights that will support your reflection on your academic professional development.

I've had several leadership roles over my career at Montclair State University, where I have been throughout my nearly thirty-year career. Montclair, a public state university in New Jersey, has experienced steady growth, nearly doubling in size over my tenure, and shifting from a regional comprehensive university to a research university while increasing its racial and ethnic diversity and its enrollment of Pell-eligible students. Today I am Associate Provost for Faculty Affairs, leading faculty development and supporting titled and untitled leaders—and an organization can only thrive when one has both kinds of leaders—helping them develop new skills and build on the skills they already have. I have discovered that many of the most adept leaders in higher education leadership are also excellent teachers.

As excellent teachers, they were not masters of all aspects of teaching; rather, they had developed the ability to exploit their strengths, but also to seek ways to view their practice from multiple angles, and then to methodically reflect not just on the effects of their efforts, but also on their interactions with others. Leaders who resist this work of what Donald Schön terms "reflection-in-action" are not very effective (1983). Schön, the twentieth-century philosopher and learning theorist whose work best informs my understanding of nurturing excellence, writes: "Whatever [the] starting point, [...professionals are] unlikely to get very far unless others help [them] see what [they have] worked to avoid seeing" (1983, 283). This is true for both teachers and leaders: we all have our weaknesses, and it takes emotional maturity and belief in the power of conversation and reflection to seek others' help in seeing ourselves and our practice more clearly, especially those aspects of our practice that we are deeply committed to and thus avoid seeing weaknesses in.

In addition to what I have learned from Schön, I learned essential leadership strategies from several teacher-scholars who work in Writing Studies and Teacher Education, people whose work I read as part of my education in Writing Studies, but who never wrote or spoke about leadership! I read their work to understand teaching, which was their primary focus. Yet these scholars—Peter Elbow, best known for *Writing without Teachers;* Anne Herrington and Marcia Curtis for *Persons in Process;* and Lisa Delpit for *Educating Other People's Children*—taught me as much about leadership as anyone else. These educators' words have functioned as "mentor texts," returning to me repeatedly, especially when I help colleagues develop as teachers and/or leaders. Their insights and strategies can have instructive value for other academic leaders as they do for me. That at least the ones I knew personally—Peter Elbow, Marcia Curtis, and Anne Herrington—were phenomenal teachers is suggestive: great teaching may be a pathway to great leadership. If we can learn to lead like these teachers teach others to teach, we can do well by those we seek to lead. While administrators are not to faculty as teachers are to students in significant ways, the work of leading is a lot like the work of teaching in that both teachers and leaders are at their best when they lean on their strengths, seek to always be learners who seek insights from varied sources, and develop and practice reflection.

I'm devoting this chapter to making the case that lessons learned from years spent teaching have valuable application to leadership development. I connect Schön's lessons on reflective practice with the teacher-educator perspectives of Elbow, Harrington and Curtis, and Delpit, to show how academic leaders can call forth the lessons they developed as teachers (or, if they don't have teaching experience, to learn from those who do). Further, I speculate on what I see as the common phenomenon of "forgetting" past lessons we've learned, particularly when faculty move into academic administration. Too many academic leaders seem to have forgotten these lessons learned, failing to study and reflect on their practice, as good teachers must.

Stay Connected to Your Pre-Leader Professional Self

We have all observed this "forgetting" phenomenon: faculty-administrators who appear unreflective and unwilling to seek others' perspectives on their leadership. Why do we fail to implement the lessons we've learned as teachers when we become administrators? Why do faculty administrators sometimes (often?) abandon the insights and practices they honed as faculty once they become administrators and leaders of faculty? (Or perhaps the question is, why do we think someone who hasn't mastered self-study and self-reflection of their primary professional practice—in my case, teaching—will be an effective leader?) For those teachers who did become good administrators, I think the answer lies in overcoming the artificial but powerful chasm between faculty (the light side) and administrators (the dark side).

That metaphor of "crossing over to the dark side" is powerful in academia, and it also has an insidious effect on our work. Too often, faculty-administrators do not reach back across the chasm and seek out faculty experiences and perspectives. We have crossed over, and we are unable to process the "back-talk" of our work—the feedback and resulting changes to our work that occur as we engage in and respond to real situations—with those who have remained firmly on the other side of the divide. We need to acknowledge and negotiate this chasm as we work to advance the mission of our institutions. How great the chasm is—how far apart we are—depends on the extent to which administrators and faculty who work together share purpose and mission and the extent to which they *believe that they share the same purpose and mission.*

As noted earlier, four of the five educators who are leadership touchstones for me are literacy educators, which is my field as well. The fifth, Donald Schön, was not. Trained as a philosopher and a student of John Dewey, Schön focused on professional education, and from this study of professionals, he drew implications for how schools might better prepare pre-professionals. Schön's best-known book, *The Reflective Practitioner: How Professionals Think in Action,* draws on professionals in engineering, urban planning, management, and psychotherapy to paint a picture of the professional who employs "reflective practice" to aid them in their advancement. I have never forgotten his language for describing the ways that successful professionals must mediate technical knowledge with the realities of "messy, confusing problems" (1987, 3). His key term is "reflection-in-action"—referring to the process of reflecting on your work while you're doing it. Reflection-in-action is when professional practitioners "turn thought back on action and on the knowing which is implicit in action" (1983, 50).

As Schön suggests, across many professions, successful practitioners' "inquiry, however it may initially have been conceived, turns into a frame experiment…the inquirer is willing to step into the problematic situation, to impose a frame on it, to follow the implications of the discipline thus established, and yet to remain open to the situation's back-talk. Reflecting on the surprising consequences of [their] efforts to shape the situation in conformity with his initially chosen frame, the inquirer frames new questions and new ends in view" (1983, 269). When we reflect in action, or as Adler-Kassner and Gallagher say in the introduction to this volume, "put [ourselves] into a learner's mindset," we connect our actions with the theories and lessons we have learned from schooling and previous experiences yet remain open and seek "back-talk" so we can reframe the challenging tasks that face us.

Build on Your Strengths

I'll begin with the most accessible but essential lesson that I learned on my journey as a teacher: build on strength. Peter Elbow, best known for his popularization of freewriting and other strategies for supporting a student-centered writing classroom where teachers are more like coaches and students discover the power of focusing on drafting, revision, and rewriting, is the author of *Writing without Teachers (1973)* and *Writing with Power (1981),* among many other books. Peter was also one of my first teachers in graduate school, and he was a great teacher to me when I began teaching. One day we were in a dusty hallway at the University of Massachusetts-Amherst. I was telling him of my novice struggles and he said to me: Do more of what you do really well. That's your gift. Do more of that. It's a lot easier to do more of what you do well than to get good at doing something you aren't already good at.

I've repeated that advice over and over again, to students in my writing classes, to new or struggling teachers, to staff, and to emerging leaders. I give myself the same advice. From writing pedagogy, a classic technique is to mark a passage of student writing and essentially say, "'Please do more of this thing you are doing here'" (Elbow 2000, 356). When I work with teachers who are struggling, I always ask them what they're good at, and then I seek to help them expand upon that strength first, spending less energy trying to compensate for or improve in the areas where they struggle. For leaders, it's the same tip. I'll use myself as an example. I tend toward enthusiasm for both projects and people, but I struggle with figuring out how people can collaborate with me on the projects. It is difficult for me to do two things: to ask for help directly and to create structures where collaborators can see how they can join me. When I'm working with a team to formulate a plan to address a problem or create a program, I focus on my enthusiasm: I tout the program and its potential, but I also call out individuals for their strengths, noting their previous contributions and abilities, which often leads them to feel more comfortable and willing to pitch in and take on responsibilities, and to help me in identifying doable chunks of work that collaborators can take on. I use my strengths and the strengths that others possess to create an environment where what I have difficulty doing is done by others (and vice versa).

When supporting teachers and leaders, it is important to be clear that what works for one person often will not work for another. Our strengths and weaknesses are not the same. An error that many novice teachers make is to attempt to adopt the strategies of a teacher they most admire, and then they are disappointed with the results. This also happens to new leaders. I have seen new chairs struggle with running faculty meetings. They tend to assume they should run their department meetings as their immediate predecessor had, and they are disappointed with the results. Discussions are not robust, volunteers do not make themselves known, and the chair's goals are not advanced. The novice chair has adopted the predecessor's strategy and format but hasn't yet considered how well it fits their skills, personality, and style. The challenge is exacerbated when leaders rise from their work group; the outsider chair is given more leeway to create their own processes and methods than an insider is given.

To know your strengths, you have to ask questions. As a teacher, your students are asked through surveys that your institution runs but you can also run your own and simply ask students directly. As a leader, you need to seek ways to understand your strengths. Ask people who know you, and don't rely on one informant. Read your performance reviews for specifics. If you can, consider requesting a 360-degree or other leader assessment, but only if you're ready to read anonymous feedback from peers, direct reports, and superiors. While our growth begins with our strengths, we need to figure out how to attend to our weaknesses, which is most possible if we think about those weaknesses within the context of our strengths, as I hope my example illustrates.

Leading from your strengths is further complicated by the fact that we are not all afforded the same authority. Our social identities influence what strategies a roomful of people—faculty or students—will support. Often novice teachers and leaders admire someone who occupies a more empowered identity. The middle-aged white professor who is self-deprecating and informal in their interactions with their students may be admired by a younger instructor of color, but that instructor of color, occupying a very different social identity, may find that self-deprecation and informality are read as weakness, not strength. Marjorie Hass, former president of three colleges, writes about how she recognized her identity as a woman shaped how she was perceived—"It might be assumed that you will automatically side with women and be too 'personally' involved to set fair policies and processes around Title IX issues or other gender-based discrimination" (2021, 37)—and how it shaped her responses to these "provocations." She describes her preferred approach as "gentle reframing" because in her experience, a more direct approach by a woman is often not well received.

The lesson here is not simply to lean on your strengths, but to analyze your strengths and understand what other people perceive as your strengths. People don't always want to tell you what your weaknesses are, but they can identify and give language to your strengths. I tend to *feel* massively disorganized, but it turns out I'm extremely organized: I know this because it's regularly cited as one of my strengths, so now I accept it and lean into it, even boast about it!

Take heed, however, as you also need to recognize that your strengths will shift as you change contexts. Most leaders will tell you that they are different when they are in a room full of faculty than when they are in a room full of staff or students. Why is that? Faculty demand a different kind of leadership style. They are skeptical if not dismissive of the hierarchy that staff and students typically accept more readily. For some higher education leaders, this means they avoid leading faculty—they prefer leading staff, or they return to the classroom where they can lead students and be colleagues with faculty. Leaders who successfully lead faculty learn to approach faculty leadership as shared or collaborative leadership, and they likely adopt a transformational approach.

Transformational leadership is about influencing others: "Transformational leadership influences followers by getting them to transcend their self-interests for the good of the group, organization, or society, while also enhancing followers' expectations and abilities, and their willingness to take risks" (Bass, Avolio, and Atwater 1996, 10). When I lead faculty, I'm at my best when I'm supporting other faculty to step up and lead; in this leadership work I play an organizing, facilitating, project-managing, and coaching role. I've come to this perspective by reading articles and books about leadership, talking with others at my university and at conferences, and critically reflecting on my experiences of relative success and failure. Situations in which I have taken on a more traditional leadership role, in which I define goals and ask others to fulfill them, have not gone as well as those in which I've been one among many—or even better, the person behind the scenes.

Seek Input from Others, Even When You Don't Think You Need It

Teachers and leaders regularly decide what course of action to take to further learning, whether that's for students in a classroom or faculty in a college. Conversant with most of the dilemmas of higher education, experienced administrators do not have difficulty coming up with plans to solve problems we face. For example, when it comes to increasing enrollment in a low-enrolled major, there's a ready set of strategies that one can pull from *The Chronicle of Higher Education* or *Inside Higher Ed*: revise the curricula to better align it with student interests; change the major's name, course titles, and marketing material; reposition your faculty so that especially appealing faculty are teaching introductory courses for undeclared majors. The challenges we face in higher education are seldom unique, and solutions and strategies are regularly showcased at administrator conferences, journals, and by higher education consultants. It's not that these plans all work—they don't!—but it's easy to read and study the problem and become convinced of a plan you have devised. Thus, it's tempting to do the planning and creating alone or just with one or two others, and then to attempt to roll out the plan and ask everyone to get to work.

And this is exactly what most novices are inclined to do both in the classroom and in our leadership roles. I have seen it repeatedly, and still today I catch myself in that inclination. We don't spend enough time understanding problems with the help of others before we implement solutions. When teachers and leaders tell me about a problem they are trying to solve, quite often they begin with what they want to do if only they can get others to go along with their plan or get out of their way. I try to slow them down: I ask them how they've sought to understand the problem and I encourage them to gain additional perspectives, resisting reliance on the most visible, "received knowledge" perspectives.

Anne Herrington and Marcia Curtis (working as a team and individually) and Lisa Delpit are literacy researchers who exemplify how to challenge and extend received knowledge—how to come to new knowledge by seeking to better understand a problem, even one that has already been frequently studied and analyzed. I think of them as experts in triangulation, that idea born from geometry and developed by social science researchers who found the geometric metaphor helpful in developing new methods to "come to know." The sociologist Norman Denzin defined triangulation as "the combination of methodologies in the study of the same phenomenon" (2009, 291). When I think about triangulation, I start by brainstorming how I can analyze what's before me from multiple angles. My questions are: how can I get another angle or perspective from the one that is most available to me? How can I see what's before me from a different angle? I also think of these literacy researchers who exemplify how to enact the principle of triangulation.

Herrington and Curtis and Delpit are teacher-scholars who suspected limitations to the received, dominant narrative they were working within, and sought to learn more through a variety of methods. Approaching their work as literacy teachers with curiosity, with a "learner's mindset," they sought triangulation strategies to better understand why dominant narratives explaining how students learn and grow didn't thoroughly match the students they encountered in their teaching and research. I'll summarize a few examples from their work for illustration.

Herrington and Curtis were writing what became an influential book in the field, *Writing in Process,* when I was Herrington's doctoral student. They intended their research to reveal how basic writers differed from mainstream "college writers" on their path through the first three semesters of college, with survey data from over 1,000 students and case studies of eighteen students. However, as they studied their collected data, working inductively, they changed their plan dramatically and instead wrote case studies of just four college students, following them longitudinally for many semesters, finding that these students' journeys provided them a perspective that was missing and needed to be heard. They write, "our ways of conceptualizing the study and our particular focus changed as we changed and learned from the students participating in our study" (2000, 7). It was risky to shift their research plan so dramatically, but it enabled them to discover new insights, allowing other teachers to understand college students' literacy development more deeply. For example, through their multiyear case studies we see how personal academic writing is, even when it doesn't appear to be, and how deeply instructors' feedback affects college writers. Herrington reinforced the lesson of triangulation that I first learned in her methods class through her regular work with me as a student and a nascent higher education administrator: she asked questions constantly, guiding me and her other students and staff to seek out fresh informants and perspectives on our research questions and in our administrative work.

Lisa Delpit emerged on the scene of literacy instruction in 1986 with the publication of "Skills and Other Dilemmas of a Progressive Black Educator" in *Harvard Educational Review*. That article and the follow-up to it, "The Silenced Dialogue: Power and Pedagogy in Educating Other People's Children," were hugely influential and remain widely cited. Delpit, a Black educator, began as an enthusiastic adherent to process-writing pedagogy (a writing pedagogy that emphasizes brainstorming and drafting to develop ideas and voice over direct instruction in writing conventions) but became more skeptical—first as a teacher, later when Black educators with whom she taught in Philadelphia took her to task, and increasingly as she conducted research on literacy education in diverse communities. In these two articles, Delpit critiqued process writing instruction as an approach designed by and for middle-class white people, with little interest in the voices of Black and other non-dominant educators. She writes: "It seems as if leaders of the writing-process movement find it difficult to develop the vocabulary to discuss the issues in ways which teachers with differing perspectives can hear them and participate in the dialogue" (1986, 383–4). Her articles and later her book *Teaching Other People's Children* do not argue for rejecting process writing pedagogy or the white middle-class educators who led the research and movement, but instead forward a much-needed correction that has enriched the discipline. She was an early voice in my development as a teacher and ultimately a leader. She asked: Who is not served by this method? Who is not at the table? To better understand the perspectives of those not at the table—in Delpit's case, working-class African Americans and Native Americans—she traveled to communities outside of the easy orbit of higher education researchers.

From these teacher-scholars, I gained a habit and appreciation for seeking to understand problems from multiple angles. This is especially useful when your analysis of a problem seems obvious. In teaching, this tendency to assume you know what students need is especially hard yet important to resist. When working with others—students, teachers, leaders—I try to bite my tongue and wait. It's hard, but I keep trying, and often succeed, or manage to ask questions, and when I do speak, to speak in clear first-person terms, telling my own stories of challenging problems. I try *not* to say what is at the tip of my tongue: "You should do this, then that, then this other thing." It gets easier with age because I have learned from experience observing how the advice I wanted to give wasn't very good. Recently a chair told me about a junior faculty member who was avoiding her advice, and an answer popped into my head related to that specific professor and situation. But I kept listening; as she continued to speak, I realized my advice would have backfired. I was about to advise on the presented problem, not the real one, which I began to suspect had more to do with the leader than with the junior faculty member.

Seeking input from multiple sources, or triangulation, is challenging for higher education leaders who are on a fast clock. Administrators encounter problems at a rapid rate and feel pressure to solve them quickly. The triangulation principle that is so useful in defining and ultimately addressing complex problems when you are a student or researcher is very hard for administrators to put into practice. I know this from experience. One solution I can recommend is to wait. If you are action-oriented like me, you need to resist action and attempt to solve fewer problems. Of course, if you have the opposite challenge, and you avoid action, my advice would be different. If you avoid action, you may be too anxious about dissent and criticism, especially from your former colleagues on the other side of the faculty-administrator chasm. For you, leaning into triangulation as a method that you can follow as you did when you were a student or researcher can provide a roadmap of discovery and learning that will lead you to more consultation and ultimately action that you can take with others.

Resist Walling Yourself Off from Those You Lead

My worst leadership experience was related to a failure to follow the principles of triangulation. When I became an associate dean, a position I took after serving as first-year writing director and chair of English, I was shocked by some of what I saw on the other side of that chasm. The veterans in my new office—the dean and the associate and assistant deans—smiled as they saw my jaw drop when I learned that many faculty did not faithfully or adequately complete required assessments, reports, and the like, and that some faculty had developed ways to deny persistent negative reviews of their teaching or to reduce workload and increase their pay through a variety of means. I was truly shocked. At a public state university with a longstanding and strong union, I thought the rules were pretty clear and that people played by them, if not because they wanted to, then because they had to.

I hadn't seen this level of rule-breaking and what I saw as a violation of the trust held in us as public university employees in my job as chair or faculty; I didn't know that so many faculty and chairs didn't follow through on problems. As associate dean for faculty affairs, I vowed to clean things up and put some order to the wayward ship. I remember feeling appalled and somewhat overwhelmed by it all. It was like I moved into a fixer-upper and I had to start with some demolition and deep cleaning, which is more or less how I approached my first administrative job taking over a first-year writing program that had been run by an absent administrator for several years. As a new associate dean, my sources for coming to understand the problems I saw were all within the dean's office; they seemed pleased by my zeal and furnished me with their knowledge of how systems and rules had come to be ignored or sidestepped by so many.

What I didn't do was try to understand these problems by talking to people outside the dean's office. I didn't talk to the chairs who had endorsed faculty research reports that were thin. I didn't talk to the faculty who hadn't completed required post-tenure reviews for years. I didn't talk to the faculty whose records suggested that their teaching was poorly received by students. I didn't triangulate! I didn't see how I had fallen into a deficit-based approach, just the kind of approach that I would criticize instructors for taking on with their students. I fell into the trap of technical rationality; as Schön writes, "Hungry for technical rigor, devoted to an image of solid professional competence, or fearful of entering a world in which they feel they do not know what they are doing, [unreflective practitioners] choose to confine themselves to a narrowly technical practice" (1983, 43).

I saw a problem and adopted a familiar and comfortable frame that I had applied to neglected administrative work previously: I set out to organize the mess and return things to order. I created tables and plans, wrote emails informing faculty of what they needed to do, reduced overload payments, etc. With support from my local colleagues and armed with data from the dean's office point of view, I sprang into action, relying on my technical expertise as a capable administrator. I wasn't able or willing to "remain open to the situation's "back-talk." Unlike Curtis and Herrington, I wasn't able to give up on my plan of action. Also, I didn't have an ally who might have encouraged me to slow down, take more time, and seek out other perspectives. I take responsibility for my rush to action, but I also think I needed leadership coaching, if only in the form of trusted colleagues who agree to work with one another much to provide feedback, much like coauthors do, and as I have done throughout my career.

I have had time to think about the first year I served as associate dean. No doubt I did many things well, but I feel regret and shame about locking into technical rationality and deciding to demand greater accountability without understanding why my colleagues were making the decisions they had made. I had been active in the college for years and had good relationships with many on the faculty. As a teacher, I had learned to seek out student perspectives when they were not doing well on assignments. I had come to know that I alone couldn't see why students weren't succeeding and that I needed to seek student insight. I could have found colleagues who were willing to serve like Donald Schön's coaches, fellow travelers who listen to their colleague's challenges, ask questions, and share their experiences with the complex work of teaching and leading.

So why didn't I seek to learn more? Why didn't I pause to reflect on the practice that I was adopting? Why did I not follow the deeply ingrained principles of triangulation and reflective practice? Why did I rely so heavily and almost exclusively on the perspectives of those who sat closest to me?

Beyond convenience and the pressure of the clock and not having a leadership community or partner, a big part of my behavior, particularly forgetting what I had learned in my development as a teacher and a teacher of teachers, has to do with what is one of the hardest parts about academic leadership: effectively traversing and managing the chasm between the light and dark side of faculty and administration.

"Crossing over to the dark side" is something faculty joke about when a colleague becomes an administrator. The dark side, the land of Darth Vader and the stormtroopers, is administration, and so naturally Luke Skywalker and the rebels are faculty. Who hasn't laughed about the dark side? But it's also serious: the divide between faculty and administrators, camouflaged as a joke, is a great challenge to effective leadership, not just because of how it leads to reflexive faculty criticism and skepticism of administrators and initiatives that are associated with them, but also because of how it shapes and influences the decisions of administrators, both staff administrators and former faculty who have crossed over. Administrative leaders, and many of the staff they work with, are also reflexive in their criticism of faculty.

Administrators are introduced to students as Darth Vadarian characters when we first start on our path toward faculty; in college and graduate school, faculty complain to students about new policies, decisions, and procedures that negatively affect faculty and students, attributing those always to "administrators" who are overpaid yet ineffective at best, and at worst, intent on evil as they crawl their careers forward. Ridiculing administrators is a quick way to gain student trust: teachers and students are bound together, struggling to cope against a common enemy, whether that is in the effort to access essential technologies, run a low-enrolled course, or overturn a negative tenure decision for a beloved instructor. Once employed as an instructor—tenure-track or not—administrators become stormtroopers, sometimes deserving but always convenient as the responsible party for all unwelcome decisions.

Returning to my story: I became a full-time administrator accidentally, as is often the case. I was a successful first-year writing director who was asked to chair the English department and then asked to become associate dean. I kept saying yes when asked, which is to say I wasn't intentional in my administrative career path. (A little discussed truth is that many of us who become administrators do so because we need, or believe we need, even just a little more money than faculty salary provides. Sometimes I feel resentful of faculty whose personal circumstances are different from mine, making it much easier for them to say no to opportunities that provide more income.) The first two administrative positions at my institution allowed me to retain my membership with the rebels. I was still in the union (at my institution department chairs remain in the faculty union), and I was sitting figuratively and literally among the faculty. But associate dean was, in retrospect, a big break. I had crossed over to the dark side, and it was hard to figure out how to cross back for visits. I lost friends when I crossed over, some through no fault of my own (literally, the cross made me unacceptable as a friend), but it was also me. I think my demeanor and approachability must have changed, that the shock and disappointment I experienced when I saw all these examples of faculty essentially rejecting the terms of their work had changed the way I saw "faculty" and how I engaged with my peers. I became just a little Darth Vadarian. Colleagues in student affairs tell me the same divide exists between student affairs staff and leaders, so perhaps all of us have our stormtrooper and rebel roles.

The dark side metaphor and all it portends is unlikely to go away: it's an old and valued trope embedded in higher education. What we can do, as leaders, is talk about it more directly, to the faculty and staff we work with, but also among ourselves. As we reflect on our actions, we need to consider whether we are letting that trope and the pain we have experienced as we crossed over unduly affect our work. Higher education leaders are guilty, too, making jokes about faculty that rely on tired stereotypes like that of the entitled scholar whose commitment to their own research and intellectual autonomy trumps all other concerns, including those related to students and their needs; or, and I know this one galls faculty especially, about "lazy" tenured full professors enjoying large paychecks with few responsibilities. The jokes come often and reflexively at administrator-only meetings, no less frequently than administrator jokes come in at faculty-only meetings. All of these jokes are problematic because the people who tell them are only half joking. We start believing the jokes, and the chasm between administrators and faculty deepens, making it more difficult for us to achieve our collective and individual goals.

I've become aware of my own participation in this dynamic of creating an us-versus-them environment and its effects on others and on me by reflecting on my experience as an associate dean. The self-reflective process was sometimes painful. As a result today, I enjoy stronger relationships with faculty, and thus I am better able to practice what I preach: doing more of what I do well, following the principles of triangulation to better see and imagine solutions, and especially seeking to listen to quieter voices of those who are often furthest away from decision-making, whether that's adjunct instructors, students, or individuals who do not volunteer to speak, but whose observations can be most valuable to learn from.

For higher education leaders, whether you've set forth on your journey into administration with deliberation or seemingly by accident, whether you're reluctant or eager, success will feel authentic to you if you can draw on the same practices that good teachers draw on. Even if you never really felt you were good in the classroom—and this is a guilty little secret few administrators share—you can still draw on the principles and practices I have outlined, and that I gained from teaching, but that you may have gained from research, particularly if you were successful working with diverse research teams. Leadership, like teaching and researching on diverse teams, is work that involves humans with all their foibles, biases, and unique experiences and perspectives. It thus requires deliberate efforts to seek greater knowledge through triangulation, to seek greater understanding by talking with people who hold diverse perspectives, and to seek novel solutions through iterative reflection, work that is greatly facilitated through conversation with oneself as well as with other leaders, in or outside of leadership programs.

References

Bass, Bernard M., Bruce J. Avolio and Leanne Atwater. 1996. "The Transformational and Transactional Leadership of Men and Women." *Applied Psychology: An International Review* 45 (1): 5-34. https://doi.org/10.1111/j.1464-0597.1996.tb00847.x.

Delpit, Lisa. 1986. "Skills and Other Dilemmas of a Progressive Black Educator." *Harvard Educational Review* 56 (4): 379-386. https://doi.org/10.17763/haer.56.4.674v5h1m125h3014.

Delpit, Lisa. 1988. "The Silenced Dialogue: Power and Pedagogy in Educating Other People's Children." *Harvard Educational Review* 58 (3): 280–298.

Delpit, Lisa. 2006. *Other People's Children: Cultural Conflict in the Classroom.* The New Press.

Denzin, Norman K. 2009. *The Research Act: A Theoretical Introduction to Sociological Methods*. Routledge.

Elbow, Peter. 1981. *Writing with Power*. Oxford University Press.

Elbow, Peter. 1973. *Writing without Teachers*. Oxford University Press.

Elbow, Peter. 2000. *Everyone Can Write: Toward a Hopeful Theory of Writing and Teaching Writing*. Oxford University Press.

Hass, Marjorie. 2021. *A Leadership Guide for Women in Higher Education.* Johns Hopkins University Press.

Herrington, Anne J. and Marcia Curtis. 2000. *Persons in Process: Four Stories of Writing and Personal Development in College.* NCTE.

Schön, Donald A. 1983. *The Reflective Practitioner: How Professionals Think in Action.* Routledge.

Schön, Donald A. 1987. *Educating the Reflective Practitioner: Toward a New Design for Teaching and Learning in the Professions.* Jossey-Bass.

CHAPTER 3

Learning to Lead without Authority

Accreditation and Assessment Mandates

Chris Blankenship, *Salt Lake Community College*

Looking back over my twenty years as a teacher of college writing, I have to appreciate just how much authority I have had. Even as a graduate TA, the writing courses I taught were mine to design and run. While I might choose to cede some of that authority, such as giving my students a say in course policies in service to a pedagogical philosophy, the largest part of my job was one in which I held that ultimate authority of the final grade.

As I have moved into administration at my open-access urban community college, I have reflected on this idea of authority as something that I no longer possess in my current role. Despite the feeling of powerlessness that many faculty feel in contemporary higher education, they often have more authority in their jobs than they care to admit: academic freedom, faculty primacy over the curriculum, grading practices in classes, choice in research projects, and so on. On the other hand, staff and administrative positions, particularly those focused on accreditation and assessment mandates, are often saddled with a great deal of responsibility but no direct power to make change, as I found when I stepped out of my tenured faculty position and took on the role of director of learning outcomes assessment.

This chapter will describe how I learned to lead these efforts without any positional authority, using lessons from my training in traditional and feminist rhetorical theory as well as writing pedagogy. As I reflected on this learning for this chapter, I was struck by how much I had to adapt this academic training for institutional leadership. Even though my background is in a communication-focused discipline, I couldn't just slap academic theory onto my work and call it a day. Learning to move past the abstraction, to think about people I sought to lead, their motivations, and the points of connection that we share—those are places where I was able to apply my knowledge to standing at the forefront of valuable institutional work, even while having no positional authority to demand that this work be done.

Institutional Power and Authority

Especially in academia's hierarchies, it may not be easy to account for authority. Department chairs, deans, provosts, or presidents might be seen to all hold direct authority over those in faculty positions, particularly when issues of evaluation, tenure, promotion, and professional conduct come by their desks; however, even these areas can be tenuous depending upon how strong the model of shared governance is within an institution. A union, a faculty senate or association, or an evaluation committee may hold more de facto power over these processes, even if the ultimate decision rests with someone in this line of authority. For example, a dean may need to weigh carefully the amount of political capital they need to spend in order to deny promotion to an influential faculty member, no matter how well justified they feel that denial may be. And when the waters are murkier—such as a disagreement over the extent to which the principle of academic freedom weighs upon a personnel decision, or the ways that budgetary priorities are determined—exercising authority that a position *technically* holds might be especially fraught.

Authority-Adjacent Leadership

Consider, then, the position of those who are adjacent to these more authoritative roles. A common misconception about anyone in an administrative position at a college or university is that they wield a similar kind of authority over faculty to those in direct supervisory lines. Although there are always exceptions, this is seldom the case. Put an "assistant" or "associate" in front of a title like "dean" or "provost," and that person is likely removed from the line of any direct supervisory authority over all but the few staff that their specific office may have. Other titles like "director" or "manager" likely have the similar challenges, despite the authority their non-academic analogs may hold.

My current position is an example. As director of learning outcomes assessment, my primary responsibilities, according to my job description, are to "work with faculty and academic administrators to plan, design and implement ongoing assessment of student learning outcomes for the improvement of teaching, learning and instructional programs" and to "lead… professional development efforts related to learning outcomes assessment." A note of explanation here: In US higher education, assessment is tied to institution-wide accreditation. This is often a high-stakes effort, particularly for schools that don't fall within the upper echelon in national rankings. In these instances, accreditation is an acknowledged marker of the quality of a credential granted by that school. Accreditation is also essential for US colleges and universities because without it, they cannot receive federal funding like student financial aid or grants.

At the comprehensive community college (i.e, two-year college) where I work, we rely on federal money much more than many other types of institutions since we receive less state money per full time equivalent student than four-year institutions (Community College Research Center 2022) and certainly don't have the endowment that most universities do. In other words, the work that faculty, staff, and administration do who work with assessment and accreditation can have an impact on whether a school has the budget to operate effectively. To be accredited, institutions demonstrate the quality of their programs and work environment through a comprehensive self-study document and follow-up investigation by external peer reviewers from other institutions. These visitations are conducted every several years, resulting in an accreditation report listing strengths and areas for improvement. Depending upon the extent to which an area needs improvement, the accreditor can issue various types of warnings, from a recommendation that must be followed up on by the next visit, up through the need for immediate action and threats of losing the institution's accredited status. Additionally, some individual programs will have specific, profession-level accreditation, often conducted through national organizations. These accreditation standards vary by discipline and only impact the specific program, not the institution as a whole, though the assessment required by professional accreditors is often even more rigorous than that required by more general accreditors and thus dovetails well with those standards reported on in the institution's self-study.

Thus, the paradox. While my position has high-profile, high-stakes responsibilities, people in positions like mine are seldom granted any kind of direct authority to mandate assessment of our programs, and any indirect authority depends entirely upon the willingness of those in formal reporting lines to take up my recommendations and hold faculty accountable to them. I report to an associate provost, who, as I outlined above, is removed from the direct lines of authority over faculty. But I do have an advantage that many others in my position don't: I am organized within the same division as the faculty, Academic Affairs. Many other staff members who are responsible for assessment practices are organized in divisions with names like "institutional effectiveness," often alongside offices of institutional research, analytics, and non-academic program review (Walvoord 2010). These professionals, despite their role in speaking to the learning that students do within their programs, are even further removed from the faculty who are (or should be) ultimately responsible for assessing the learning of their students.

Even with my organizational advantage, however, I still found myself at somewhat of a loss at how to proceed with the responsibilities of my new position when I stepped into the job. Prior to this position I had served as the director of faculty development for the 2020-21 academic year. My predecessor affectionately referred that role as a "yes job": I had the autonomy and budget to bring in interesting speakers, provide books for discussion groups, organize workshops on salient pedagogical topics, pay faculty to develop open educational resources for their students, and give out awards for excellent work. I had no real authority beyond my own staff, but I didn't need any. I simply had to ask faculty what they wanted to fulfill their professional activity requirements for yearly evaluation, tenure, and promotion, and then work with my staff on providing those opportunities. Where we didn't have clear answers, my staff and I (all teachers before our work in the Faculty Development office) came up with ideas based on the prevailing pedagogical trends in higher education. Even as the COVID-19 pandemic shut down our campus a few months into the year, our role remained largely the same. We supported our eLearning office in helping faculty move classes online and pivoted our work to focus on asynchronous and broadcast instructional methods. My position remained a "yes job" even throughout the crisis, and when I transitioned out of the predetermined year of this interim position and back to faculty the following spring, I felt a sense of accomplishment that I had been successful in my first administrative role at my new institution.

That feeling of accomplishment was the catalyst for my application to my current role. As faculty, my penchant for doing a disproportionate amount of institutional service kept me involved in both department and college-wide faculty leadership, culminating in my service as chair of the Faculty Senate Student Learning Outcomes Assessment Committee. I came to this position the very semester that our accreditation review cycle had come up and when our college assessment coordinator (the only administrative-level assessment specialist on campus) had abruptly retired. It quickly became clear that even the longstanding members of the committee weren't prepared to effectively step in and address our peer reviewers' questions about how the college was addressing the newly updated standards of our accreditor, the Northwest Commission on Colleges and Universities (NWCCU). These new standards required all colleges and universities to assess student learning in entire majors (hence the term "program learning outcomes assessment"), rather than assessing learning in individual courses (or "course level learning outcomes").

Because the visiting team did not believe we had a systematic enough process for program learning outcomes assessment, the NWCCU issued our college a "recommendation" rather than reaffirm our accreditation fully. This meant that we were expected to address the problem and would be formally reevaluated three years later during our next mid-cycle visit. As happens so often in the wake of accreditation issues, upper administration jumped into action. The now vacant assessment coordinator position was moved from the division of Institutional Effectiveness into Academic Affairs, elevated to a director level, and rewritten to require teaching experience in addition to assessment expertise. Seeing what I felt were very positive changes in the approach to assessment at the college, and remembering fondly my time in Faculty Development, I applied for the position and was hired at the end of the spring semester in 2022.

Upon getting access to all the records and resources of the Learning Outcomes Assessment Office, though, I quickly realized that I had a very different task ahead of me than I had in either of my prior leadership positions. First, I was under a critical institutional mandate. As I described earlier, accreditation is serious business for any college or university. While a "recommendation" is the lightest of the criticisms that our accreditor can offer, if it goes unaddressed, it can lead to stronger reprimands. Our president was taking this recommendation to heart, thus the reorganization and additional resources put towards the office.

Second, the faculty were burnt out on assessment changes. My predecessor, a knowledgeable psychometrician, had done a great deal of top-down institutional assessment, and expectations of faculty involvement and data collection/analysis methods changed multiple times. As a faculty member at the college for six years, I had personally witnessed at least three different assessment processes, some of which I had been philosophically or methodologically opposed to. Especially following all the shifts in teaching due to the pandemic, faculty simply didn't have the will to learn yet another assessment protocol. It was clear that the faculty saw assessment exclusively as an exercise in compliance: conducted solely to show those in power, particularly accreditors, that assessment is happening. This compliance mindset completely disconnects assessment from the culture of continuous improvement in teaching and learning that is often cited as the primary pedagogical goal of assessment in the first place (Suskie 2018).

Third, I had no authority to require anyone to do anything. Reporting to an associate provost, I was completely outside any chain of command of faculty. The best that I could do was report to the provost, who could then require action from the deans, who could then require action from the departments. But, as I outlined above, even those in positions of positional authority have limitations with faculty, particularly when it comes to issues that touch on curriculum and instruction, like assessment does.

Ultimately, the purely compliance mindset was a large part of what had driven our problems with assessment in the first place. While I could potentially entreat the provost/deans/chairs to wield their positional authority on my behalf to attempt to ensure that faculty conducted assessment, that would only reinforce the framework of compliance that I was trying to get away from. I knew that I needed a different tactic to emphasize assessment as a tool for improving teaching and student learning, which is when I started to reflect on what I had learned about rhetoric and conceptual framing as entry points.

Motivating Faculty Engagement

The first task in my new position was to get the lay of the land. I knew, both from experience and from our accreditation report, that we had no systematic way of conducting program assessment across the college. As a comprehensive community college, some of our programs with accreditation from professional organizations (Accreditation Commission for Education in Nursing, ABET, etc.) were conducting some kinds of assessment each year. Beyond these programs, though, regular, systematic learning outcomes assessment at the program level was sparse. These programs would need to do something that they hadn't done before. But with multiple assessment methods having been passed down over the last several years, asking faculty to do yet another new thing would be difficult at best.

My first thought was to return to the very basics of traditional rhetoric that I had been steeped in since my earliest college courses in the field. Aristotle (2006) outlined rhetoric as a way to examine the available means of persuasion in contexts where the authority lay elsewhere, such as a vote in the Assembly or a judge in a courtroom, and thus persuasion was needed to drive the motivation of those with the power to make a decision. Aristotle's artistic proofs, sometimes referred to as his appeals to audience, are *logos*, the appeal to the audience's sense of reason; *pathos*, the appeal to the audience's emotions, and *ethos*, the appeal to the audience's sense of the writer/speaker's credibility. There's certainly more to Aristotelian rhetorical theory than just these simple terms, but they form the core of so much of my academic training that they made an excellent frame for my approach to leading in a role where my ability to enact positional authority would be associated with my ability to persuade.

Appealing to Reason: Logos

In the academic world, it's often the appeal to reason that takes center stage: lines of logic, rigorous methods, detailed analyses—the belief that the best ideas will win out, even if we have to go through vigorous debate to figure out which ones are the best. Everyone who has worked in academia knows otherwise, though. There aren't always clear answers to questions, and certainly emotions can run high and hot. This is especially the case for questions of workload and the tensions between academic freedom and accountability, which are so prevalent in assessment. In thinking through my understanding of the traditional rhetorical framework of the three appeals, it quickly became clear that reasoning simply wouldn't be the driving force behind how I needed to learn to lead through this change.

When it came to program learning outcomes assessment, most faculty already knew some of the reasoning behind doing the compliance aspect of the work. Why did we need to do it? Because our accreditor demanded it of us, and therefore, the president and all other academic administrators on down from there demanded it of faculty.

Reasons beyond accreditor compliance for doing learning outcomes assessment may not be as readily apparent, but are difficult to argue with when presented: Why should we assess the learning outcomes of our programs? Because we believe that the credentials that we confer are valuable, as we can see from the learning outcomes that ground our programs and curricula. We should be able to demonstrate what students who earn these credentials know and are able to do upon earning these degrees and certificates. Why should our learning assessments not just be our course grades? Because individual courses cover more than one learning outcome in the vast majority of our programs, and we want to be able to say, specifically, what our students are doing well and what they aren't doing well. Having this data will allow us to make meaningful changes to our curricula or make evidence-based arguments on why what we're already doing is working well. Also, because many of us use factors in our grading that are related to, but ultimately not the same as, the learning we want to see in our students. If a student can pass every exam in a course but still fail due to attendance, then unless there is a learning outcome that is directly about showing up to class, that course grade isn't exclusively about learning.

Faculty already knew or readily accepted this reasoning, but that didn't drive motivation or engagement in ways that would be meaningful or sustainable. To lead through this change, I had to learn to appeal to them in different ways.

Appealing to Emotions: Pathos

Appealing to an audience's emotions is often given a bad rap. It's associated with manipulation, playing off feelings like pity, fear, anger, or disgust to bypass rationality, despite being quite a reductive way of thinking about how emotion factors into our reasoning. We know, physiologically and neurologically, that human brains don't separate reason and emotion but integrate them as part of overarching cognitive processing (Damasio 2005), so I felt that it was best to lean into this fact when it came to attempting to lead from this new role. I knew I needed to speak to the affective elements of the teaching profession that

I know so well myself. I wanted to emphasize the positive feelings surrounding being not just an educator, but one who is engaged in always working to improve student learning through meaningful changes to our teaching.

The emotion that was most relevant to my audience was their devotion to their students. Few faculty who choose to teach at a community college come here without a passion for teaching. There are few resources for faculty to conduct research, and many of those are for Scholarship of Teaching and Learning projects; similarly, the pay for community college professors is often substantially lower than our four-year university counterparts in all but the most strongly unionized states. Even in the trades programs that don't exist at the universities, our faculty could generally be making more money working directly in their trade than as a professor. What brings faculty to open-access, community-focused institutions is the desire to teach.

To tap into this energy around students, though, I had to be able to show that participating in program learning outcomes assessment was about even more effective teaching. This involved appealing to faculty to shift their thinking about the foundational purposes of assessment. Natasha Jankowski describes four philosophies for thinking about these purposes: (1) compliance/reporting, or assessment purely for the sake of accountability to entities like boards of education and accreditors; (2) measurement, or assessment focused on valid, quantitative methods and accurate measures to document and record learning; (3) teaching and learning, or assessment as part of effective pedagogy that is formative and intended to improve teaching and learning; and (4) student-centered, assessment as a reflective practice where students actively participate in the assessment process, "not simply the object of assessment, but the primary beneficiaries" (Jankowski 2017, 11).

I needed to change the discourse around assessment to one of the latter two philosophies, and while student-centered assessment is an ideal goal, it would be a much more difficult shift in culture and implementation, especially at a college that works exclusively in smaller credentials (15-60 credit-hour associate's degrees and certificates), serving largely students who don't attend full-time due to family and work obligations. The teaching and learning philosophy seemed like a natural fit since it was already aligned so well with our college mission, the inclinations of those who choose to work at a teaching-focused institution (myself included), and the robust Faculty Development and eLearning offices on our campus.

To attempt the cultural change, I needed to shift the way that we talked about assessment. My research as a graduate student dealt with the ways that we teach argumentation in writing, and in particular, the conceptual metaphors and cognitive frames that we use to discuss what argumentation is and does. George Lakoff and Mark Johnson in *Metaphors We Live By* argue that the language we use around certain ideas conceptually maps one concept onto another (2003). For example, if we describe argument as "attacking a weak point" or "defending a position," with ideas being "weaponized" or a tactic being "scorched earth," then we see the mapping "*argument* is *war*." Lakoff extends this theory to political discourse in his books *Moral Politics* (2002) and *Don't Think of an Elephant* (2004), where he discusses the broader implications of how choices in language can reframe or reinforce systems of values. In this case, I wanted to emphasize the values underlying choosing to become a teacher at an open-access institution. I learned early on in my study of traditional rhetoric that coming back to these positive emotions that drive initial motivation, especially for something as fundamental as a career choice, can build a more sustained commitment to change.

As I prepared for the responsibilities of my new position, I began to change both internal resources and public-facing documents away from accountability and reporting back to teaching and learning. Assessment was not just something we needed to do for the Board of Education; it was something we should be doing for our students. Assessment didn't just result in a report renewing our accreditation; it resulted in actionable information to allow us to improve our students' experience in our classes. Assessment wasn't just a part of institutional success; it was a part of effective pedagogy and thus an essential part of being an active, engaged teacher.

Perhaps most important, though, was my decision to eschew the pervasive idea of a "culture of assessment" (Ikenberry and Kuh 2015). This approach appears in a great deal of contemporary scholarship on institutional assessment to describe infusing assessment into most standard practices. The intent here is a good one: to always be considering how we know a practice is an effective one and in what ways. But for my campus, there was so much exhaustion around assessment and its constant changes that I wanted to avoid the word as much as possible, especially as a justification for the changes that we had to undergo as part of the accreditation recommendation. So, instead, I chose to use the idea of "a culture of curiosity" to highlight the actual pedagogical purpose of learning outcomes assessment, using the phrase "I wonder..." when talking to faculty and academic leadership about the assessment work to be done. "I wonder how students are reading these outcomes when they encounter your program documents?" "I wonder how this outcome could be looked at directly in one of your courses?" "I wonder if a timed in-class exam is the most effective way to see how students are learning this thing you want them to learn?" Emphasizing the curiosity that goes into being both a good teacher and a good learner, I hoped, would effectively reframe what was previously considered an onerous task. Framing myself and other faculty as learners in this new process as well also helped to smooth these paths.

Once I had the framing language figured out, I knew I also needed to convince faculty to come along with me on this change, despite the work that it would entail. For this, I looked further into my training in feminist rhetoric, specifically, in what I learned about alternatives to the "*argument* is *war*" framing. My introduction to feminist rhetorics, and one that created a lasting impression on how I approach persuasion, is Foss and Griffin's 1995 work on what they call "invitational rhetoric." In this article, they present the idea that persuasion for conversion to a point of view may be harmful and not truly result in a meaningful understanding. Instead, they advocate for the presentation of perspectives under the principles of "equality, immanent value, and self-determination" (2) with the goal of achieving understanding and collaboration. Setting aside the accountability framing was one step in this rhetorical move. Faculty already knew about it; they had been operating under it for years now. But over the years, I had learned that respect is key in creating sustainable change. Traditional rhetoric gave me a process for constructing effective arguments, but feminist rhetorics, and in particular, invitational rhetoric, gave me a framework to acknowledge an individual's autonomy and value their experience within whatever topic we were discussing. By setting aside the pure goal of persuasion to focus on collaboration, I found new ground on which to push the conversation forward while still meeting the requirements of my job.

So, when I began meeting with faculty in the first months of my new position, I didn't focus on the institutional assessment mandate, the literature on pedagogy, or any other tactic relying on traditional persuasion. Instead, I told them stories about how I thought about my classes and my students, how I saw changes in their confidence and skill as I looked at data I gathered on their learning and made changes in cycles. I described what I wanted my students to learn and how that was demonstrated in their work under a variety of different grading systems and with iterations of assignments that I continued to develop over several semesters. I talked about gathering with my colleagues who taught in the same associate's granting programs I worked in, how we collaborated on defining learning goals for the program, and how the individual courses that we taught all worked together to create a cohesive curriculum that spoke to those program learning outcomes. Then, I asked faculty questions about their own students, what they wanted them to know and be able to do when they complete a course or a program, how they know that students have accomplished these learning goals, how this information helps them to improve their students' experiences from semester to semester.

By focusing on the students, the real reason to look at learning outcomes in the first place, I was able to start showing faculty that the college's new approach to assessment was a positive one that already aligned with their own devotion to student learning. And as I created resources, presented at meetings, and continued to listen and learn about how this approach landed with faculty, I started to see less resistance and apathy to doing the work. I had people reaching out, wanting to know more about how to use assessment to improve their teaching. It wasn't a groundswell, but it was a marked improvement from the attitudes I experienced before I took the position.

Appealing to Credibility: Ethos

Ultimately, I believe that at the heart of leadership lies ethos, the appeal to the audience's sense of the writer/speaker's credibility and character. Nobody looks to leaders for guidance, no matter what level of official authority you may have, unless they believe that you know what you're doing and trust that you have their best interests at heart. I was very fortunate to have some credibility with faculty at my college when I began my new position. Thanks to my visibility as the interim director of faculty development a few years earlier and my more recent work on the Faculty Senate Leadership Committee, I managed to make connections across campus in ways that faculty who remained siloed in their own departments aren't often able to do. That said, I knew that I could lose that goodwill I had accumulated if I were to sweep in and try to demand huge changes in service to the accreditor recommendation we received, even though there was pressure from the college president to do exactly that. At heart, I was and remain a teacher, someone devoted to education, and I believe this regardless of what my job title says; however, much like many faculty who move into administration, I had to show that my character remained unchanged.

I wanted faculty to know that I was with them, that I was one of them. The division between faculty and administration, between compliance and academic freedom, is a common tension in higher education. Part of my attempt to move beyond this tension with faculty was demonstrating shared positive values, like my devotion to teaching through my stories of student learning; however, I also wanted faculty to know that I shared their frustrations as well. In an article that has stuck with me since graduate school, Barry Kroll (2008) likens effective rhetoric to aikido, which, while a form of martial arts and therefore somewhat at odds with the philosophy of invitational rhetoric, provided me a helpful frame for addressing resistance. As Kroll describes, aikido is the "art of peace," focused on principles to do the least amount of harm in a situation where a person cannot back down to defuse a conflict. In my case, despite my wanting faculty to *want* to do assessment as part of effective pedagogy, I knew that the assessment mandate, ultimately, would require faculty to do the work. So, when faculty expressed frustration with assessment, I would agree, that yes, assessment as it had been done, with my predecessor's standardized rubrics and reports that didn't speak to student learning, was a major problem. But, just like faculty do in their departments, we could solve this problem together. I encouraged them to look to their own needs as faculty, at what information could they gather that would help them be better teachers, and I encouraged them to collect this information in systematic ways. Similarly, I acknowledged the shifting assessment expectations over the years, which created uncertainty and new labor every time. I invited faculty to collaborate with me, working through existing power structures and shared governance to create a series of policies and practices that would be codified and enduring. At every step, whether dealing with apathy or outright resistance, I learned that I had to be at the forefront of the change in order to make space for the voices of the teachers that assessment is meant to serve.

In addition to reinforcing my identification with faculty values, I also wanted to bolster my ethos by respecting faculty agency in determining what they felt was valuable. Instead of attempting to impose standardized methods or measures across such a diverse array of programs, thus flattening any meaning the data might have at the individual or program levels, I encouraged faculty to develop their own metrics and instruments that spoke to the epistemologies and methodologies that were meaningful to their own disciplines. As I told our director of institutional research, who expressed some skepticism about this approach's ability to produce quantitatively valid data, our accreditor just requires us to have a system, and this type of assessment could be systematic without being normative. What our campus needed wasn't a simple table of results; it needed an overall picture of student learning, and this could be done with an approach I learned of only after I started my new position. Called "evidence-based storytelling," it emphasizes the use of data, from assessment and other related measures of student success, to present a narrative of institutional learning rather than just a list of decontextualized metrics (Jankowski and Baker 2019). Hearing about this method in a workshop, I was immediately interested in learning more. It seemed to mesh so nicely with the rhetorical framing that I had already been adapting that I quickly found the article (and others that cited it) and integrated the concept into my discussions with faculty. This approach allows me to bring together disparate types of evidence to form a cohesive and coherent view of learning in our programs, emphasizing the teaching and learning philosophy of assessment as well as my character as a teacher, while also speaking to our accreditation compliance needs. Learning that assessment scholarship, which I had previously found to be overly quantitative and prescriptive, could dovetail so nicely with my rhetorical training, encouraged me to dig deeper into the literature and continue to find new ways to adapt to this leadership challenge.

Takeaways

While I addressed individual faculty, faculty senate, and department leadership during that first year, I found my approach turned their skepticism, concern, and frustration into focus and resolve. Upper administration had already made our need clear, but rather than leaning on that mandate to attempt to borrow authority that I didn't hold myself, I kept to my stories as a teacher, my shared frustrations as a faculty member, and my respect for shared governance and faculty expertise. What started as just a few highly motivated individuals approaching me for guidance turned into a flood of emails, phone calls, and invitations to meetings. Assessment processes within departments and on college-wide committees were discussed and revised independently of my intervention, and I saw the culture of curiosity start to gain a foothold through these revisions.

Currently, I am beginning my third year in this position, and we have just finished our mid-cycle accreditation report where our peer reviewers will specifically investigate how well we have addressed this recommendation. Reaching this point hasn't been easy. Adapting the abstraction of rhetorical theory and the very different audience of writing pedagogy to academic leadership took a lot of careful thought and plenty of mistakes along the way. But I've learned that this adaptation is part of becoming a leader. I'm convinced that everyone entering positions like mine, where there is plenty of responsibility but little authority, has a lot that they can bring from their disciplinary training, whatever that might be. We just have to be willing to let go of what we think we know and ask ourselves, "How does this speak to the challenges in front of me?"

As for me, although there have been plenty of bumps along the road, we've made substantial progress towards turning assessment into a meaningful part of teaching and learning at the college. But nothing has made me prouder than a recent note from our director of strategic analysis and accreditation, who is leading the preparation for our evaluation: "I just wanted to let you know I've had meetings with faculty leadership and Chairs' Council to get feedback on the mid-cycle report over the last week and they have a lot to say about every section *except* L[earning] O[outcomes]A[ssessment]. They're always like "Oh, it's been fine, Chris is great, no notes." If that is the current response to the previously onerous task of assessment, I'll take it as lessons well learned and a job well done.

References

Aristotle. 2006. *On Rhetoric: A Theory of Civic Discourse*. Trans. George A. Kennedy. 2nd ed. Oxford University Press.

Community College Research Center. 2022. "Public Funding of Community Colleges." https://ccrc.tc.columbia.edu/publications/public-funding-community-colleges.html.

Council for Higher Education Accreditation. n.d. "Accreditation and Recognition." Accessed November 6, 2024. https://www.chea.org/about-accreditation.

Damasio, Antonio. 2005. *Descartes' Error: Emotion, Reason, and the Human Brain*. Penguin Books.

Foss, Sonja K. and Cindy L. Griffin. 1995. "Beyond Persuasion: A Proposal for an Invitational Rhetoric." *Communication Monographs* 62 (1): 2–18. https://doi.org/10.1080/03637759509376345.

Ikenberry, Stanley O. and George D. Kuh. 2015. "From Compliance to Ownership." In *Using Evidence of Student Learning to Improve Higher Education*, edited by George D., Stanley O. Ikenberry, Natasha A. Jankowski, Timothy Reese Cain, Peter T. Ewell, Pat Hutchings, and Jillian Kinzie. Jossey-Bass.

Jankowski, Natasha A. 2017. "Moving Towards a Philosophy of Assessment." *Assessment Update* 29 (3): 10–11. https://doi.org/10.1002/au.30096.

Jankowski, Natasha A. and Gianina R. Baker. 2019. *Building a Narrative Via Evidence-Based Storytelling: A Toolkit for Practice*. University of Illinois and Indiana University, National Institute for Learning Outcomes Assessment.

Kroll, Barry. 2008. "Arguing with Adversaries: Aikido, Rhetoric, and the Art of Peace." *College Composition and Communication* 59 (3): 451–472. https://doi.org/10.58680/ccc20086407.

Lakoff, George. 2002. *Moral Politics: How Liberals and Conservatives Think*. 3rd ed. University of Chicago Press.

Lakoff, George. 2004. *Don't Think of an Elephant! Know Your Values and Frame the Debate*. Chelsea Green Publishing.

Lakoff, George and Mark Johnson. 2003. *Metaphors We Live By*. University of Chicago Press.

NWCCU (Northwest Commission on Colleges and Universities). 2020. "NWCCU 2020 Standards." https://nwccu.org/standards/.

Suskie, Linda. 2018. *Assessing Student Learning: A Common Sense Guide*. 3rd ed.Jossey-Bass.

Walvoord, Barbara E. 2010. *Assessment Clear and Simple: A Practical Guide for Institutions, Departments, and General Education*. 2nd edition. Jossey-Bass.

CHAPTER 4

Academic Leadership Beyond the Academy

Heidi Estrem, *Idaho State Board of Education*

When I moved from my campus office to the government building that houses the Idaho State Board of Education just over a mile away, I was crossing more than a physical distance. This transition from twenty-two years as a faculty member and writing program leader at a university to the Associate Academic Officer position at a state governing agency would reshape and is reshaping my understanding of what it means to lead in academic contexts. I had spent my career working to thoughtfully advocate for first-year college students through writing program leadership. I was now embracing the opportunity to advocate for all college students in Idaho through work that took me further away from the classroom and closer to the legislative environment.

I initially hesitated to apply for the position. The prospect of year-round, in-person work in a government building seemed constraining compared to the flexibility of faculty life. I loved my work on campus; I had thoughtful, dedicated colleagues, and students continued to amaze and energize me. I enjoyed leading initiatives in first-year writing because our work together was deeply collaborative, and it directly impacted students. Yet I was also thirsty for a new challenge and felt a little too settled in my role. In a state office, I would be physically removed from a university, but I would have the opportunity to serve on behalf of students from an entirely new perspective.

Elaine Maimon, initially a writing scholar and later a university president, writes that presidential leadership must be "transformative rather than transactional" (2018, xvii). Transformative leadership, she writes, "is about shared ownership—buy-in, rather than buying ... transformative leadership is more focused on relationships, more open to multiple interpretations, more adaptable to new situations . . . and capable of paying attention to both the goals themselves and to the process for achieving those goals" (Maimon 2018, 5). adrienne maree brown encourages leaders to focus on love, noting that "the strength of our movement is in the strength of our relationships, which could only be measured by their depth" (2017, 10). This chapter traces echoes of these ideas about transformational, relational leadership through exploring what learning to lead in an educational setting beyond a university looks like. I reflect on what the leadership approaches developed in college writing program leadership have taught me for my work now in broader educational leadership roles.

Learning Through Writing Program Leadership

Early in a PhD program in Composition and Rhetoric, influenced by texts like Elspeth Stuckey's *The Violence of Literacy* (1990) and Paolo Freire's *Pedagogy of Hope* (1990), I realized that there was positive, impactful work to do in the academy beyond the individual classroom or research project. I was drawn to positions where I could influence and improve institutional policies and pedagogies that negatively impact students. I am not a solitary scholar; I thrive most when I'm talking and learning with others. I like to look for "the conversation in the room that only these people at this moment can have," to sharpen ideas through collaboration, to shape large-scale work (such as a college writing curriculum) through small-scale discussions (brown 2017, 41).

Fortuitously, I was hired into an unexpected collaboration in my first academic position as an assistant professor and assistant writing program director at Eastern Michigan University. While only one position was advertised, they were able to hire two of us, and Linda Adler-Kassner joined as the writing program director at the same time.

Our tenure-track faculty positions included reassigned time (from teaching or research) for writing program leadership, and we dove in. I brought with me a hopeful, asset-based view of students from my graduate school experience, and that continued to deepen through extended collaborative leadership work with Linda. In the US context, a "first-year writing program" refers to courses that students complete as part of their general education requirements. In some US institutions, such as the one where Linda and I worked together, these programs are directed by tenure-line (or full-time) faculty. However, because of the large number of courses included in the programs—courses required of many first-year students in large universities—they are often taught by a combination of contingent faculty, tenure-line faculty, and/or graduate students.

Changing the curriculum of a writing program without any additional funding and while mostly relying on the goodwill of everyone involved requires that leaders have the willingness to listen and learn from instructors with widely differing backgrounds and commitments, to look for the conversation that only the "people in the room at that moment" can have. I have good memories of hosting pizza-and-curriculum afternoons in Linda's backyard, encouraging interested instructors to engage and share how and why they taught as they did. Those informal meetings led us to drafting possible approaches, sharing them back with the instructors, listening to input, and drafting again. Linda and I spent hours over tabouli talking and writing and rewriting plans. We encouraged instructors to pilot new approaches and share their results. It was uneven and challenging work, and it engaged me with a wider variety of instructors than I'd previously encountered. Through co-leading that program, I learned that people need multiple ways to be included and engaged; instructors could live with compromise if they also felt truly heard. I also experienced how leading a writing program is a blend of thoughtful cheerleading, pragmatic compromises (we did not implement a perfect curriculum), and joy.

I moved to Boise State in 2006, entering as the director of the first-year writing program and a faculty member in the English Department, a position I held until 2022. I followed a mostly traditional tenure-track academic journey there, earning tenure; researching issues that mattered to me; leading a writing program that was directly connected with student belonging, learning, and retention initiatives; and serving in my university and in national professional organizations. Two leadership projects at the university were especially transformative for me: our statewide work on writing placement and a curriculum project within our program.

Writing placement—how students' capacities are assessed and then how students are "placed" into a first-year writing program—is often represented by a few lines, or maybe a chart, in a university's policy catalog. However, placement can have a substantial impact on students, requiring them to take courses that do not count toward their degree, for example. At Eastern Michigan, I had collaborated with colleagues from across campus to change and improve our writing placement processes, and so when I arrived at Boise State, I saw that the then-required approach, which used standardized tests only, was negatively impacting some students.

First-year writing courses, due to their particular location within a US university as a set of general education courses that are often also graduation requirements, are among those most regularly transferred to other institutions. These courses have a rich disciplinary history of their own and yet are often subject to state placement and credit policies (see Estrem, shepherd, and Duman 2014). This complicated location means that any change in first-year writing requires input and buy-in—not just from the instructors teaching the courses, but also often from external communities like the registrar's office, the provost, advising, and even other community colleges or universities in the area.

Because we were bound by state policy, before I could change writing placement at my institution, I quickly realized that we would also need to engage in this work at the other seven public postsecondary institutions in Idaho. At that time, the English Department chairs and writing program leaders from each institution were meeting annually to discuss various issues of concern. Our conversations shifted from lament into collective action; we worked hard to listen to each other and compromise while also developing a common writing framework that could work for open-access community colleges and research universities (Estrem, shepherd, and Sturman 2018 and 2020). This work unfolded over years, requiring patience and careful listening. We presented plans to the State Board of Education office staff (yes, the place where I now work); we learned about each other's institutional uniqueness and specific student populations. We conducted pilot placement projects and then reported on them to our statewide provosts' council. We wrote together and took those ideas back to our institutions; just as writing is a "social and rhetorical activity," as Kevin Roozen describes, so too is writing leadership (2015). Further, first-year writing curriculum is a "social and rhetorical" enterprise itself, as it is highly contextual—intentional, deliberate, designed for the students and the institutions within them—and it must be "social" in many ways since it is so intertwined with transfer of learning. These years of conversation, experimentation, and proposals resulted in some changed lines in state policy. They also engaged me in a transformative leadership experience that unfolded over time and through compromise and shared trust.

While the placement work took place across the state, another key leadership experience was situated directly within our own first-year writing program. About seven years ago, the associate director of the first-year writing program, dawn shepherd, and I facilitated a years-long curriculum change project at Boise State. Drawing on our commitments to learn better together, we hosted workshops, discussions, and professional learning communities. We sought to lead with humility—"enough humility to learn, to be taught, to have teachers" in our colleagues even as they learned from us (brown 2017, 10). While this change process was quite different from what I'd experienced a decade earlier at Eastern Michigan—it unfolded over years; internal department turmoil added layers of struggle to the work—we sought to hold on to whatever trust we had through conversation and discussion and encouragement. Without shared trust, change becomes nearly impossible (we explore this experience further in Estrem, shepherd, and Shadle 2019).

When our curricular discussions stalled around issues of perceived standardization and a loss of autonomy—a moment that felt loud, messy, and personal—I initially retreated to reflect, process my frustration, and regroup alone. After reminding myself that "adaptive and relational" leadership was what I really valued and wanted to embody, dawn shepherd and I co-wrote course guidance documents with input from others and invited instructors to experiment with them and give feedback (brown 2017, 23). Then, the COVID-19 pandemic hit, and the fragile trust that had been established grew stronger as instructors generously and quickly shared materials, ideas, and strategies for moving to fully online instruction. However, some threads of tension remained, and our "reflexiveness and self-questioning" led to many hours of discussion among the writing program leadership team (Adler-Kassner 2008, 32). This wasn't a seamless leadership experience, and while there were some gains, there was not the widespread impact or buy-in that we'd worked so hard to attain.

Not long after that experience, I read Annie Duke's book *Thinking in Bets (2018).* Her description of how decision-making unfolds in poker helped to frame the curriculum project work for me: "What makes a decision great is not that it has a great outcome. A great decision is the result of a good process, and that process must include an attempt to accurately represent our own state of knowledge. That state of knowledge, in turn, is some variation of 'I'm not sure'" (2019, 27). An effort that felt like a leadership failure ensured that I experienced firsthand how to separate the process from the results. I left that experience with a different kind of humility, deepened through realizing that even the best intentions and the most thoughtful process will lead in unanticipated directions. The lingering regrets helped deepen my empathy for all involved—including myself. My commitments to "consensus-based, systematic, thoughtful processes" as well as to "ongoing, loud, sometimes messy dialogue...to ensure everyone is heard and, hopefully, represented" hadn't been implemented perfectly, but the uneven experience likely taught me more than a "successful" one would have (Adler-Kassner 2008, 32–33).

The State Educational Policy Context

How, then, does my proclivity for collaboration, conversation, and leading with both humility and commitment unfold in a new context here in the office of the State Board of Education? Because most readers of this collection will be more familiar with campus contexts but less so with state agencies, I will briefly describe this aspect of the educational ecosystem before exploring what I continue to learn about leadership in this context.

Idaho is unique in that we have one governing board for all public education. The State Board of Education has constitutional oversight over K–12 education, governs our four public four-year institutions as their Boards of Trustees or Regents, *and* serves as the coordinating board for our four community colleges. So, the full K–PhD span of public education is governed by one board (community colleges also have local governing boards and regularly report to both). Additionally, the State Board of Education governs the Division of Career and Technical Education, Idaho Public Television, and the Division of Vocational Rehabilitation.

The State Board of Education is composed of seven governor-appointed members and the elected superintendent; the Office of the Board of Education (OSBE) is made up of staff like me who support a wide variety of educational initiatives. The Executive Director of OSBE is appointed by the governor and serves as an ex-officio member of the Board. The workload for this part-time volunteer board is staggering: every two months, they read, synthesize, and make decisions that encompass everything from early literacy goal setting to contracts for university buildings to degree program approvals to annual agency reports. In a state like Idaho, where all of education (but especially higher education) is viewed with skepticism and is subject to shrinking state funding, the leadership and vision of the Board is critically important (see Hebel and Smallwood 2021, Jedeed 2024, Guido 2024).

OSBE has teams that focus on academic affairs (the higher education team), planning, policy and government affairs, college and career access, technology, research, finance, and school safety (see "Board Facts"). Within academic affairs, my colleagues and I provide leadership, coordination, and support on a wide range of issues that affect all eight public postsecondary institutions. For example, people on the team I co-lead are responsible for areas including:

- proprietary and online school registrations;
- systemwide academic technologies;
- state research grant funding;
- postsecondary academic program review/approval process; and
- student affairs and dual credit.

The Chief Academic Officer and I facilitate a number of cross-state initiatives, policy development, and implementation projects. He leads the higher education portion of a statewide health care workforce committee, for example; I lead our statewide general education committee and AI professional development coordination. We both coordinate revisions to higher education policy when needed, and we both provide input to the executive director on a wide range of issues impacting higher education, and higher education funding, in our state.

The rhythm of work has shifted for me from the academic calendar to one driven by board meeting cycles and legislative sessions. Instead of semesters—the rhythms of which were very familiar to me—I now work in a two-month Board meeting cadence. While our academic affairs team isn't directly involved in legislative work, we closely monitor education-related bills and provide input when requested. Our physical proximity to the capitol—our building is connected via an underground tunnel—serves as a constant reminder of the political context surrounding our work.

Collaborative State Educational Policy Revision

To illustrate how leadership learning manifests in practice, I'll detail a recent policy revision process that exemplifies both the application of my writing program-developed approaches and the unique demands of state-level leadership. In early 2023, I was asked to initiate a revision of Board Policy III.Q, Admissions Standards. Even though this policy wasn't on our annual review schedule, it was brought to our attention through an Admissions Director at one of our state universities, who met with us to explain that the policy hindered his work with a particular student population. The policy had been written in such a way that highly prepared students had to be admitted through an "alternative admissions" process, which was affecting their recruiting and engagement with these students. Drawing on approaches I had developed through years of facilitating change in and across writing programs, I began by mapping the policy's impact across different stakeholder groups. Just as writing program changes affect students, faculty, and administrators differently, I knew this policy touched multiple constituencies:

- students interested in going on to college;
- high school counselors;
- postsecondary academic advisors;
- admissions officers;
- provosts responsible for institutional planning; and
- board members concerned with system-wide effectiveness.

This stakeholder mapping, informed by Adrianna Kezar and Daniel Maxey's (2016) emphasis on understanding organizational networks, helped me identify potential allies and resistance points before beginning the revision process. The process also highlights how policy revision work at its best is deeply rhetorical and social.

The earlier leadership experiences had taught me that more conversation is better than less, and that a shared governance approach—which we had explicitly committed to on our academic affairs team here at OSBE—meant that I needed to deliberately work around the hierarchy embedded in a Board staff's relationship to the institutions. So first, I met with admissions leaders, as one of them had surfaced the need for a revision. The conversations revealed how current policy was affecting all of our institutions—we just hadn't asked and hadn't realized its impact. Next, I drafted revisions to the policy and sought feedback from those within my office. With a full revision completed, I met again with constituency groups: in this case, admissions officers, and then registrars, and then provosts. As in my earlier work, I found that everyone was willing to engage honestly when they felt their expertise was valued.

The drafting process exemplified what Kezar (2018) calls "convergent leadership": bringing together top-down and bottom-up perspectives. I developed multiple drafts based on community group feedback from registrars and admissions officers, tested proposed language with real-world scenarios, and refined based on practical considerations. Throughout this process, I drew on skills developed through years of writing program leadership. The ability to synthesize multiple perspectives, anticipate implementation challenges, engage community groups to provide purposeful input, and craft language that serves multiple audiences—all crucial writing program leadership skills—proved invaluable in policy development.

I recognized that policy change requires careful attention to rollout and support. In many ways, this policy revision and implementation process was relatively simple; since community groups had been engaged early in the process, they were ready to work within this policy as soon as it was approved. It now moves onto our schedule for regular policy review every few years.

Continuing Leadership Education

Through these experiences, I've deepened several leadership approaches that guide my work. These strategies, while grounded in specific contexts, continue to build from broader themes in Writing Studies scholarship and Kezar's (2018) research on institutional change.

Linda Adler-Kassner's (2008) framework for writing program advocacy provides a useful model for state-level work. She emphasizes the importance of understanding and using institutional narratives, building strategic alliances, connecting local concerns to broader educational values, and using research purposefully, and those strategies—which I practiced in writing programs for decades—also inform my work here. For example, when addressing Board member questions about the role of general education, I used Adler-Kassner's approach to story-changing, helping reframe the narrative from one of inefficiency to one of student success and engagement—and workforce development. I have led an effort to infuse "durable skills" into content-rich general education courses at all eight institutions—starting with pedagogy and curricula before moving to policy revisions—and this work has enabled many external groups to better understand the role and purpose of general education. Writing program leadership is steeped in pragmatic compromise, state leadership even more so. I work and interact with a much wider variety of people with various entry points for understanding postsecondary education. I've come to enjoy this rhetorical challenge.

Adrianna Kezar's (2018) research has been particularly relevant to state-level leadership. Her emphasis on developing "multi-hub networks" that connect different types of change agents resonates with how I have structured statewide initiatives with more communication and more input than I might think is necessary. Our general education reform work now intentionally connects faculty discipline groups, their faculty communities at their home institutions, and the state general education committee (which includes representatives from other groups impacted by general education: dual credit, open educational resources, digital pedagogy, registrars, and technical colleges). All of these networks and interactions swirl to support any change initiatives.

Do leadership and advocacy unfold similarly on campus and in a state educational policy office? In some ways, yes: my commitments to conversation, shared governance, and engaging with stakeholders remains constant. In practice, though, this work feels different in a number of ways. First, writing program leadership takes place in a setting where there is generally a shared discipline and/or commitment to one critical component of the college landscape: first-year writing. When my colleagues and I were working together on curriculum, for example, we might disagree about specific approaches, but we have the shared experience of teaching and learning within first-year writing that informs our discussions. Here in the state office, our networks are differently distributed and cast more widely across eight institutions. Each institution has a different funding capacity, distinct student body populations, and particular local contexts within which they work.

Within a writing program, practice—teaching writing—is the heart of the mission. Curricular guides, program policies, or institutional processes arise in support of that mission. Here in the Board office, policy is more prominent in our work because that is the main way the Board communicates its values and expectations for the postsecondary institutions it governs. There is sometimes a tension between an institution's preference for what is best for its own students and our Board's statewide responsibility to all students, many of whom move across multiple institutions. Part of my job description is to assess how institutions are meeting state policies and address areas where there are gaps—a supervisory role that does not always sit comfortably for me, just as the supervisory aspects of writing leadership were not those that I enjoyed the most. Still, my OSBE colleagues and I work hard to position ourselves as allies and advocates far beyond any role in policy enforcement. Policy is rhetorical; like any public-facing texts, its polish sometimes belies the deeply contextual, relational, and conversational work behind it.

As I continue to settle into this role, I am grateful for the ways in which my decades of campus-level leadership inform what I do and how I do it. Here in the Board office, I am afforded glimpses into the larger educational landscape of our state, and I share Elaine Maimon's perspective that pragmatic liberal education is "essential to democracy" and that is what our state institutions are best at (2018, 127). I feel fortunate to be able to learn from and with colleagues from across eight institutions, all striving to engage students in postsecondary education in ways that are personally relevant and socially meaningful.

References

Adler-Kassner, Linda. 2008. *The Activist WPA*. Utah State University Press.

brown, adrienne maree. 2017. *Emergent Strategy: Shaping Change, Changing Worlds*. AK Press.

Duke, Annie. 2018. *Thinking in Bets: Making Smarter Decisions When You Don't Have All the Facts*. Random House.

Estrem, Heidi, dawn shepherd, and Samantha Sturman. 2018. "Reclaiming Writing Placement." *WPA: Writing Program Administration* 40 (3): 56–71.

Estrem, Heidi, dawn shepherd, and Samantha Sturman. 2020. "Corequisite Writing Courses: Equity and Access." *Composition Studies* 48 (2): 9–17.

Estrem, Heidi, dawn shepherd, and Susan Shadle. 2019. "From Threshold Concepts to Learning Outcomes: Developing a Shared Framework for First Year Writing." In *(Re)Considering What We Know: Theory and Practice of Threshold Concepts in Writing Studies*, edited by Linda Adler-Kassner and Elizabeth Wardle. Utah State University Press.

Estrem, Heidi, dawn shepherd, and Lloyd Duman. 2014. "Relentless Engagement with State Educational Policy Reform." *WPA: Writing Program Administration* 38 (1): 88–128.

Freire, Paulo. 1995. *Pedagogy of Hope*. Continuum.

Guido, Laura. October 24, 2024. "DEI Task Force Focuses on Higher Ed and Limiting 'Social Justice Ideology.'" *KTVB*. https://www.ktvb.com/article/news/local/idaho-press/dei-task-force-higher-ed-limiting-social-justice-ideology/277-2df7ee99-9faf-4d72-b083-e04221b6102c.

Hebel, Sarah and Scott Smallwood. 2021. "What A Deep Distrust of Higher Ed Looks Like." *Open Campus Media*. March 18. https://www.opencampusmedia.org/2021/03/18/what-a-deep-mistrust-of-higher-ed-looks-like/.

Idaho State Board of Education. n.d. "Board Facts." Accessed January 12, 2024. https://boardofed.idaho.gov/board-facts/.

Jedeed, Laura. 2024. "North Idaho College Was Taken Over by the Far-Right—It's a Warning for the Future of Higher Ed" *Teen Vogue*. October 16. https://www.teenvogue.com/story/north-idaho-college-far-right.

Kezar, Adrianna. 2018. *How Colleges Change: Understanding, Leading, and Enacting Change*. Routledge.

Kezar, Adrianna J. and Daniel Maxey. 2016. *Envisioning the Faculty for the Twenty-First Century: Moving to a Mission-Oriented and Learner-Centered Model*. Rutgers University Press.

Maimon, Elaine M. 2018. *Leading Academic Change: Vision, Strategy, Transformation*. Stylus.

Roozen, Kevin. 2015. "Writing is a Social and Rhetorical Activity." In *Naming What We Know*, edited by Linda Adler-Kassner and Elizabeth Wardle. Utah State University Press.

Stuckey, Elspeth. 1990. *The Violence of Literacy*. Heinemann.

CHAPTER 5

Practice Giving as a Way of Learning Leadership

Jeffrey T. Grabill, *University at Buffalo, State University of New York*

The week I sat down to write the first draft of this chapter, I was in a meeting on "listening and leadership," and I had a conversation there with a colleague who asked me a question about where and how I learned to be a leader. The question and the conversation focused on how and where academics learn to lead and made me think about where in my career I learned to lead.

There was never any direct instruction. I taught for a long time, including, delightfully, lots of first-year students. I researched, wrote, revised, and resubmitted. I started and led a research center. I became a department chair not because I wanted to but because I felt I needed to, and that kicked off a set of more senior roles that weren't part of a plan but have been fun and educational. Along the way, I have been led, ably and clumsily, and I have led myself, ably and clumsily. As a way into this chapter and drawing from those experiences, let me start with some patterns that have been descriptive of my experiences in higher education and that have become resources for how I think about leadership.

1. We tend to confuse management and leadership. These are two different and often complementary ways of thinking and behaving, and most leadership development in higher education that I have seen or experienced is focused on management. That is, the programming is likely to cover issues like budgeting basics, managing promotion and tenure processes, hiring, or

performance reviews and not the leadership issues I will address in this chapter. Academic cultures in the UK are heavily focused on management to the detriment of leadership conversations. Academics need both the tactical management skills and leadership skills that I would associate with what Beronda Montgomery describes as "cultivation and enactment of leadership philosophies and progressive vision" (2020, 1). We need higher education institutions to match the significant investments other organizations make in their people to develop effective leaders. We rarely see those investments.

2. For our most senior leaders, we want, as a former president of Georgetown University is said to have quipped, "God on a good day." This expectation is perhaps one reason why we are so disappointed with our leaders. This might also be one reason that senior roles are unattractive to those who might be good at them—and why those same roles burn out those who take them. This speaks to the need for higher education to understand leadership and its development as part of everyone's career pathway. Doing so would provide us with a shared language, a shared sense of purpose, and hopefully shared humility about how difficult it is to lead and be led.
3. Leadership is a team sport, not an individual sport. If we select leaders focused primarily on their own goals and outcomes and reward that way of leading, we should expect outcomes directed toward individual rather than community advancement. This insight matters because we need leaders committed to making those around us better, building teams, and creating strong communities.
4. All work begins and ends in relationships. Break relationships, and there is nothing.

These patterns are foundational for how I think about leadership in higher education. Put simply, leadership is not management. Leaders create conditions for others to thrive. Leadership can never be transactional. It must be relational. This last issue, relationships, has been bedrock for my entire career as a teacher, a researcher, a leader, and a human being. It is also the most fragile of principles because more often than not, the transactional trumps the relational. More challenging still, "short termism," or the drive to return immediate term results over longer term investments, dominates leadership and management incentives. Managing short-term outcomes may produce efficiency but is unlikely to produce effectiveness or community. If, as Paul LeBlanc (2020) argues, we live in a moment in which our social systems, including higher education, are fundamentally broken, then the way to put them together again requires leaders to dwell in the relational and long-term.

Effective leadership requires that we have ideas about how to lead and who we want to be, what I will call "dispositions" in this chapter. But for the most part, leadership lives in our behaviors, and ultimately it is our behaviors that tell others who we really are and which dispositions we embody. The nice thing is that we can practice behaviors, and in practicing, we learn and become. We can learn to lead by practicing, too, and one outcome of intentional practice (and learning) is that we become different sorts of people. We become leaders. To be concrete and focused in this chapter, I choose one behavior, and that is *to give*, which is something we can practice at any point in our career.

Dispositions as a Leadership Foundation

I spent nearly twenty years of my career at Michigan State University (MSU), and in that time, as noted above, I was able to experience much of what higher education has to offer an academic. But I also had some unusual experiences, such as starting an educational technology company. Late in my time there, the provost asked me to take on a new role as an associate provost for teaching, learning, and technology. In my last year at MSU, influenced by the experience of the COVID-19 pandemic and leadership failures at that university (and my experience of how people responded to those failures), I decided to run an experimental version of one of our internal leadership development programs. That program was in my portfolio as an associate provost. I didn't think our existing approach, which was focused on didactic experiences and content that

I'd term management-focused, was appropriate for the moment. So we crafted an experience focused on an unusual (for MSU) set of leadership dispositions, cohort activities centered on reflection, and—since participants were in leadership roles—connecting our reflections to our day-to-day work as leaders.

The program started with some work on "leadership as learning," which established the program as genuinely developmental. In other words, the goal of the program and the work we did together was to enable participants "to *practice* and/or *perform* leadership" as our way to realize this developmental goal of leading and learning at the same time. What that meant varied by the participant, but one thing was shared. We wanted each participant to explore how to help *others* grow and improve. We then went on to work through the following dispositions:

- Purpose and vision
- Integrity and trust
- Curiosity

To which I will add here *kindness*, which I wish we'd included at the time. This list of dispositions is a good foundation for leadership if we are going to lead in ways focused on relationships and longer-term outcomes. But we would struggle to find these dispositions listed together in any "position description" for a senior leadership role at a college or university.

We spent the most time on purpose and vision in our program. With purpose and vision, our reading and reflection focused on the need to be clear with regard to purpose, both for oneself and with others, and on how to develop a shared vision related to that purpose. Purpose is a story about why we exist, and vision tells us where we are headed together. A focus on purpose was initially experienced as odd because in higher education our purpose, to many, seemed obvious. Yet upon reflection, it became clear that universities have many purposes, and they are sometimes in conflict.

We braided together integrity and trust because building trust requires acting with integrity. Trust seems such a rare commodity in the workplace (sadly), including academic workplaces, and building trust requires overcoming skepticism if not also cynicism via behaviors such as predictability and consistency, listening well (see curiosity below), and connecting transparency with accountability. This last issue is particularly challenging in an organization with talented and creative people accustomed to high levels of autonomy and who want transparency but are less keen on accountability. When transparency and accountability are braided together, it can really supercharge a team or organization. As my colleague Michelle Hayward at Bluedog Design writes, "transparency fuels accountability. Talented people cannot be accountable for what they can't see or understand. The more effort that goes into fueling their ability to make great decisions for the business, given their proximity to the client outcomes, the greater our collective success" (Weiner 2018). That is, people in a team or organization need to be able to see and understand purpose and how the organization is trying to achieve that purpose in order for them to carry out their work effectively.

Curiosity is the leadership disposition that most surprised participants. It was not a disposition participants immediately associated with leadership (in contrast with something like "courage"). And upon reflection, we found it rare in our lived experiences of leadership.

We grounded our reading in the experiences of people in creative industries and those who work with creative professionals because that is the place to find a conversation about the role of creativity in effective teams. Yet I think it's obviously the case that people in higher education are highly creative, and literature on creativity in teams and organizations is insightful (e.g., Kelly and Kelly, 2015). In practice and as a set of behaviors, curiosity is often visible in those who listen well, those who seek to understand, and in those who ask genuine questions.

While we didn't reflect on kindness in that program, it is the disposition that I would add here based in particular on my leadership experiences post-pandemic. Kindness is a forgotten virtue and easily dismissed. It is not niceness (though being nice is, well, nice). Kindness requires us to be vulnerable. Kindness, as Barbara Phillips and Adam Taylor write in their book *On Kindness*, is "the ability to bear the vulnerability of others, and therefore of oneself" (Phillips and Taylor 2010, 6). It is a virtue grounded in empathy, curiosity, and perhaps most importantly, imagination, specifically "our imaginative capacity to identify with other people" (Phillips and Taylor 2010, 54). Kindness is one of the virtues that returns more than we give (more on giving below). That is, in imagining the lives of others, in identifying with what they might need from us, and in trying to provide that to them, we feel and become more fully human.

The leadership literature is full of dispositions, so they must clearly matter, though the relationship between dispositions and behaviors is sometimes challenging to see in that literature. I'd suggest that dispositions are essential because they index values. That is, dispositions point to or indicate values, and if one is practicing (and learning) leadership by way of a set of dispositions, there will be attendant values that should be visible in behaviors. Dispositions might constitute, along with other issues (e.g., good management guidance), part of a conceptual understanding of leadership. But I think it is important to understand *how* dispositions mean in leadership development and practice. They can be practiced and developed. They are both learned and revealed as a function of behaviors. Leadership is a *verb*. Our leadership dispositions (and cultures) live in our behaviors. The ways in which we behave don't simply express a set of dispositions. They are how we come to have them. Dispositions and leadership can be developed. They can be learned.

Learning Leadership by Practicing Giving

The way that I think about learning leadership is shaped by my own intellectual history as a student of rhetoric, which is relevant in terms of how I will frame learning as having artistic qualities. By "artistic" I don't mean something like aesthetics. I mean *techne*: a transferrable body of knowledge that is typically composed of theoretical concepts to be learned, methods to guide practice, and lots of practice to realize benefits. Leadership is artistic in the sense that it has (any number of) theoretical frameworks and orientations (any leadership reading list would suggest so) and methods to guide practice. And like many such things, leadership is learned by practicing: writing and revising, making and remaking, acting and reacting.

One pathway to learn to lead is for a learner to move from conceptual understanding (belief) into habits (behaviors) that become internalized, and based on that, transformation (becoming). This is an artistic pathway for the embodiment of a virtue: believe, behave, become. It is not a linear pathway—what we become is as much about our behavior as it is about what we believe. Dispositions are important because they are part of a conceptual understanding of what it means to be a leader or what leadership looks like. Dispositions started, at least for me, as ideas. But for a leadership identity to be coherent and fully artistic, those same dispositions must live in our behaviors. That is, if curiosity is part of our leadership practice, it's not enough to simply be an idea we believe in. We must behave with curiosity. If we do this enough (if we practice enough), then we are curious.

The answer to my colleague's question at the start of this chapter about how I learned to lead is "to practice," which should be understood in two ways: (1) as a habitual pattern of activity, and (2) as doing something again and again, to learn. I will focus more on the second meaning here. Practicing is the only way that behaviors become habitual. Practicing is the only way that the ideas we believe about leadership become part of our identity as a leader. Indeed, when we experience a gap between what a leader says they believe and what we observe in their behaviors, we are seeing something real. We are seeing, perhaps, an individual whose leadership practice and identity are in development. Or someone on a bad day. We might also be seeing a leadership practice that will be experienced as confusing and contradictory. What and how we practice determines who we become as leaders. If we aspire to lead with curiosity, for example, then we need to practice it. We can say we believe in curiosity all we want—we can claim the disposition—but we only become curious by behaving curious. We practice that curiosity as leaders by taking the time to get to know our colleagues, how they experience their work, and what motivates them. We practice curiosity by seeking to understand why people make the choices they make or why systems produce the outcomes they produce before moving too quickly to solutions. Who we are as leaders is determined by the dispositions we express and the cultures we model via our behaviors.

To be clear, I want others to practice the behaviors that align with the dispositions I've shared in this chapter. I want my colleagues to be that kind of leader. I want to be led by that kind of a leader. In that regard, I am making an argument here for a set of leadership ideas. Yet the challenging part of the answer to my colleague's question that opens this chapter is located in what to practice as a way to *learn* leadership. There are any number of appropriate behaviors to practice that align with the dispositions above. I'm choosing giving here because giving is accessible to each of us. The barrier to practice is low.

In making that choice, I am guided here, as we were in that leadership program at MSU, by work such as Adam Grant's on giving. He provides an extended example. In his book *Give and Take: Why Helping Others Drives Our Success* (2013), Grant focuses on our interactions with others—what he calls, perhaps surprisingly, a neglected variable in success or failure. The fact that he names interactions between people as a neglected variable should tell us a great deal about why organizations and systems might be broken. He writes that "every time we interact with another person at work, we have a choice to make: do we try to claim as much value as we can, or contribute value without worrying about what we receive in return?" (Grant 2013, 4). Grant goes on to note that in the workplace, givers are rare. More common by far are takers or matchers (those who seek always to balance the scales). Givers are just as intentional as takers or matchers. Grant notes that if you're a giver at work, "you simply strive to be generous in sharing your time, energy, knowledge, skills, ideas, and connections with other people who can benefit from them" (Grant 2013, 5). Yet while givers are inclined to help others without expecting anything in return, that isn't always the case. They also do cost-benefit analyses and have their limits (I've learned that transactional people and relationships eventually drive me to set boundaries, for instance).

In a transactional workplace (and world), does giving give one an advantage? Does it win? Or is it for losers, just as kindness is wrongly thought to be for losers? Grant wrote a book on givers because it is valuable. But giving is complicated. As he works through some of the evidence early in his book for why giving might be useful, Grant notes that both the best and worst performers are givers. He notes that "the answer [to if it "works"] is less about raw talent or aptitude [among the givers], and more about the strategies givers use and the choices they make" (Grant 2013, 10). He goes on, "successful givers are every bit as ambitious as takers and matchers. They simply have a different way of pursuing their goals" (Grant 2013, 10).

To illustrate, Grant tells the story of a venture capitalist (VC) who is a giver—intentionally so—in a context in which there is lots of transactional, taking behavior. I want to use this story to provide more detail on what giving behaviors look like. I have no idea what dispositions our VC has or what he believes in. I don't know if he is curious or kind, though I suspect he might be. What we can see from this story is the intentional way that an individual *practices behaviors*.

As a giver, the VC shares ideas and insights. He gives away more time and attention than others. He invites competitors to share platforms with him. He takes less value in companies than other investors. Yet despite this—or maybe because of it, at least initially—the VC is rejected by an entrepreneur in whom he really wanted to invest and to whom he had given a great deal of time and a number of ideas. The entrepreneur felt our VC wouldn't challenge him enough.

Eventually the entrepreneur reconsiders his original decision and invites the VC to invest in a second (and typically less valuable) round. Our VC accepts the offer to invest in that second round, and not long after, he significantly contributes to the company's success. As we might expect given the argument of Grant's book, the VC's success isn't unique. Our giving VC is highly successful. He doesn't approach his work in this way because he is a good person or a nice person (he may be). It's not about his personality or his leadership dispositions, which are unknown to us. The VC behaves in this way because it works to help others grow and develop, which is the core of his leadership practice (to help others succeed). For him, giving wins, and he practices it with intentionality.

Grant notes that most organizations approach leadership development by identifying high potential individuals and providing them with the support they need to develop. This seems reasonable, yet in an organization full of talented professionals, careful attention needs to be paid to what constitutes "talent." The talent that is in evidence in a successful researcher or a remarkable teacher might not be the same talents that align with the leadership behaviors and outcomes we want in our organizations. As we might expect, Grant isn't a fan of a talent-first approach to identifying leaders. For him, motivation to learn and grow is far more important. For me, I've learned to look for givers and for those with a record of building strong teams. They make others around them better. Grant argues that those who developed into high performers didn't necessarily start that way and weren't often identified early. That is, they didn't present as "talented," particularly early in their lives and careers. Instead, these individuals were often deeply interested in the work or craft or sport—we might say they were deeply *curious*—and they had teachers who were caring, kind, patient and made learning fun (Grant 2013, 104–105). That is, they were well led.

Grant's argument is that the best leaders are those capable of developing people into high performers and leaders, and again, that is certainly what I have learned in my own practice. The takeaway for organizations is to think differently about those we identify for leadership development and how we coach and support people into role-based leadership. Following Grant's lead, I wouldn't necessarily start with the "high performers," which in higher education is likely to be those with the strongest research metrics. I'd look for the dispositions that I've argued for here. I would look for those with purpose and vision, those who act with integrity, those who demonstrate curiosity, and those trusted by others. We see dispositions most clearly in behaviors, so what people do would be more important than what people say. I'd seek to develop those dispositions by providing people with opportunities to practice in contexts that are caring, kind, patient, and risk tolerant.

Giving can be practiced, and I do believe that if one wants to learn to lead, practicing giving is the place to start. We can model and coach behaviors like giving. We can reward and reinforce them organizationally. In fact, we should be good at this in higher education because in many ways, giving runs deep in academic value systems. Most academics give away their intellectual capital every day. We teach. We are eager to publish our ideas and share them as widely as possible. For free. Many of us have made giving things away an explicit operating principle. The research center I ran with Bill Hart-Davidson for years at MSU was explicit in this regard, and that was one of the primary places in which we tried to model, mentor, and develop people.[1] We were intentional about creating platforms for people to share. We gave ideas away willingly in the expectation that in the end, much more would come back to us. And it did, mostly in the form of people who were curious and kind and loving.

Most importantly, one does not need to have a leadership role to practice a powerful leadership behavior. No matter who we are, no matter where we are located in higher education, and no matter what we do, we can choose to be a giver and practice giving each day in our work because leadership and its development must be part of everyone's career pathway. When we do that, we will learn a great deal about ourselves and others. We will learn what works and doesn't. We will learn when to stop giving. We will learn so much about the teams we are part of and the organizations we work in. In our teams and organizations, we will develop a shared language, a shared sense of purpose, and hopefully shared humility about how difficult it is to lead and be led. And if we

1 Bill was the Associate Dean of Research and Graduate Studies and a Professor in the Department of Writing, Rhetoric, and Cultures at Michigan State. We worked together for more than twenty years until he passed away suddenly and far too young in 2024. Bill was a giver, which can clearly be seen in this tribute to him: https://cal.msu.edu/news/associate-dean-remembered-for-personal-and-professional-impact-at-msu-and-beyond/.

stick with it, we will become a different sort of person. Perhaps a better person. Perhaps a leader.

References

Grant, Adam. 2013. *Give and Take: Why Helping Others Drives Our Success.* Penguin Press.

Kelly, Tom, and David Kelly. 2015. *Creative Confidence: Unleashing the Creative Potential within Us All.* Harper Collins.

LeBlanc, Paul. 2022. *Broken: How Our Social Systems are Failing Us and How We Can Fix Them.* Matt Holt.

Montgomery, Beronda L. 2020. "Academic Leadership: Gatekeeping or Groundskeeping?" *The Journal of Values-Based Leadership* 13 (2): 1–15. https://doi.org/10.22543/0733.132.1316.

Phillips, Adam, and Barbara Taylor. 2010. *On Kindness.* Penguin.

Weiner, Yitzi. 2018. "Michelle Hayward of Bluedog Design: Why You Need to Drive Transparency Through the Organization." *Medium.* January 8. https://medium.com/thrive-global/drive-transparency-through-the-organization-words-of-wisdom-with-michelle-hayward-founder-and-f2e1f20558d6.

CHAPTER 6

Lessons from a Black Feminist (Interim) Dean

Can I Bring My Authentic Self?

Staci Perryman-Clark, *Western Michigan University*

If I were to answer the question posed by the subtitle of this chapter, today's answer would be "no," or at least "not yet." This is a story with lessons learned from serving as the interim dean of my institution's university college, Merze Tate College. Merze Tate College was named after the first Black woman to earn a bachelor's degree from Western Michigan University. It is a story of pain, strength, and healing. It is a reality for Black women in leadership. It is accurate; it is true.

This chapter addresses double standards in Black women's leadership and examines instances of pushback, resistance, and hostility related to leadership. I also critique diversity, equity, and inclusion (DEI) performance rhetoric, a performance that I argue brings "lip service" (Perryman-Clark 2023) to DEI advocacy yet does not seek to dismantle systemic oppression. Finally, I offer cautions learned for Black women leaders and accomplices who desire to see Black women succeed within the academy. With these cautions, I strongly recommend leaders make space to journal what they observe and feel and then take moments to provide advice for future leaders based on their journaling.

What Did I Learn about Leadership Before Becoming an Interim Dean?

During my first year as a doctoral student, I took a Contemporary Issues in Composition Studies course, where the faculty member invited any interested graduate students to tag along with her as she did a workshop on administrative work at a regional campus. Thinking any job-shadowing opportunity would be useful, I was the only student to volunteer despite not really knowing much about administrative work. This experience led to being an assistant director for first-year writing, an experience I've written about with my colleague, Colin Craig, in previous writing program administration (WPA) scholarship (Craig and Perryman-Clark 2011). My work with WPA scholarship provided a substantial foundation for understanding leadership, starting with my experience as director of first-year writing as a new tenure-track professor, a role I held for eight years at Western Michigan University (WMU), my current institution.

While serving as WPA, I took on an additional leadership opportunity as the associate director of the Office of Faculty Development (OFD), where I strategized developing writing across the curriculum (WAC) with diversity, equity and inclusion (DEI) programming, an experience I've written about previously when discussing implications for leadership, DEI, and WAC programs (Perryman-Clark 2023). The visibility of administrative leadership outside of a department or academic program would shape the leadership opportunities I was afforded to grow, advancing to an associate dean, a department chair, and eventually an interim dean.

Beyond these opportunities, I also sought campus and national leadership development programs. Based on my work with the OFD, I was selected to complete WMU's Academic Leadership Academy, where the curriculum focused on understanding the national higher education landscape, the campus landscape and community, and theories of leadership, including emotional intelligence. During my first year as an associate dean of WMU's Lee Honors College, I completed administrative training for new department chairs and associate deans.

After briefly returning to faculty, my then-provost sponsored my participation in the HERS Leadership Institute for women looking to advance in higher education leadership. As interim dean of Merze Tate College, I returned to HERS once again to complete the Next Stages program for women looking to advance into higher levels of senior leadership. I found Next Stages beneficial because it gave me an opportunity to prepare job application material and learn tips on interviewing; it even addressed how internal and interim candidates should conduct themselves during the search process. One key piece of advice that they provided for internal/interim candidates was not to campaign for the position. At the time, I disagreed with this advice, believing I needed to know where my support was. In hindsight, though, this advice was sound, and I wish I had listened. As I will share via my experiences as interim dean, the vocal support I believed to be there actually was not. Perhaps I campaigned too hard and made staff feel uncomfortable by knowing my interests and how much I really wanted to be their dean. But I wanted to demonstrate the transparency that many staff felt lacked with senior leadership. Nonetheless, in retrospect, I find myself wanting to find the balance between transparency and being too loose or too revealing.

While I went by the book (for the most part), taking opportunities to participate in campus and national leadership development programs as recommended by various provosts and academic administrators at my institution, which were often framed as prerequisites for future campus leadership opportunities, none of these formalized programs prepared me adequately to think about leadership from the perspective of a Black woman. I even attempted to design a campus leadership program built around DEI issues, but even the leadership program I developed for my campus could not replace the experience of being a Black woman leader. When I went through leadership programs and developed my own, there were no handbooks or manuals to consult when actively dealing with microaggressions. In fact, one leadership program simply acknowledged that while biases exist, academia is very traditional, and they expect traditional decorum. One leadership consultant even admitted that despite institutions' willingness to consider non-traditional qualifications, academics remain snobbish and expect traditional academic rank. Amplifying this assertion to me suggests clear biases against women and racial minorities who don't have the same access to traditional opportunities. I took away the idea that I would have to assimilate to be successful, but I resisted assimilationist discourse and vowed to be true to my values and convictions, especially given that I possessed a traditional academic background with substantial leadership experience and the academic rank of full professor. In my own hiring decisions, I vowed not to be solely focused on tradition and would adopt practices that looked beyond tradition, a framework that led to quite a few successful hires under my leadership. Still, based on my own consequences, I learned that perhaps there is a double standard for Black women leaders.

What a Story It Would Be...

One of the most challenging times I've had as a Black woman leader occurred when a new provost arrived at my institution. Upon meeting him shortly after his arrival, the first thing he said to me was that he had heard wonderful things about me and he needed to get me "more money," without me even asking him for a higher salary or more leadership opportunities. I expressed to him my interest in a newly created associate provost for DEI position he created after his arrival.

Fast forward to May 2023, when I was a finalist for the new position: the inaugural associate provost for equity-centered initiatives. Given my experience in DEI and the work stemming from my 2023 book, *The New Work of Writing Across the Curriculum: Diversity and Inclusion, Collaborative Partnerships, and Faculty Development*, I felt more than prepared to serve. The provost and many others on campus encouraged me to apply. In 2023, I was stunned to receive a phone call from the same provost asking me to consider serving as Interim Dean of Merze Tate College because the then-dean resigned to take a provost role at another institution. He asked me about my long-term aspirations. I shared that I had provostial and presidential aspirations. He told me that if I wanted to be a provost, a dean's role would prepare me better than the associate provost role, for which I was a finalist. I asked him point blank if I should withdraw my application, and the provost (as he often would say) said he could not tell me what to do but to consider it as a plan B option if I was not selected for the associate provost role he created.

As the process progressed, I received a few additional calls from the provost, letting me know he knew how competitive the pool was for the associate provost role. He acknowledged that he knew candidates personally in the pool and told me it included many "heavy hitters." At the time, I didn't let this shake my confidence; I remember telling him to "bring it on" because I also considered my work comparable to the work of a heavy hitter as someone who had previously served as an acting dean, associate dean, department chair, and chair of the Conference on College Composition and Communication (CCCC), the flagship organization in Writing Studies. Though confident, a small part of me felt insulted by the insinuation that there *could be* heavier hitters in the pool with whom I wasn't competitive. I decided to complete my finalist presentation and trust the process.

In June 2023, the provost's office formally called for nominations for interim dean. I was informed that I was nominated and asked to submit a cover letter and CV, and I submitted my materials as requested. Unusual for the process the institution used for appointing interims, the provost asked me to give a public presentation of my vision for the college, a request given while I was vacationing in Saint Thomas, US Virgin Islands, and celebrating my twentieth wedding anniversary. At the same time, I learned that I would have to have my gallbladder removed. Uncertain of the potential impact of the upcoming medical procedure, I spent part of my vacation preparing a public presentation and delivered the presentation the day before my surgery.

I will be the first to admit that while competent, the presentation was not my strongest, considering the time I was given to prepare. But I learned that I was the only candidate who submitted materials offering to serve as the interim dean. In the meantime, I heard cautionary tales from colleagues across campus about why I should not take the position. Some claimed that staff were used to doing whatever they wanted, that it was toxic. But I am (for better or for worse) drawn to opportunities where problems are to be addressed and things to be fixed, so I didn't consider withdrawing, despite the warnings.

The day after the presentation, I missed a call from the provost on the way home from the hospital from my outpatient procedure. Still woozy, I sent a text reply that I'd just had surgery and was going home to recover, to which he told me to focus on my recovery. A few days later, I returned his call, and he informed me that he wanted to debrief my presentation. He said that while I provided a clear and powerful vision for the college, the feedback expressed that I was not a viable candidate because I was "arrogant" and only talked about myself (even though I laid out a clear vision and structure for the college absent of any mentioning of me). The feedback also said that I had made a comment that I was "famous" for specific research and scholarship, which was a put-off to attendees. I was then coached to limit the frequency of talking about myself to one slide and to change language referring to "fame." In other words, I was told to minimize my accomplishments to appease the college staff I would work with. The provost said that only 25 percent of the feedback saw me as a viable candidate despite being the only candidate and that if I assumed the role, I would need to win them over. Given the feedback, I initially decided that I would not take on the role of interim dean and would remain a candidate for the associate provost for equity-centered initiatives.

A few days later, though, the associate dean and assistant dean of Merze Tate College contacted me, pleading with me not to let the naysayers win. Both were strong Black women who vowed to work collaboratively with me, promising to place sisterhood over white supremacy. One of the two had a contract up for renewal, which had been in jeopardy after the college staff completed a 360-degree review and survey for her with strongly negative results. Given the biases associated with evaluations of women faculty of color, in addition to the fact that systemically, Black women are often targeted in evaluations (Bell et al. 2021), I was not at all surprised to hear about her feedback. The same personnel evaluated my presentation poorly without having even met or interviewed me. Given my strong commitment to sisterhood, I decided to take a risk and serve as interim dean and withdrew from the associate provost role, a decision that pleased the provost, who said the interim dean role would be a wonderful opportunity for me.

As I prepared to serve as interim dean, the provost promised the role under a few conditions but refused to put any promise in writing. Because the college's infrastructure was important for helping the institution meet its retention goals, the provost said that I could serve in the role permanently if (1) I didn't "piss the staff off," and (2) I kept the retention metrics for the university moving in a positive direction, promises I kept until leaving the role. He urged me to "win these people over" and that everything would be fine. To persuade me to choose Merze Tate College, the provost said, "Wouldn't you want to make history as the first Black woman to lead a college named after a Black woman? What naysayers would challenge that narrative? I'm not going to tell you what to do, though. It must be your decision." I hoped for the best but prepared for the worst. I was becoming increasingly uncomfortable with the political maneuvering as if people's lives were simply chess pieces to place strategically on a game board. My intuition would later prove accurate. Trust your gut and see the warning signs early, even if you are optimistic about the work and the experience.

Life as an Interim Dean and the Red Flags

Despite the promises of a permanent dean role, I began to see quickly how my time as an interim dean would be temporary. First, I was required to apply for the permanent dean position. At the same time, a man, white and cis-hetero, was given a different permanent position without any prior higher education experience, knowledge or service to my institution and without having to apply for his position—yet I was required to apply for the dean role despite past higher education leadership experience at the same institution. My predecessor had occupied two administrative roles: the Dean of Merze Tate College and the vice provost for teaching and learning. The provost clarified that he planned to split this role into two positions, staffed by two personnel. The provost did not conduct a formal search for the vice provost for teaching and learning, instead appointing an acquaintance from the provost's past institution, despite said candidate lacking higher education experience. While the provost brought the person to campus to meet staff and leaders, the provost offered him a permanent position without posting the position or seeking nominations. He did not qualify for a tenured position because he had no prior higher education experience, which is perhaps why the role was changed from a vice provost role to an associate vice president. In contrast, I was a full professor with multiple years of leadership experience who was relegated to an interim role. I was also qualified to assume an associate or vice provost role in teaching and learning given my previous experience and scholarship in faculty development.

When the time came for office assignments, I did not have a dedicated office or space. The office occupied by the former dean of Merze Tate College was reserved for the new associate vice president for teaching and learning, even though it would be three months before he would arrive. A staff member in Merze Tate College vacated space on the third floor in a separate staff wing for me to occupy. Thus, the dean's office was a former staff member's office down the hall, tucked away in a difficult place to find. A couple of months into my interim tenure, I identified a space owned by the college that was no longer occupied. After consultation with my associate dean and assistant dean, we agreed that it would be an appropriate space to transform into a dean's suite like other colleges at the institution had. The former dean had earmarked carryforward funds and fundraised money to redesign the college's designated space and signage. While some staff questioned the appropriateness of an interim dean renovating and designing a dean's suite, the bottom line was that any dean would need a designated space for their office, their executive assistant's office (I shared an executive assistant with the associate vice president for teaching and learning for six months, but was in the process of hiring my own), a new business manager (this position was shared with the associate vice president for teaching and learning as well), and a conference room for meetings (the college had no designated space for meetings, and we had to request to meet in borrowed spaces for all meetings). So, even if I would not reap the benefits of working in a dean's suite (and I didn't), the new or permanent dean would need this space. At the end of the day, the provost approved using funds to renovate the space, even though the process of obtaining approval seemed like sharecropping all over again.

Another red flag concerned transparency and trust by the dean's leadership team members. Shortly after I arrived at the college, I was briefed on complaints from one of the departments concerning a hostile work environment, workplace bullying, and other toxic behaviors. Several of the complaints identified racism and microaggressions as the cause. Given the information I was provided in writing, I alerted the provost, who suggested I contact our institution's office of institutional equity. I followed the process. From institutional equity's perspective, they identified the matter as a human resources issue and not an equity issue. Their finding did not surprise me; as I have argued with colleagues elsewhere, "Institutions need to equip diversity and institutional equity offices with the authority and independence to identify and respond to complaints and prioritize justice more than protecting the institution from potential lawsuits" (Richardson et al. 2024, 144).

Because the unit in question also reported to my associate dean, I gathered information from her. I trusted her assessment, as she had supervised the unit from day one. She decided to investigate the matter and stated she was working with human resources during the process. She also hired a DEI consultant (approved by the former dean) to work with the unit. The problem with the consultant was that she brought in another employee, the spouse of the department's director, who had been identified as the problem. After learning this, I contacted the provost and general counsel to discuss potential conflicts of interest. When I shared the responsibility of reporting this with my associate dean, she chastised me and said I didn't need to tattle everything to the provost, stop micromanaging her, and let her handle it. We had a lengthy discussion and disagreement about my handling of the matter. Upon finding out the nature of the consultant relationship, I learned that the consultant was a friend of the associate dean who hired her, which is perhaps why she did not want me to refer the matter to the provost.

The lack of transparency recurred throughout my relationship with my associate dean. I pride myself on not being a micromanager, but I did expect less secrecy and more transparency from her. When I arrived, I shared my calendar with the entire leadership team; however, she never shared her calendar back with me. I chalked it up to perhaps it being her personal preference since she had an administrative assistant with access to her calendar. I also wanted to give grace because she was a Black woman in leadership, and college members forged forward with a survey to show a lack of support for her leadership. Given the cultural biases associated with the evaluation of Black women leaders, I decided to renew her contract. I wanted to provide the college with stable leadership despite prior attempts to remove her from this role, so I overlooked secrecy associated with meetings she attended, some of which I thought would be more appropriate for the dean to participate in than the associate dean. I aimed to create a sisterhood that supports Black women leaders.

Another series of events would prompt me to question the degree to which sisterhood was reciprocated among Black women leaders. The first event was MTC's annual Giving Day, where each unit was expected to fundraise as much money as possible. The institution gave incentivized challenges for institutions to add more money to the totals previously raised. While MTC's Giving Day raised a record amount of money, I noticed that unique donors from employees and staff decreased. I was alarmed that only one person in college leadership contributed even though they served on fundraising committees and shared about Giving Day within their networks. More surprisingly, though, was that neither my assistant nor associate dean (my sisters in the academy) contributed to Giving Day, even though they had in the past. I recognize that I don't know everyone's financial situation, and there could be valid reasons why neither gave. But it did seem to me to be a slap in the face, knowing that my leadership was under a microscope and I was expected to produce. After observing that they didn't make a financial contribution, I made a mental note to see if their lack of support would continue, and it did.

Can I Be Myself? The Answer Right Now is No ...

Around the end of the academic year, I received a late evening call from my associate dean asking me if I withdrew from the search as a candidate for the permanent dean of MTC. I told her I hadn't and asked for more context. She then asked me if I made a joke about a chicken bone on Facebook and tagged MTC in the joke. I told her I didn't tag any staff. However, I referenced an inside joke about my preoccupation with eating all the meat from chicken wing bones at a staff lunch that the associate dean hadn't bothered to attend until shortly before the event ended. The caption simply referenced teaching my staff how to eat a wing with a cleaned chicken bone. Most social media followers know my joking about chicken wings, so I thought nothing of it. When I explained the context, my associate dean scolded me and told me to take the post down immediately; she said she was contacted by multiple staff who thought the post was tacky. Frustrated and already stressed at the time, I removed the post. Still, I felt a clear line had been crossed when she lectured me on the appropriate ways to use and not use social media, referencing her use as an example to emulate. My approach to social media is quite different: I never post negativity about my job, but I post casual humor to be approachable as a leader/public figure and not take myself too seriously. And to be clear, I get the stereotypes associated with Black people and chicken. Still, I'm pretty sure I am not the first Black person to talk about chicken on social media (I mean, how else do you think Popeye's crispy chicken sandwich became viral!). At the same time, I realized that if I must censor myself about something as simple as a chicken bone with folks who claimed to be my sisters in the academy, where could I be my authentic self? I experienced a valuable lesson that the elders in my family had always taught me: Not all skin folk are kin folk.

The intraracial conflict I experienced does not let white people, including white women, off the hook, though. As interim dean, another experience consisted of a litany letter sent to me by my former dean (and now current supervisor again, for which our working relationship has improved tremendously) on behalf of chairs from the college where I formerly served as chair. About three months into my tenure, I received this eight-page, single-spaced letter complaining about the university's new student success portal (Student Success Hub) implemented by a collaborative team across academic affairs, student affairs, and the office of diversity and inclusion for Merze Tate College to oversee. In addition to complaints associated with the portal, the letter shared disdain for the fact that a similar portal wasn't available for graduate students (even though Merze Tate College only serves undergraduate students, and the university has a graduate college), among other things beyond my control. When I expressed concerns about the over-surveillance of things I could not change, in addition to my former dean copying every member of the provost's council on the letter (which greatly embarrassed me), the provost simply told me that I get paid to take attacks and to respond to all of the complaints. After much back and forth about how to navigate the issue, the provost sent me an email asking me to limit text and phone conversations with him and to work with a veteran dean (who was new to campus) to problem solve, as he did not have the time to focus solely on my issues, even though part of the agreement in my assuming the interim role was bi-weekly meetings (which were not happening) and mentoring from him. Interestingly enough, though, the provost still called and texted me whenever he felt the need to, yet I was supposed to limit communications (he rarely responds to emails) with him.

The conflict between me and my now-supervisor would occur throughout my interim dean appointment. First, one of the academic advisors in her college repeatedly became disruptive toward my assistant dean at monthly advising leadership meetings. It progressed so severely that the staff member began foaming at the mouth after one of the meetings. Another staff member, an assistant dean from the Honors College (see Chapter 5 in Richardson et al.), became hostile at a meeting because my assistant dean shut down his agenda when he attempted to undermine her authority in setting academic advising leadership agendas. After he reported her alleged rudeness and disrespect to his dean, I met dean-to-dean with his dean. Before the meeting, however, I sought solutions from the provost. My assistant dean requested that I ask the two disruptive staff members to stop attending meetings, at least for now. The provost agreed but said the decision had to be mine. I requested that the two staff take time out from meetings to support my academic sister. I clarified that this was only a temporary solution, but I believed it was appropriate, given the behavior I witnessed.

After making this decision, I was called into a meeting with the two deans of the disruptive staff members and the senior vice provost, where I was informed that each of them consulted with HR. As dean, I was not allowed to move anyone from meetings my college holds, and this form of corrective action is not one the university provides (though I am sure that people have been uninvited to meetings in the past). The real kicker, though, was when I recommended both staff participate in cultural humility and DEI training, given their hostility toward a Black woman leader and record of microaggressions toward her. In one instance, I noted an assistant dean referring to another Black administrator simply by his last name, which happened to be "Cotton." I found this offensive and offered that given that he has an earned doctorate, calling him "Dr. Cotton" or by first name would be more appropriate. Both deans defended him and said that what he did was culturally relevant and not a DEI issue. HR agreed. Ironically, no one thought to consult with our vice president for diversity and inclusion.

On Merze Tate Day (a day we set aside to honor Dr. Tate on her birthday), which also corresponds with Black History Month, the college organized a series of events for the campus where the community could learn more about Dr. Tate's legacy. On this same day, I received an email from the same dean/my current supervisor who sent the previous litany letter. This time, she marked the email with high priority and said she was concerned about an email our college put out on behalf of all academic advisors to students. The email, she determined, had been written too casually and was unprofessional, and she didn't want advisors' names attached to it. The email simply took a more approachable tone, reminding students to make an advising appointment if they hadn't done so already. To be fair, other college staff and associate deans expressed similar complaints. But, in responding to said dean/supervisor, I explained that it was Merze Tate Day, I would focus on my staff and events of the day, and I would get back to her later. She replied that my initial response wasn't acceptable, the issue needed to be addressed urgently and that if I didn't address her complaint, she would escalate the incident above me, to the provost. I did not react but informed the provost that threatening colleagues was unacceptable.

As a result of my concern about said dean's threat to escalate the issue, the provost sent a letter requiring both said dean and me to attend mediation. It seemed to me that I was disciplined for reporting workplace bullying, and after mediation, said dean and I didn't work collaboratively on MTC and university initiatives until I was informed by the provost that I did not have "the strongest support" to be named dean of the college and that I would return to my department chair position under said dean.

...But I Can Share Some Cautions for Prospective Leaders of Color

As leaders, it is always important to keep a journal of what you observe and experience, especially when going through new experiences. The act of journaling has helped me reflect on some cautions I would provide to prospective leaders, especially women of color. Keep a journal, document everything, and keep receipts. As I reflect on the past year, I want to share ten insights from my experience:

1. *Even though interim means temporary, I have zero regrets about advancing the organization, giving 100 percent, and leading with a vision beyond simply keeping the lights on.* Leaders have varying interpretations of what it means to be an interim leader. Some believe that the organization stays still to provide stability, and new initiatives and visions should be left for the permanent dean. In contrast, others believe that interim leadership is the leadership that still has the responsibility to move the

organization forward. I took the latter approach. In my time, I created a new Merze Tate Honor the Legacy initiative through a series of working groups to honor Dr. Tate's namesake and elevate the contributions of Black women. When I arrived, Merze Tate's artifacts and proclamations were stored in a closet that used to be a women's bathroom. As dedicated staff, we owe Dr. Tate better recognition than that.

2. *Build a solid structure of expertise, knowledge, and a foundation, even if temporary. Fake it 'til you make it is not for the excellent; it only advances mediocrity.* Since arriving at MTC, critics continuously said I was arrogant or too much of this or that. And while I won't say much here about the finalist candidates and the one who ultimately received the position, I will not apologize for being the candidate with the most leadership experience, most knowledge of the college, most peer-reviewed publications, most national recognition, and most demonstrated data-driven accomplishments in terms of retention and fundraising. While other candidates lauded their ability to build a plane by flying it, I celebrate that I did the intellectual work to lay the foundation, craft and cultivate the builders, test the operations, and equip all with the ability to take off *before* flying the plane.
3. *Friendships and partnerships are earned. Keep your circle of friends and support very small despite shared collective understandings and subject positions with the people on your team. These boundaries aren't simply about trust but more about being definitive about what relationships do and mean.* This may be the most painful lesson for me. I developed what I thought would be a close sisterhood with my assistant and associate dean, often treating them to lunch and sharing parts of my personal life and family with them. When we experienced clear microaggressions, we cried and strategized together. On holidays, we shared meals and baked goods. I considered both true friends even before working together. But as a leader, it's challenging to lead friends and sisters. When the assistant dean was a search committee member, she was clear about establishing

boundaries concerning future lunch dates and even gave me rides home. I respected her boundaries. In hindsight, as the dean, I should have set the limits from the beginning.

4. *Generosity, fairness, and integrity must mark every move you make, even if the consequences appear to be adverse in the short term. Do not regret giving your heart to people and fighting for their livelihoods, even if that devotion is not consistently recognized, valued, or reciprocated.* When boundaries of relationships are established from the beginning, one protects oneself from the personal hurt and pain associated with unreciprocated support. Both my assistant dean and associate dean had multiple complaints about their tone and behavior, complaints I considered mainly to stem from biases toward Black women. Both leaders had contracts in danger of not being renewed. In one case, the associate dean had an impromptu 360-degree evaluation so negative that staff thought her contract would not be renewed. Focusing on her work record, I chose to renew her contract. When I shared with both the assistant associate dean that I would not be named the permanent dean, I was ghosted, and even before the decision, both stopped communicating with me via phone or text. Even though their support for me wasn't returned, I can at least have the consciousness that I made the decision I believed to be correct and just.
5. *The spaces we belong in are the spaces where we can bring our authentic selves without hyper scrutiny or backbiting.* On multiple occasions, I found myself the brunt of over-scrutinization. Everything from the handbags I wore to the car in which people saw my husband drop me off were causes for snared remarks about my material possessions. To be fair, other leaders carried luxury bags, and I'm sure criticism was also hurled at them. Beyond the bags carried, however, I received criticism about various statements I made. For example, when I boasted about the staff doing outstanding work, I called it the work being done in "my college." Staff criticized why I didn't say "our

college," but the context of my dean's boast was a meeting in which deans were sharing their colleges' accomplishments with each other. In another instance, I introduced a staff member to another leader by joking, "Here's one of my staff who likes me," when the point was simply to show that I have excellent support and not to insinuate that there are staff who don't like me. The sad thing was that most of this criticism was derived from Black women, with whom I thought we shared a sisterhood. In fairness, I think it's appropriate to have conversations about how what leaders may say can offend staff, provided that the space is safe. However, given that people rarely provided positive reinforcement despite what I had accomplished as their leader, the feedback was unbalanced. I mean, I did get chastised for posting a chicken bone on my personal social media page.

6. *Moments of prioritizing self over community are not necessarily bad, especially for Black women who are called upon to clean, fix, and nurture others while also sacrificing their own needs being met.* Another word of caution is about how to reconcile the level of support Black women give to institutions, expecting that the same support will most likely not be reciprocated. I gave women, people of color, and especially Black faculty and staff over fourteen years at WMU. I advocated to save people's jobs, to appeal biased tenure and promotion decisions, to recommend for career advancement and promotions, and even wrote endorsements and letters of concern to cabinet leaders on behalf of Black organizations on campus. But when it came time for a coalition to support me, Black organizations declined to help me and write endorsements. Again, the same level of support was not reciprocated. I faced significant criticism for my advocacy, which perhaps hurt my candidacy as the permanent dean. In the next phase of professional advancement, I am no longer willing to sacrifice myself for others who aren't willing to do the same for me.
7. *Observe patterns early and write consistently in a journal what you have experienced.* Take those journals and pursue publication

opportunities to train leaders of the next generation. Early on, I observed patterns I was reluctant to address because of my vulnerability as an interim dean; nonetheless, I wrote copious notes in my journals about the patterns I observed that questioned my lack of character and support. Of the provost, I observed his strategic maneuvering to get me out of the way of positions where he wanted to hire his friends. He did not conduct a formal search for a position for which I was highly qualified. He hired a friend from his past role with no higher education experience. He also promised to do an internal search for my position (manipulating the word "internal" as one without a search firm). A clear pattern of the provost is not to use a search firm when he has friends he wants to hire. He did not use a search firm for the associate provost of equity-centered initiatives, for which I was a finalist. Still, he promised me the dean role if I withdrew from that search only to hire his friend, who had also been a former graduate student (and left his past institution because he was found responsible for plagiarizing a journal article). When it came time to search for the permanent dean, a trusted colleague shared that he asked another Black woman (with whom I had a friendship) with limited experience and without full professor rank to apply to replace me. When leaders do not make the most ethical decisions in their previous work, do not expect them to treat you ethically.

8. *The ability to lead is not simply a popularity contest; if it becomes that way, there's a better space for you to be.* The provost scheduled a meeting with me to discuss his decision not to hire me while I was on vacation with my family; in the meeting, he never turned his camera on, so I knew the decision was adverse. He shared his reasoning for not hiring me by saying that while recognizing my contributions, he is one of many on this campus to weigh in. Unfortunately, I did not have the strongest support based on feedback. This rationale had nothing to do with my qualifications or accomplishments. While leaders should have the support

of their constituents, leadership should not be a popularity contest, especially when there are systemic biases in the representation of Black women. And replacing me with another Black woman who is more palatable to the masses does more harm than good in terms of solidarity, competence, and action. I learned that if you are promised a job based on popularity, run for the hills, for that stipulation will significantly undermine your effectiveness.

9. *There will be no pity parties when you know you've fought the good fight and you have a record of achievement and accomplishments that tell the story for you.* Others' validation doesn't measure your value. When I lost a previous deanship, I went into a lengthy depression and had to take medical leave. This time was different. I was intent on showing my face and moving on instead of going into hiding. I take pride in that nobody can say they accomplished what I did as interim dean, and I put the college in a better position to meet retention goals than I found it. The metrics and data provide more robust validation of effectiveness than what popularity can offer.
10. *Finally, family above all. Find a good work/life balance.* Reflecting on the past year also taught me to focus more on family. Many hobbies like cooking and baking fell to the wayside while I was interim dean. During the next year, my daughter would be starting a new high school emphasizing college prep. She would take multiple advanced courses while balancing her time as a competitive dancer. Fewer professional obligations would enable me to be more present as she navigates new transitions and offers emotional support and intellectual advice.

In summary, no interim leadership experience is ever easy, especially as the first Black woman to lead a college. The treatment I endured functions less and less as disappointment and more and more as a series of teachable moments and experiences I can bring to a new environment. I hope this story does not discourage anyone from pursuing future leadership; instead, it should serve as a series of lessons learned to help others with similar subject positions to navigate new leadership challenges.

References

Bell, Myrtle P, Daphne Berry, Joy Leopold, and Stella Nkomo S. 2021. "Making Black Lives Matter in Academia: A Black Feminist Call for Collective Action against Anti-Blackness in the Academy." *Gender, Work & Organization* 28: 39–57. https://doi.org/10.1111/gwao.12555.

Craig, Collin L. and Staci M. Perryman-Clark. 2011. "Troubling the Boundaries: (De)Constructing WPA Identities at the Intersections of Race and Gender." *WPA Journal* 34 (2): 37–58.

Perryman-Clark, Staci. M. 2023. *The New Work of Writing Across the Curriculum: Diversity and Inclusion, Collaborative Partnerships, and Faculty Development.* Utah State University/University of Colorado Press.

Richardson, Jennifer, Mariam Konaté, Staci Perryman-Clark, McLaughlin, Olivia, Grace Keiondra. 2024. *The Black Feminist Coup: Black Women's Lived Experiences in White Supremacist Feminist Academic Spaces.* Peter Lang Academic Publishing.

CHAPTER 7

Learning to Navigate Online Leadership

An Invitation to Collaborate for Group Project Skeptics

Erin Lehman, *Ivy Tech Community College*

Maybe you hated group projects in school because you are a high achiever and you don't like working with people you consider "slackers" or "procrastinators." Or perhaps you feel that you work better on your own—though you accomplish less and take on more, you believe those sacrifices are worth avoiding uncertainty and conflict. Both of these sentiments describe me when I was asked to serve as the academic voice for the implementation of a new centralized online delivery hub at Ivy Tech Community College, the statewide community college system in Indiana. But being challenged by such a collaborative and fast-paced professional project expanded my capacity and curiosity. By meeting IvyOnline's fast implementation speed and high volume of sections, I learned to collaborate, communicate, and rely upon others to shoulder an incredible lift and navigate an uncertain path.

Understanding Today's Online Department

Within Ivy Tech Community College, IvyOnline supports about 45,000 online seats (this is duplicated headcount) every semester. This volume of students and sections makes the enrollment and sections management process demanding. Additionally, as a centralized hub, IvyOnline has stakeholders throughout the system, requiring collaboration with nineteen distinct campuses across the state—each campus with its own set of vice-chancellors, deans, chairs, faculty and academic advisors. Within the IvyOnline unit, there are six schools: the School of Advanced Manufacturing, Engineering, and Applied Sciences; the School of Arts, Sciences, and Education; the School of Business, Logistics, and Supply Chain; the School of Health Sciences; the School of Information Technology; and the School of Public Affairs and Social Services. All six schools work together to streamline and update processes and discuss how we should manage various situations and events, such as our annual online conference.

My area of responsibility within IvyOnline is the School of Arts, Sciences, and Education, which accounts for 35,000 of the 45,000 enrollments across seventy different courses. I lead a team of ten "assistant faculty leads" (AFLs) who serve as statewide, online department chairs representing the major disciplines across liberal arts and sciences. An important component of our work is ongoing team building and community building practices, which I've found are particularly important as an entirely virtual team spread across Indiana. Because of this ongoing virtual team building, we are strong, capable, and able to respond to a high number of individual student requests and complaints throughout each term. We review online course success rates each term and connect outcomes to weekly literature review sessions to engage with current teaching and learning scholarship in online course delivery. We create and host weekly professional development offerings tailored to online faculty and regularly meet with our online faculty for hundreds of performance evaluations and teaching observations each year.

Leading this effort is a big job, and when I describe the scope and volume of my role to other administrators, their eyes go wide. They wonder how I manage it all. The truth is that I rely upon my team of AFLs to be successful, something I learned the hard way—by initially avoiding delegation and promising my direct supervisor and my team that I could and should handle everything they could throw at me. To understand how I landed in that difficult spot, you should understand a little bit about my bookish background.

Winding My Way to Online Learning

Prior to joining IvyOnline, I was a traditional department chair for English and education at a rural campus location of Ivy Tech. I spent most days alone in my office grading papers, engaged in individual reading and responding labor (Giordano and Wegner 2020). I was advised by colleagues that I should spend more time in the hallways talking to people, and was told it was a shame I spent so much time at my desk. I had worked my way from faculty to program chair to assistant chair and then department chair by being detailed, organized, and reasonable—not necessarily because of any refined leadership skills. I didn't see my journey as unique; this career path was a typical route for someone who wanted to land in academic leadership. I enjoyed the balance of teaching, staffing, and working with the small group of early childhood education, education, and English chairs who reported to me within the department. The administrative role felt manageable, even as I continued to teach three classes a semester and, after five years, I fell into a comfortable and predictable routine. Staff up for classes in August, complete program reviews in December, conduct performance evaluations in February, and assist with Capstone courses, student awards and graduation in May. Though I was in my early thirties at this time, I assumed I would continue this cyclical and relatively solitary routine until retirement.

Throughout this period, I taught online throughout the academic year—at first because teaching online suited my personality and weekly (administrative meeting-heavy) schedule better, and then because I found ways to become more effective and grew to truly enjoy online teaching and felt "engaged" by my online students (Hewett 2015, 70). Around this time, institutions were beginning to shift their online course delivery from multiple campus sites to one centralized hub to improve efficiency and save money (Bailey et al. 2018). Though Ivy Tech had unsuccessfully attempted a similar centralization about ten years earlier, again in early

2019, the goal was announced that the institution would be moving to a single delivery hub for all online courses.

A mentor encouraged me to apply for the interim "faculty lead" assignment that had been posted. The role was loosely defined and tasked with voicing the faculty perspective as the institution built a centralized online department. The College assumed that the faculty lead role was temporary and, after the set-up of IvyOnline, the faculty member would return to their previous position because their set-up work would provide the necessary structure to run online courses. (Since then, the faculty lead and AFL roles have become the primary permanent, full-time roles within IvyOnline.) I was offered the position, a one-year reassignment which came with no increase in pay and no title change—merely the chance to try something different and to influence the future of the online department. I accepted the assignment with curiosity.

Attempting to Exit the Comfort Zone of One

At the start of my interim assignment the last week of May, my supervisor and I had less than three months to figure out how to navigate the process to build the foundation for IvyOnline and launch forty individual courses (which ended up being 532 sections). We started the staffing process in June, and our first online courses would go live that August. Though this project would be a big lift, it was initially handled through 1:1s or small-group work—my preferred way of operating at the time. The situation felt manageable because *I touched everything and I could therefore quality control everything. I didn't have to negotiate my ideas with other departments or stakeholders but could create the ideal situation with the support of a close collaborator.*

But as IvyOnline began scaling and staffing up, the volume of sections prevented me from continuing to operate in my comfort zone. I learned that I needed to develop the skills to collaborate with other professionals as equals. Rather than next steps being directives, there was discussion and negotiation. That uncertainty bothered me because I couldn't plan my way out of these situations or account for every variable.

IvyOnline's leadership meetings became a critical place where I began to learn how to work differently—where I needed to grow, how to advocate across departments, and more. These meetings were held every Monday morning and grew to include additional staff: our assistant vice president, educational technology lead, instructional design lead, and me. Rather than the cyclical routine I was familiar with as a department chair, the meetings had start-up energy where every week brought new and complex issues. For example, we would hash out several impactful decisions at each: on what date course shells would be released to faculty; whether courses would have a mid-semester correction and reload; which department would receive and respond to course errors; how we would communicate bookstore changes to faculty and who would be responsible for these; how accessibility issues would be resolved; how we would share out professional development and event information and who would be responsible for this communication; who would draft a team presentation; who would represent IvyOnline on relevant committees and why. Because of the number of decisions and the stakeholders in the room, the environment in these meetings was challenging and, depending on the participants and the task, could become combative. As temporary faculty lead, I would often be put on the spot to speak for faculty. If I didn't persuade the permanent IvyOnline staff with backgrounds in technology and instructional design to see my perspective, then I would easily be outvoted and outmaneuvered in the meeting.

As someone who had hated the friction and uncertainty of group projects as a kid, I found Mondays were days of intense pressure for me as I started this new role. It was hard to gain my footing in high-stakes discussions where I was often the last person to speak up and voice my opinion. I learned that one reason I disliked group projects and avoided combative environments was because I was sensitive to the power dynamics that often put me at a disadvantage. I didn't want to dominate the conversation, and I didn't want to create unnecessary conflict. Sometimes the conversation and the takeaways would become jumbled for me—either because the conversation was moving too swiftly among the virtual and live attendees, or there were technical terms or jargon I didn't understand.

The "4 Disciplines of Execution" (4DX) podcast, which I was listening to for work because our institution was using the 4DX platform for project management, offered me a lifeline for the challenging power dynamics I was facing. The podcast host explained his method of pausing the conversation to gain clarity by summarizing what was said and asking the listener or group if that summary was correct (McChesney and Downs 2021). It is a simple step that never occurred to me. But as a minority woman working in higher education, it was often hard for me to take up meeting space and verify my (mis)understanding. I was the only non-white individual in these leadership meetings, one of the youngest people in the room, and a woman. Pausing the conversation to summarize what I thought I heard as well as expected next steps, which were often unspoken, was a game changer. Advocating for my own comprehension built my confidence as a leader.

Struggling Against a Workload Fit for Many

Navigating communication across departments was one challenge, but I was also trying to build the structure, processes, and team culture for my school. I still have the 1:1 notes from my first year in this position. In them, I see someone thinking through the practical steps of a large group project and the challenges of trying to manage a growing list of tasks and responsibilities without anyone to delegate to. For example, I asked how to offer adjunct faculty members course assignments. Without an HR team, we weren't sure how to write and send contracts for those course offers once accepted. In our early notes, I had questions about hiring and communicating, and discussed creating a communication plan, creating a shell of resources for faculty, staffing online courses, ways to meet and get to know faculty, how to audit online sections with Educational Technology department, and how to create a scoring system for faculty that would create transparency around the course offer process.

One of the unspoken responsibilities of my temporary position was to onboard liberal arts and sciences faculty and encourage them to engage with this new online unit. I decided to meet 1:1 with all faculty who would be in my online department, which ended up being seventy individual meetings via Zoom that first fall semester. Based upon feedback from dozens of faculty, I started developing and managing a Canvas course shell of resources. I uploaded resources, links, and dozens of in-house created videos to this Canvas shell and started directing faculty to it. Today, the shell has become a rich course site that my team continues to maintain for faculty. The content is readily available. Plus, since the shell can function like an online course, we model the behaviors we are hoping to see in online faculty—posting weekly announcements, facilitating discussion boards, posting relevant recorded videos, and updating resources connecting content to current events.

If this sounds like an incredible amount of work for one person to take on, it was. During this first year, I strained to keep up with my ballooning workload and complete tasks I had promised to do. I also struggled to say no or to express that I had hit my maximum workload capacity as more tasks (anything faculty-facing) were directed my way. Looking ahead, the volume and demands would only increase because additional courses would be shifted to our centralized unit each semester until the entire college catalog was available through IvyOnline. But eventually, because of the anticipated volume, I asked for additional help and ended up hiring eight new part-time AFLs. These were chairs and faculty at an Ivy Tech campus who also applied, interviewed for, and accepted an interim assignment with IvyOnline.

It made sense to hire additional help, but it was difficult to move from my individual, start-up mindset to instead put my energy into building and training a team. Because I had already taken on so much to avoid the potential conflict of more group work, I had little time and capacity to train the new team so they could do the job effectively. Diverting from the tasks at hand felt impossible, like an indulgent decision that would only create more work later. Plus, as someone who understood the drowning feeling of work, it felt unfair for me to land my work with my new and inexperienced team. This was a period where I felt drained by Teams messages and notifications, the influx of constant emails, and back-to-back Zoom meetings scheduled for hours of every workday. I had too few boundaries and devoured lunch in the two minutes I would get between scheduled Zoom meetings. My eyes, neck, and back ached from long hours sitting stiffly in the same position, and at the end of most days, I felt sick looking at a screen.

Here is an example of my mindset a year into the faculty lead role. The excerpt below comes from a Google form that I set up to try to capture my thoughts and experiences during this implementation project. However, I was so overwhelmed by other tasks that I only submitted two entries to the form. You will see that the numbers are different from what I've mentioned in this piece so far because all online courses were transitioning to IvyOnline over a two-year period, and the numbers reflect the summer term:

> The biggest challenge in my role these past few weeks has just been the workload...my small team is working with 12,000 students/seats and over 450 sections this semester. It's hard to even wrap my head around those numbers. I know that my team of mostly part-time AFLs is overworked at this point, and I am starting to feel bad about the workload that I have assigned to them. At the same time, I've had a difficult time completing my own workload as well—and I need the AFLs to continue to get caught up and pick up the pace. Scaling up has been the biggest challenge this semester by far. I didn't realize the volume of courses I would be dealing with. Frankly, it's been a steep learning curve. (Collection Point for IvyOnline Leadership, June 22, 2020)

In this short reflection, I see a leader struggling to figure out how she will lead. I hear a leader who is buried in work and trying to get ahead of her team so that she can lead effectively. Someone who has difficulty delegating and knowing when and how much to challenge her team. Throughout my education and career, I declined to rely on others because I thought I preferred and found success by doing tasks myself. But to build IvyOnline, I had to change my mind and my inclination to do it all myself. As you can see, I learned this lesson the hard way—by trying to power through the work, rather than listening and being strategic with my time and energy.

Humbly Inviting in Others

A key moment in my leadership trajectory is when I was so overwhelmed with daily tasks that I couldn't provide any vision for my team and department. I was meeting with the lead AFL on my team who had incredible leadership experience—Dr. Marsha Turner-Shear was a former K–12 school superintendent—and I shared that I wanted to hold a few events during the summer for the team to connect, build relationships with each other, and establish our own leadership philosophy and team guidelines. I could see that these items were missing but had no capacity to develop a way to counter the situation. Dr. Turner-Shear said she enjoyed this type of work and asked to plan the event. Though I was hesitant—I wanted to plan the event by myself because I thought that I *should*—I was so time poor that there was no other option. Dr. Turner-Shear put together this simple but effective agenda:

Topic: *Leadership Philosophy* (3.5 hours, Zoom) Thursday or Friday morning or afternoon

- Icebreaker: Describe one of your proudest accomplishments from high school or undergrad college years.
- Favorite leadership book (Advance Assignment)
- Share title, author, etc.
- Main take-aways
- How it has influenced your leadership style
- Brainstorm ASE leadership philosophy together

During the Zoom session, each person shared one leadership book that shaped them and explained what they learned from that item—leadership lessons and experiences that were funny, shocking, engrossing, or wise. Dr. Turner-Shear facilitated the session, and her plan and approach modeled the way a leader invites others to bring their expertise into a space to enrich the community and learn from each other. She demonstrated the assurance and trust that is needed to develop a team on their own terms.

The experience of participating in this first "Summer Session" humbled me and opened my eyes to the deep talent the team already had, as well as their potential. I underestimated the skill, ambition, and capabilities of my team. I underestimated how strong they were. I failed to realize that for them, most opportunities are good and desired, not dumping my work onto them. This event resituated my leadership approach. I saw clearly that every professional on my team already had the leadership skills they needed and so didn't need my protection from the big scary IvyOnline group project.

This first event and our subsequent "Summer Sessions" (we have several every year as a team that AFLs help plan) helped me muster the confidence to develop a shared vision to motivate my team, despite challenges and uncertainty in our new online department. I learned to lead by encouraging and supporting the people around me and highlighting their voices and their abilities. I learned to trust my team and to work on ways to earn their trust. This trust isn't always returned "purely" and openly. There have been times that colleagues have taken advantage of my trust and goodwill in the workplace—and this is painful to experience. But I've also come to terms with the vulnerability of my trust because I've learned what type of leader I aspire to be. I want to be someone who invites people in, acknowledges their skills and potential, and elevates others' voices. Through the challenges I faced building IvyOnline, I've learned that I have the strength and capacity to aim to lead with generosity, kindness, and trust.

In order to succeed in leadership, I needed to overcome my fear of group projects and collaboration. I thought I preferred working on my own because this approach was functional in my early career, and it helped me avoid conflict. But I'm not conflict averse. Instead, it turns out that I feel discomfort in combative environments where power dynamics put me at a disadvantage. Perhaps the same is true for you, fellow group project skeptic. I encourage you to reframe your perspective to be a group project leader who invites in every voice and perspective, who has the strength to rely on the expertise of others; who reads the room and listens carefully to the stories, lessons, and ambition that every person already has. You might find that you enjoy group projects after all.

References

Bailey, Allison, Nithya Vaduganathan, Tyce Henry, Renee Laverdiere, and Lou Pugliese. 2018. *Making Digital Learning Work: Success Strategies from Six Leading Universities and Community Colleges*. The Boston Consulting Group. https://edplus.asu.edu/sites/default/files/BCG-Making-Digital-Learning-Work-Apr-2018%20.pdf.

Giordano, Joanne, and McKenna Wegner. 2020. *TYCA Working Paper #3: Workload Management Strategies for Teaching English at Two-Year Colleges*. Two-Year College English Association. https://ncte.org/wpcontent/uploads/2020/11/TYCA_Working_Paper_3.pdf.

Hewett, Beth. 2015. *The Online Writing Conference: A Guide for Teachers and Tutors*. Bedford/St. Martin's.

McChesney, Chris and Jeffery Downs. 2021. *Episode 3: Engaging Your Teams*, The 4 Disciplines of Execution Podcast, podcast audio, September 22, 2021. Streaking LLC.

CHAPTER 8

Listening as a(n Incomplete) Leader

Beth Brunk, *University of Texas at El Paso*

> *"Learning to lead is hard, and it takes a long time."*—with credit to Stephen North (2000)

While some people appear to be natural born leaders, many of us need guidance, experience with successes and failures, reflection, and plenty of time to become effective. The leadership style I have learned and strive to practice did not happen overnight, and if anything, I've learned that this thing called leadership is tricky at best. Amid the ever-changing landscape of leadership in the senior administrative levels of higher education, this chapter provides me with the opportunity to reflect on my leadership experience at my institution, consider what I learned from a year-long leadership workshop, and note some practices I have learned that have led to successful outcomes.

Accepting Invitations to Leadership

The path to my current leadership position may *appear* straightforward and deliberate. In retrospect, and in the short summary below, it seems like I could make that case. However, throughout the last fifteen years, it did not seem that way. Rather, invitations to leadership opportunities were often surprises that were the result of passion for my academic discipline and commitment to my university's dual mission of access and excellence. I in no way planned, or even imagined, that I would be a dean and be leading an organization of more than sixty people with six direct reports charged with supporting the mission of expanding access to the institution through online learning, continuing education, and other "non-traditional" initiatives. Perhaps behaviors that I assumed were intrinsic to doing any job well—such as openness to people and ideas, continuous learning, calm demeanor, going above-and-beyond—were perceived as essential leadership qualities. I have been fortunate that campus leaders who were dedicated to cultivating the next generation of leadership recognized those characteristics in me and invited me to participate in leadership roles.

My professional leadership journey began as a writing program administrator. In this role, a faculty member serves as the leader of a group of other writing instructors and is responsible for a number of academic and administrative decisions. These include designing and/or revising curriculum as well as the modalities it may be taught in (classroom, computer lab, online, or hybrid), hiring instructors, preparing new instructors to teach the curriculum in different modalities, providing professional development for the instructors, scheduling courses, staying within the budget, assessing student learning, evaluating transfer credits that students bring from other institutions, addressing student concerns, and other assorted duties. In this role, one begins to understand the importance of working with and supporting multiple stakeholders: the instructors who are teaching in the program, the department chair, the dean, the registrar's office, the technology support office, the bookstore, sometimes parents, and most importantly, students.

This first official university leadership experience was both rewarding and challenging. It was rewarding because the work was relevant to my academic interests, and it allowed me to gain a better understanding of the university ecosystem and all its moving parts. However, it was also challenging because it put me in the position of leading a group that I had, just a semester previously, worked with as a peer. While most instructors were open and collaborative, it took me some time to appreciate that I was now the one to make decisions about the writing program. Because of this, I soon learned the importance of listening to multiple and sometimes competing voices and how to make decisions based on this input balanced with what I determined to be best for the program, the people who worked in it, and the students we served.

Three years into directing the writing program, I was asked by the dean of the College of Liberal Arts about my interest in joining his office as an associate dean. While I was surprised to be asked, I accepted the position while continuing to work as the director of the writing program. I admittedly had very little knowledge about what the role of an associate dean looked like, but I quickly learned that it included meeting with students individually for a range of concerns that could include academic probation, issues with classes they were taking, and a variety of personal matters—some being quite serious. However, rather than seeing these concerns as issues requiring swift resolutions, I engaged with students as individuals with unique challenges that could often become opportunities if students could be directed toward the appropriate resources. Again, I learned to listen carefully, to locate the best resources, and present the best options at the time. In this role, I learned to advocate for students in ways I had not understood previously.

In addition to working with students, as associate dean I was also asked to participate in projects that served the mission of the college and the university. At the time, there was a developing interest in the strategic offering of online courses and the development of online concentrations, minors, and majors. Leading this work provided me with the opportunity to learn how to work across many departments, collaborate with support services, build a student-serving infrastructure, and make decisions about the best path for the university and its students. I learned that I had the ability to establish a vision for the college while managing the many challenging details of how to make that vision happen.

When our provost launched an initiative to organize and establish a new unit to support all the university's online programs, I was asked to join that unit, Extended University, as a senior associate dean. My work here built upon what I had learned as a writing program administrator and associate dean to focus on working with the faculty who were engaged in online program development and to build knowledge bases for enrollment counselors and student success advisors to assist fully online students. This work also built upon the collaborative networks I had established in both previous roles, as I would be the liaison to various Faculty Senate committees and work with support staff to establish processes and logistics of running fully online degree programs.

About a year into this work, at a crucial time in the program's development, the dean I was working for stepped down and recommended me for the role. I have stayed in this position as Dean of Extended University and oversee the online program portfolio, continuing education, youth programming support, the online course instructional design team, and senior adult education. As the scope of my organization expanded and the pressures to perform increased, I realized that I still had much to learn about being an effective leader.

Seeking Time to Learn and Reflect

Recognizing that I had over a decade of leadership experience but minimal leadership education and training, I sought the opportunity to participate in a selective national leadership academy. The Academy for Innovative Higher Education Leadership, a partnership between Arizona State University and Georgetown University, brought together more than thirty higher education leaders from across the United States. Participants came from various types of institutions, with different levels of experience, but all with the expressed interest in developing innovative ways to improve the quality of and access to higher education. We evaluated articles, listened to podcasts, met individually with our leadership coach, discussed leadership topics in large and small groups, engaged with guest speakers, wrote about our leadership journeys, and worked on an innovation challenge for our current institution. Over the course of a year, these experiences provided me with the opportunity to think deeply about how I operate as a leader, what I value in my work, what rubrics I employ to make decisions big and small, and how to innovate within the university by employing equity-centered design thinking.

Our first assignment after being accepted into the leadership program was to participate in a leadership survey for which a minimum of thirty people would respond to questions about my leadership style: myself, my boss, my boss's boss, my colleagues, and my direct reports. One of the questions was: *In your opinion, what is the leader's greatest leadership asset, skill, or talent, and what suggestions do you have for leveraging it?* Four of the comments that stood out most for me were:

> "She maintains an even balanced approach, can listen, and is a team player."
>
> "She advocates for important assets by listening carefully to all points of view, proposing creative solutions that include others, and by keeping a calm yet strong demeanor."
>
> "My observations in some situations are that Beth is almost too accommodating both to her peers and to those who report to her. She is extremely smart and perceptive. She is also compassionate and it seems that she could take the opportunity to be more assertive to ensure decisions are made the ways she knows are best for her area and the institution."
>
> "She can voice her opinions more frequently as they will be strongly considered by leadership based on her record of success and talent."

I appreciated that my colleagues recognized and respected my efforts to be a thoughtful and inclusive leader through listening to all parties, balancing diverse perspectives, and collaborating to achieve goals. What I was a bit surprised about was my leadership coach's big takeaway, which was that "your colleagues think you are smart and want to hear from you more often." I wondered, then, if my leadership style leaned too much on listening and inclusiveness and that perhaps my colleagues might sometimes wonder what, if anything, I had to say.

With that feedback in mind, a few months later, we were asked to participate in an exercise that helped us to identify and define our core leadership values. The four that rose to the top for me were:

- **Integrity**: I use integrity to guide big and small decisions and strive for transparency so that decisions won't be questioned for their ethics and consistency.
- **Harmony:** I do not like unnecessary conflict, prefer to work with people who respect each other, and seek common ground by giving others their say.
- **Compassion/empathy**: I strive to be kind, caring, and involved and try to read, appreciate, and consider others' emotions.
- **Collaboration:** I feel that better products result when working with others, I request input and feedback, and I feel isolated and unsure when working in solitude.

My colleagues' responses illustrated that they recognize the leadership traits that reflect my core values of integrity, harmony, compassion/empathy, and collaboration. Their feedback and the reflection exercise simultaneously identified the challenges that can sometimes make me uncomfortable as a leader, such as voicing thoughts more frequently and more assertively, making difficult decisions, and addressing conflict directly.

The remainder of this chapter will reflect on the advantages of being a listening and collaborative leader across networks and over time while also embracing moments where it is important to speak up and address conflict head on. It will connect the power of listening to a leadership style that prioritizes what we learn together and emphasizes that leadership does not depend on knowing everything. In fact, as I have learned, the incomplete leader is often the most effective one.

Realizing that I'm an Incomplete Leader

One particularly impactful article we reviewed in the Academy for Innovative Higher Education Leadership was "In Praise of the Incomplete Leader." In it, Deborah Ancona, Thomas W. Malone, Wanda J. Orlinkowski, and Peter M. Senge (2007), faculty in the MIT

Sloan School of Management, take the position that "it's time to end the myth of the complete leader: the flawless person at the top who's got it all figured out" (1). There is a distinction to be made between an *incomplete* and an *incompetent* leader. An *incompetent leader* will attempt to hide or disguise any weaknesses, insist on being the authority on all matters, make final decisions without input, and the like, whereas an *incomplete leader* will have an honest understanding of their strengths and their weaknesses and "have good judgment about how they can work with others to build on their strengths and offset their limitations" (2). In other words, being an incomplete leader is potentially a good thing, and recognizing that one is, in fact, an incomplete leader affords one the ability to establish a common vision and inspire others to enjoy the work to attain it.

With the understanding that one person simply cannot do everything well, Ancona et. al. (2007) developed a model of distributed leadership that utilizes a set of four capabilities. The first two, sensemaking and relating—what they call "enabling capabilities" (4)—help an incomplete leader understand the organization's environment and the people who work there. The second two, visioning and inventing, are "creative and action oriented: They produce the needed to make change happen" (5). Their argument is that an incomplete leader who genuinely employs these capabilities will excel in their ability to effectively lead the organization.

What I have learned in my leadership positions, most certainly in my current one, is that the incomplete leader can draw upon their recognized and believed strengths and challenges to lead their institution in both small and significant ways. In the remainder of this chapter, I will employ the four enabling capabilities to illustrate how I have learned to do this.

Sensemaking to Understand Organizational Context

As Peter Eckel and Adrianna Kezar found, "deep changes in higher education require people to undergo a meaning construction process and rethink existing understandings, a process known as organizational sensemaking" (Kezar 2012, 764). Sensemaking, coined by organizational psychologist Karl Weick, is a process by which leaders work with others to understand their organizational contexts—to make sense of them. Ancona et al. (2007) note that strong leaders use sensemaking to capture the complexities of their organization, determine what factors are most relevant to addressing change, and work with others to develop a common map that will assist in "planning for the journey ahead" (2). Sensemaking, they argue, is "more than an act of analysis; it's an act of creativity" (2).

Sensemaking is not something that can be done on day one, and it's not something that is one-and-done. Rather, say Ancona et al., it is "a continuous process; [leaders] let the map emerge from a melding of observations, data, experiences, conversations, and analyses" (3). It requires "involv[ing] others, say[ing] what you are seeing, and check[ing] with people who have different perspectives" (3). Sensemaking requires rising above the distraction of the details, continually asking "What am I missing?," having ongoing dialogues, interpreting, and collaborating on a shared map or vision.

Sensemaking, then, is highly dependent upon listening. We might think of the act of listening as flipping a light switch. It's on or off. You are either listening or you are not. The difference from simply hearing, a more passive, almost reflexive, activity, and listening implies a level of engagement that can be amplified with the practices of active listening as well as rhetorical listening, which attempts to not only hear but also identify with others' perspectives. *Rhetorical Listening in Action: A Concept-tactic Approach* (2022), coauthored by Krista Ratcliff and Kyle Jensen, provides strategies for effective rhetorical listening, even in "difficult-to-listen-to situations" that may become polarizing (1). It can be used to "identify and navigate rhetorical problems and their situations, which are either situations in which speakers or writers must express their ideas, feelings, values, and beliefs in ways that audiences can actually hear them *or* situations in which audiences must open themselves to actually hear ideas, feelings, values, and beliefs, even those with which they disagree" (21). It provides us with a strategy to "listen across differences in preparing for communicating and acting within and across those differences" (3) and can be achieved through assuming an open stance, balancing competing claims, pausing, analyzing and reflecting for understanding of yourself and others, and the goal of arriving at win-win solutions (21). If we think again about sensemaking as gathering data from multiple sources, checking in with others who may have differing perspectives from yours and each other, regularly asking, "What am I missing?" and being open to new possibilities, much of this depends heavily on rhetorical listening, as the following experience illustrates.

In the late 2000s, our provost developed a strategy to expand access and grow enrollment through the development of an online program portfolio. To achieve this heavy lift, we contracted for a shared services model with an online program manager. While several deans and department chairs were invited to discussions, many faculty were not included in the conversations and learned about the agreement after it had been signed. They were not happy. Enough discontent was expressed that the provost invited faculty to a town hall that was met with a standing-room-only, highly engaged audience. I had just recently transitioned into my position as the senior associate dean in Extended University, so I did not have a speaking role. However, as a member of this leadership team, I was the only one who had the advantage of having been a faculty member at the university. I was able to use my empathetic experience as well as my position of observer to make better sense of the faculty's concern. I did not need to be in a position to respond, at least not at that moment. Rather, I had the opportunity to rhetorically listen for understanding. While some of the faculty's questions were perfectly reasonable, some comments were hyperbolic, almost antagonistic. There was a disconnect between what they understood as the exigence for this project versus what they thought they needed to protect as faculty. Again, instead of coming back with a quick response about why they were wrong or misguided, I was able to decenter myself and suspend my instinct to correct and defend in order to practice rhetorical listening.

To follow Ratcliff and Jensen's stages of rhetorical listening, one must be quiet and attend to not just the words being conveyed but also to others' tones and mannerisms. Distractions should be minimized or removed. The urge to interrupt should be avoided. Following these principles enabled me to learn from the faculty and to understand their perspective. From the faculty's perspective, sensemaking also allowed them to "change the way they perceive their roles, skills, and approaches/philosophies ... consistent with the realities the changing institution" (Kezar and Eckel 2002, 303). Sensemaking, assisted by rhetorical listening, helped "determine what would be a useful map given [our] particular goals and then to draw one that adequately represents the situation" (Ancona et al. 2) that the institution was facing. It also provided the space to learn how to shift from reactive defenses to purposeful and productive conversations—in effect, to relate to one another.

Relating to Understand Colleagues

Ancona et al. (2007) note that many leaders "who attempt to foster trust, optimism, and consensus often reap anger, cynicism, and conflict instead" (3). This is a result of the inability to relate "to others, especially those who don't make sense of the world the way they do" (3). Most of us are familiar with this dynamic. It may well be one of the largest complaints that faculty have about administrators and that administrators have about faculty: that they are out of touch with the realities of the day-to-day experiences, the operations, and the mission of the institution.

Being in the position of half-time faculty and half-time administrator afforded me the opportunity to maximize Ancona et al.'s second capability, relating, which is focused on building relationships. The three ways the authors suggest accomplishing this goal are through inquiring, advocating, and connecting.

Inquiring is "listening with the intention of genuinely understanding the thoughts and feelings of the speaker" (3). To continue the example above, the town hall was successful at delivering information about the initiative, but it may not have been effective at helping faculty feel comfortable about their role in it. That's where my choice to inquire, to continue listening and relating to the faculty's concerns and experiences, became effective. Doing this work on a smaller scale, which I'm much more comfortable with anyway, such as with departments, college representatives, and individual faculty, began to have some impact in our conversations. I could use what I learned through rhetorical listening at the town hall and other conversations to ask similar but new questions about their concerns and continue to listen without judgment—as much as possible. Ancona et al. suggest that part of relating to others is considering how others will react to your ideas before you present them and using that knowledge to shape and deliver that message. I was able to listen and learn from those conversations to discuss the online program in a productive manner.

Advocating is explaining one's position while making "clear to others how [one has] reached their interpretations and conclusions" (Ancona et al. 3). Acknowledging the process of sensemaking provided me with the opportunity to relate to faculty in a productive manner versus the somewhat contentious tone that the project had assumed at the beginning. It was time to (re)articulate and advocate for the larger vision of online programming and "make clear to others" how we made the decisions to establish this initiative—this all with the knowledge, perspective, and understanding of their point of view.

Finally, connecting is developing a network of support. In other words, the purpose of relating is to create connections and enable open and frequent two-way communication channels. These iterations of asking questions, rhetorically listening for understanding, and advocating for this new method of providing students with expanded access to high quality education helped to establish a more collaborative vision for this change. Concerns were addressed and colleagues appreciated the efforts, even if their departments chose not to participate.

The process of relating to colleagues across the university contributed to the creative and iterative process of sensemaking. Throughout these meetings and one-on-one conversations, I would ask myself, "What am I missing here?" in order to revise the map and focus our vision.

Visioning and Inventing to Create Institutional Change

Visioning and inventing are most effective when the processes of sensemaking and relating are thoughtfully, thoroughly, and continuously engaged. Successful leaders look to "create compelling images of the future"; this is called visioning. Visioning "gives people a sense of meaning in their work" (Ancona et al. 2007 3). It gives them something to be excited about and work toward beyond maintaining the day-to-do status quo. Engaging in visioning invites colleagues to participate in fine tuning and crystallizing the vision of the future. In doing so, others will find opportunities to generate ideas and contribute to the work needed to achieve the vision.

Lastly, inventing is the way that leaders move "from the abstract world of ideas to the concrete world of implementation" (6). Ancona et al. (2007) prefer *inventing* over the term *execution* because it "emphasizes that this process often requires creativity to help people figure out new ways of working together" (6). Rather than "executing a plan" that is already developed and documented, inventing allows for more creative, responsive, and iterative ways to make the shared vision a shared reality.

I mentioned earlier that I had been in my senior associate dean role for about one year before the dean stepped down. Before that, the provost who launched the online program initiative moved to another institution. In his place was an interim provost who was willing to support the initiative but did not have the same commitment and nuanced understanding of it. Shortly after moving into the dean's office, a series of unfortunate events occurred that led to the termination of our relationship with the online program manager. At a small meeting in the university president's private conference room, I was asked: "Can you still deliver the online programs without the support of the online program manager, Beth?" My answer was: "Yes, of course." Was I 100 percent confident in my response? No. No way. Here we were with a significant investment of time and resources in building an online program infrastructure, several of the programs launched, several more in process, and no outside support to continue the work. But I could say yes because not only was I fully committed to the vision, but through sensemaking, relating, and visioning, we now had a significant mass of faculty and staff who were equally so. It was time to simultaneously develop this shared vision for online learning and (re) invent how that vision would be achieved.

Establishing, securing support for, and reinforcing a vision can be a heavy lift, but even heavier is all the work required to make the vision reality. The building of an online portfolio—something this large-scale that touches all aspects of the institution—requires logic, strategy, process, procedures, new policies, revised policies, a whole lot of positive networking based on well-established and new relationships, and the ability to encourage others to break outside of the tradition of how things have always been done. Listening rhetorically allowed me to use my voice and vision to engage in conversations about the new reality I hoped to develop and to encourage others to be excited about the possibilities to change and expand the way my university provides educational opportunities. With the university staff who have well-established processes, I rhetorically listened to understand what limitations they envisioned and to express appreciation for time and effort it would take to transition those workstreams to one that would be accessible for online students. With faculty, I rhetorically listened to their concerns about how this might change the university in unproductive ways, how their roles as instructors might change, and the amount of time it would take for them to make these shifts. Continually asking, "What am I missing?" enabled my team to move through the process of sensemaking the current situation, relating to our colleagues' perspectives without judgment, sharing the vision we were trying to achieve, and then working together to invent a new process to create and build a desirable, detailed, and compelling picture of the future that we worked collaboratively to make a reality.

An Incomplete Leader Keeps Asking "What Am I Missing Here?"

While the example of building and sustaining a university-wide online program portfolio illustrates well my leadership experience, this is not to say that most leadership challenges are easily narrated. It's much easier to tell the story and trace the line in retrospect than it would have seemed in the chaos of it all when nothing seemed particularly clear or manageable: when I was all but certain that the whole thing was going to fall apart. The reality is that everyday leadership brings a little bit of everything—and some days more than others. Every challenge brings the opportunity to listen and to advocate, to relate and to invent. Leadership is a continuation of successes and failures, all of which is and should be handled with a dynamic and flexible approach. Leadership can bring a lot of restless nights as you mull over words your colleagues said, or their silence, as well as words you said or should not have said.

In "Innovation Strategies to Address Challenges Facing Higher Education" (2019), Sukhwant Jhaj states that the work of university administrators "is no longer to identify a problem, propose a solution, and then bring a team together to implement the solutions. Instead, administrators help others realize their ideas to transform the institution. They must do this without initially knowing the right problems and solutions" (29). Based on what I have learned, this observation seems accurate and incredibly challenging, but it resonates with me as I continue to apply what I have learned through experiences and the leadership workshop to other potentially transformative projects such as the implementation of generative artificial intelligence and the integration of microcredentials into students' educational experiences. These types of projects can be achieved by realizing that we do not have all the answers.

And there is no way that we can have all the answers. It's tempting to relate the concept of the incomplete leader to imposter syndrome—that feeling that we will be exposed for not being as good as others might think we are. We might wonder if we are capable of, or even allowed to make big decisions (I did when I was the writing program administrator), how we got picked to step up to a new leadership position (I did when I accepted the invitation to serve as an associate dean of the College of Liberal Arts), if we are able to work on something completely new to our institution (I did when I accepted the invitation to serve as the senior associate dean of Extended University), or if we are ready and capable of leading a large organization with multiple units and pressures to succeed (I certainly did when I accepted the invitation to be dean of Extended University). However, if we accept that these feelings of self-doubt and anxiety are less about imposter syndrome and more about the productive realization of both our assets and challenges as an incomplete leader, we can accept and assume leadership roles more effectively. We don't need to be incapacitated by what we don't know and by the feeling that we should know everything. For me, much of that realization came through what I saw as one of my strengths—listening—and overcoming one of my challenges: finding my leadership voice.

Note: I'd like to thank Linda Adler-Kassner, Chris Gallagher, and Brian O'Reilly for their helpful feedback and conversations about what leadership looks like for me.

References

Ancona, Deborah, Thomas W. Malone, Wanda J. Orlikowski, and Peter M. Senge. 2007. "In Praise of the Incomplete Leader." *The Harvard Business Review* 2, 1–8.

Sukhwant, Jhaj. 2019. "Innovation Strategies to Address Challenges Facing Higher Education." *The International Journal of Design in Society* 13 (1): 21–33.

Kezar, Adrianna. 2012. "Understanding Sensemaking/Sensegiving in Transformational Change Processes from the Bottom Up." *Higher Education* 65, 761–780.

Kezar, Adrianna, and Peter Ekel. 2002. "Examining the Institutional Transformation Process: The Importance of Sensemaking, Interrelated Strategies, and Balance." *Research in Higher Education* 43 (3): 295–328.

North, Stephen. 2000. "Learning to Write is Hard and It Takes a Long Time." Lecture at Spilman Symposium, Virginia Military Institute, Lexington, VA, October 14.

Ratcliff, Krista, and Kyle Jensen. 2022. *Rhetorical Listening in Action: A Concept-Tactic Approach.* Parlor Press.

CHAPTER 9

Lessons Learned about Leadership

Duane Roen, *Arizona State University*

> *"Some of the most important qualities you may have been born with or you can develop are humility, empathy, resilience, self-awareness, self-reflection, the ability to communicate, and the willingness to take a risk because the ambition for the greater good has become more important for you than the ambition for yourself."*—Doris Kearns Goodwin, *The Leadership Journey* (Goodwin 2005, 5)

There is no shortage of books, articles, podcasts, blogs, vlogs, and professional development seminars on leadership in a wide range of fields. Some of them—such as Goodwin's—resonate with what I have learned to value; some don't. Although some of what I've learned about leadership appears in these kinds of sources, I have learned much more by listening to the words and watching the behaviors of people. I have observed how others have responded to those words and behaviors—much as Aristotle did when he crafted *Rhetoric* (Aristotle 1932). That is, for decades I have engaged in a form of participant-observation ethnography (Whitehead 2005) in which I have learned from the groups that I have been a member of and/or interacting with. My observations have moved back and forth along a continuum with "covert" at one end and "overt" at the other. That is, sometimes people didn't realize that I was making mental notes or even written notes on their behavior. At other times they did know that I was reflecting on their behavior because I commented on it and asked them about it. However, I realize that humans should be aware that others are observing—and learning from—human behavior whenever that behavior is on display. People notice what others do and say.

As I reflect on what I have learned, I draw on my forty-five years of experience in higher education as a teacher and an administrator at large research universities, with roles including program director, department chair, college dean, campus vice provost, and faculty senate president. During those years, I interacted with and observed colleagues; students; administrators at every level in the university; business, government, and educational leaders; and many members of the general public. From engaging with these people, I observed all the leadership qualities that I write about in this chapter. I also draw on my five years of teaching high school English and leading a group of K-12 language arts teachers in Wisconsin in the 1970s, where I learned from supervisors, fellow teachers, students, parents, and other members of the community in which I lived. Further, I draw on my experience growing up on a Wisconsin dairy farm, where leadership skills were expected at an early age. Finally, I draw on volunteer work teaching memoir writing in men's and women's prisons in Arizona since 2022. Incarcerated women and men inspire me with their resilience and their commitments to helping others. When I reflect on what I have learned from all of these people, I am overwhelmed by how much they have enriched my life with invaluable lessons. I am fortunate to have had such positive mentors and role models.

I also am grateful for a resource that has helped me hundreds of times—the Greater Good Science Center at the University of California, Berkeley, which "studies the psychology, sociology, and neuroscience of well-being and teaches skills that foster a thriving, resilient, and compassionate society." By frequently using their resources, I have come to appreciate that learning to be a leader is also about learning to "foster a thriving, resilient, and compassionate society" (Greater Good Science Center, n.d.).

The following list of lessons is by no means complete—I frequently talk to groups about more than thirty leadership lessons that I have learned. The list here focuses on the leadership qualities that I value most, and I realize that some readers of this chapter may not share my perspectives. My list also exemplifies Kenneth Gergen's (1991) observation that "persons exist in a state of continuous construction and reconstruction" (7). That is, my list may change a few more times before my life comes to a close because as Gergen further notes, "Each reality of self gives way to reflection, questioning, irony, and ultimately the playful probing of yet another reality" (7). I realize that this is anecdotal, but in those conversations, participants have frequently shared stories about how these leadership characteristics resonate with their experiences in a range of organizations. Further, when I have interviewed candidates for senior leadership positions, they have frequently talked about their own commitments to these characteristics.

If I were to synthesize the lessons into a single statement, it would be this: "How we treat people matters." During my life, no one has done more than Fred Rogers to raise my awareness of this principle. When my children were small from the late 1970s to the early 1980s, I watched *Mister Rogers' Neighborhood* with them when I could, and in every episode, in his gentle way, Fred Rogers showed millions of people, including me, how to treat others. And in the movie *A Beautiful Day in the Neighborhood* (Heller 2019), we see the power of how Fred Rogers treated others. An acquaintance of mine lived in Fred Rogers' real-life neighborhood in Pittsburgh. When I asked him what Fred Rogers was like in his daily life, my acquaintance smiled as he said, "The same as he is on his TV show."

With that in mind, I offer the following:

Lesson One: We should all be leaders every day of our lives.

Leadership is not tied to a job title—or to any job, for that matter. For organizations and communities to function effectively, every member of any organization or community can contribute to that functionality by engaging in the kinds of behaviors described in the lessons outlined in this chapter. That community could be a group of people in a business, a college or university, a unit within a college or university, a classroom, professional organization, a playground, or some other place where individuals work, learn, play, or engage in other activities.

I've learned this lesson—that we should be leaders every day of our lives—many times over in my life, from both negative and positive models. On the negative side, I have too often seen the adverse consequences when people have not taken needed action because they have thought that someone with more authority should do what needs to be done or because they were not able to muster the courage to do what needed to be done. On the positive side, I have witnessed instances when people of all ages, including children, have stepped forward to make others feel welcomed, included, valued, respected, and that they belong. And I have seen how these words and deeds have made others feel.

Lesson Two: Every organization and community benefits from having effective leaders at every level in the organizational chart.

Too often, people think that those who reside higher in an organization's org chart will provide the leadership that will make the organization function well. Although it is necessary for people higher in the organization to exhibit the qualities, characteristics, and behaviors described in this chapter, their leadership alone is not sufficient for effective functioning. There is a multiplier or synergistic effect when others in the organization—the more the merrier—engage in these ways.

I have learned this lesson in a wide range of organizations. For example, when I grew up on a dairy farm in Wisconsin in the 1950s, everyone, regardless of age, was expected to take responsibility to make certain that all the farm tasks got done—especially during the planting and harvest seasons. Likewise, when we farm kids were in a 4-H club, every member of the club was expected to pitch in to make the organization function. And now that I'm a member of a local branch of the NAACP, I see what can be accomplished when rank-and-file members serve on committees, staff tables at public events, and volunteer for other work that needs to be done. Of course, this lesson was reinforced every day when I worked at Arizona State University, where I saw so many students, staff, and faculty step up to make certain that the institution was making a difference in the lives of students and community members.

Lesson Three: Effective leaders listen with empathy and act with compassion.

To develop empathy, we need to listen to others so that we can learn more about how they have experienced life. On the basis of empathy, we can then act with compassion to respond in ways that are helpful to others. Isabel Wilkerson emphasizes that empathy needs to be "radical" if it is to make a meaningful difference in the lives of others:

> Radical empathy… means putting in the work to educate oneself and to listen with a humble heart to understand another's experience from their perspective, not as we imagine we would feel. Radical empathy is not about you and what you think you would do in a situation you have never been in and perhaps never will. It is the kindred connection from a place of deep knowing that opens your spirit to the pain of another as they perceive it.
>
> Empathy is no substitute for the experience itself. We don't get to tell a person with a broken leg or a bullet wound that they are not in pain. And people who have hit the caste lottery are not in a position to tell a person who has suffered under the tyranny of caste what is offensive or hurtful or demeaning to those at the bottom. The price of privilege is the moral duty to act when one sees another person treated unfairly. And the least that a person in the dominant caste can do is not make the pain any worse. (Wilkerson 2023, 386)

I'm going to be vague in describing a moment when this lesson was driven home vividly for me. I am frequently haunted by the memory. After a fire destroyed the barn on my family's dairy farm when I was in eighth grade, I went to work on neighborhood farms. One day on one of these farms, another hired-hand teenager was horsing around with the owner's young son as we were relaxing on the lawn after lunch. As the two of them were playing, the other teenager inadvertently scratched the owner's son's back with his fingernail. When the son went crying to his father, the father asked what had happened. The other teenager explained that he had accidentally scratched the son as they were running around. When the farmer asked me to confirm that, I stood there silently. The other teenager lost his job because I failed to act with the empathy and compassion that the moment called for. I learned from that incident, but I am still haunted by it.

Lesson Four: Effective leaders value, embrace, and practice humility.

Humility comes in many forms, but one that matters a great deal is intellectual humility, understanding that I as an individual don't know all that I need to know. Worthington et al. note the importance of humility in building community:

> In fact, humility—with its emphasis on accurate self-perception, modest self-portrayal, and other-oriented relational stance, as well as a penchant for showing up (or hiding) when egos are strained—is at the core of a cluster of virtues that bind society together, including love, compassion, forgiveness, altruism, generosity, gratitude, and empathy. All of those virtues have at their base the other-orientedness that is facilitated by humility. (Worthington et al. 2017, 3)

Without intellectual humility, we don't learn very much, and for people in higher education, that is particularly ironic.

When I was growing up on the dairy farm, I learned every day that intellectual humility is not only desirable but also essential. Because I was given adult responsibilities on the farm when I was six years old, I encountered problems to be solved every day. In some cases, I figured out the solutions on my own—e.g., find the right wood screw in the workshop to secure that hinge. In many more cases, though, I lacked the experience to puzzle through the problem, so I had to ask my dad or my farmer uncles how to repair a machine or how to help a sick animal. Seeking the knowledge of others became a way of life.

The importance of intellectual humility was probably most salient to me when I worked with a wide range of business owners and local government leaders in my role as vice provost of Arizona State University's (ASU) Polytechnic campus. Listening to them share their experiences in the world outside the academy did much to help me understand how educational institutions can more effectively support students as they prepare for their careers. I learned that academics don't know all that they need to know about the world outside the academy.

Since 2005, I have facilitated more than a thousand workshops (333 last year alone) in which participants discuss and write about life experiences. I offer these workshops in libraries, community centers, retirement communities, life-long learning programs, schools, and in both men's and women's prisons in Arizona, mostly in the Phoenix area. In facilitating these workshops, I have come to realize that I am learning much more from the participants than they are learning from me as we talk about a wide range of life's experiences. And I think that it's important to note that I have learned the most from incarcerated men and women because they—especially the women—have experienced life in ways that I have not. I tell all the workshop participants that I am grateful for the opportunity to learn from them at this stage in my life. I also thank them for supporting one another when their stories evoke strong emotions and tears in all of us.

Lesson Five: Effective leaders seek and value ideas from everyone in the organization.

With humility in hand, leaders see and value ideas from everyone in the organization—the department, the college, the institution. It took me a while to learn that lesson. Early in my career, I sought ideas from those whom I considered "in the know." However, that often yielded fairly modest lists of ideas. It took me a while to learn what Bill Nye the Science Guy observes: "Everyone you will ever meet knows something you don't" (Nye 2014). It can be a challenge to listen to ideas from people in organizations or communities with different ideas and even a bigger hurdle to take them seriously or to avoid responding defensively. However, Monica Guzman suggests that a productive way to respond is to be consistently curious and to say, "I never thought of it that way" (Guzman 2022, 57). We also need to add, "Tell me more." This response demonstrates intellectual humility and lets people know that we value a wide range of perspectives, as well as the people who offer those perspectives.

Lesson Six: Effective leaders value and practice effective communication.

Once there is consensus about priorities and goals for the organization, people need frequent reminders so that the priorities and goals aren't neglected. For example, Arizona State University's charter is a mantra that guides the work of faculty, staff, and administrators: "ASU is a comprehensive public research university, measured not by whom we exclude, but rather by whom we include and how they succeed; advancing research and discovery of public value; and assuming fundamental responsibility for the economic, social, cultural and overall health of the communities it serves" (Arizona State University Charter, n.d.).

ASU's charter is omnipresent, appearing in many places on the institution's website, in public documents, in many presentations, and even on granite monuments on each of ASU's four campuses in the Phoenix area. Because the charter is invoked so frequently (I did so multiple times each day when I was a dean and vice provost), most ASU employees know it and can explain its impact. I appreciate the communicative power of the charter inside and outside the institution because it emphasizes ASU's commitment to making a difference in the lives of students and in the community writ large. The charter consistently made it easier for me to communicate with a wide range of stakeholders because it exemplifies the kinds of ethos and pathos that work with so many people.

Since August 2024, I have been learning more about effective communication by listening to Nick Saban, former head football coach at the University of Alabama. On ESPN's *College GameDay* each Saturday morning in the fall, he regularly talks about how he communicated with football players to help them grow as students, athletes, and citizens of the world. As I listen and learn, I understand why he was so successful as a coach. He understands the impact of the words that he uses, and his sense of humor effectively complements those words when that is what's needed. Saban also consistently exemplifies the other characteristics that I describe in this chapter. And as I watch more YouTube videos of press conferences with ASU head football coach Kenny Dillingham, who was hired for the position at the age of 32, I increasingly value how he communicates with players and with just about everyone else in the world, for that matter. And his early-career success speaks for itself.

When the COVID-19 pandemic hit in March of 2020, I was a dean. I immediately scheduled two open Zoom sessions each week for any faculty or staff who wished to participate. Usually several dozen faculty and staff colleagues joined me. At the very first meeting, I learned how valuable these conversations were. Early on, the meetings focused on questions about policies, procedures, and resources related to the pandemic; often it meant that I'd explain things that may have needed further clarification, and others would share their ideas. After a while, though, the sessions included conversations about all sorts of topics related to teaching and learning, everyone's well-being, the university's sports teams, and more. I continued those twice-weekly sessions until I stepped down from serving as a dean in June 2021. Coworkers frequently told me how much they needed this kind of communication with me and with one another.

Lesson Seven: Effective leaders strive to motivate and inspire others.

Relatively early in life, I learned about the many ways that I could be motivated and inspired. For example, when my dad affirmed the value of the work that I did on the dairy farm when I was as young as six years old, that motivated me to do more because I felt that I was making a positive difference. In school when I read books about real people and fictional characters who had made a difference in the lives of others (e.g., Lincoln, Einstein, Franklin, Antigone), those stories inspired me, and they still do. When I watched the Harlem Globetrotters as a child, their athletic skills and their joy inspired me. And when I listened to people who talked about their experiences, I learned that they too were motivated and inspired in diverse ways. When I think about the people who have motivated and inspired me along the way, they are people who treated me and others in ways that are consistent with the leadership characteristics that I describe in this chapter.

A common method for motivating people is to praise their ideas and service—to compliment them for performance. However, as sports psychologist Stephen Rollnick observes, praise has limitations because it is "a judgment you pass down" on performance. Because performance varies from one event to another, praise often varies too, which can affect self-esteem—both positively and negatively. But as Rollnick observes:

> Affirmation, on the other hand, occurs when you acknowledge something inside the player that's already there, which cannot be taken away, like shining a light on something positive that you've noticed. It's something for them to notice too, take ownership of and be inspired by. If praise is a judgment you pass down, affirmation is something you notice, an observation you share, about

> positive things in their performance, ability, attitude or behaviour that they can take ownership of and can feel proud about. (Rollnick n.d.)

Another way to motivate and inspire is to remind members of the organization why their work is important. For example, for those of us who work in secondary and postsecondary education, the US Bureau of Labor Statistics each year provides data that reminds us why our work makes a difference in the lives of students. There is a table on the US Bureau of Labor Statistics website that vividly indicates the correlation between greater educational attainment, higher earnings, and lower rates of unemployment. In recent years, I have shared these data with colleagues and with the public. Every time I have done so, other people in the room have chimed in with comments that indicate how the data have inspired them to help students complete some form of postsecondary education, including vocational education.

Lesson Eight: Effective leaders understand their weaknesses and work to overcome them.

To understand our weaknesses, we need to be self-aware and reflective. Developing self-awareness is not always easy because we often are so busy living life that it can be difficult to find time to engage in reflection: "Active, persistent, and careful consideration of any belief or supposed form of knowledge in the light of the grounds that support it, and the further conclusions to which it tends, constitute reflective thought" (Dewey 1933, 9). However, as Kathleen Blake Yancey explains, reflection is formative:

> To reflect, as to learn, we set a problem for ourselves, we try to conceptualize that problem from diverse perspectives—the scientific and the spontaneous—for it is in seeing something from divergent perspectives that we see it more fully. Along the way, we check and confirm, as we seek

> to reach goals that we have set for ourselves. Reflection becomes a habit of mind, one that transforms. (Yancey 1998, 12)

If we seek role models for being aware of their weaknesses, Abraham Lincoln surfaces for me. In *Team of Rivals*, Doris Kearns Goodwin describes how "Lincoln possessed an uncanny understanding of his shifting moods, a profound self-awareness that enabled him to find constructive ways to alleviate sadness and stress" (Goodwin 2005, xvii).

When I was a child, I don't think that I was all that self-aware of how I was treating people. As a result, I think that I sometimes treated people well in the ways that I value today. However, I think that I sometimes did not treat people as well as I should have. By the time I was a teenager, though, I learned what it meant to treat people well even if I didn't always translate that learning into words and actions. Later in life, I developed the habit of reflecting on experience each day. That is, since October of 1978, my wife, Maureen, and I have written in a daily journal, and now (January 2025) we have written more than 21,000 pages of journal entries. The entries focus a lot on our experiences with our children, grandchildren, and other family members, but they also include details about what's happening in the world that day. As we write these daily narratives, I think about my role in each narrative. I frequently think about what I learned from the day's experiences and how I can do things more thoughtfully next time. Incidentally, keeping a daily journal is a gift to the journal writer and to future generations. When I read an entry from forty-five years ago, it brings back a flood of details about that day.

Lesson Nine: Effective leaders strive to develop their emotional intelligence.

Emotional intelligence is "the ability to manage both your own emotions and understand the emotions of people around you. There are five key elements to EI: self-awareness, self-regulation, motivation, empathy, and social skills" (Mental Health America n.d.). Emotional intelligence entails a fairly complex constellation of characteristics and skills, which explains why it can be so challenging to develop. It requires the same kinds of reflection and introspection needed to understand one's own strengths and weaknesses.

In leadership roles, as elsewhere in life, emotional intelligence is essential. It helps leaders to avoid letting their own perspectives overshadow or overwhelm the perspectives of others, and that helps to foster a culture in which others in the organization feel valued, which can enhance morale and collaboration (Cole, Cox, and Stavos 2016). In my own experience, I have seen how underdeveloped emotional intelligence can negatively affect working relationships to the point where people dread working with the individual. A vivid example stands out for me. During my second year of teaching in a high school, my Grandpa Roen passed away. When I asked my supervisor for a personal-leave day to be a pallbearer for Grandpa, he said, "A grandparent isn't close enough to you to warrant a personal-leave day." Of course, he did not ask me how emotionally close I was to Grandpa Roen, someone whom I had spent much time with for more than two decades and with whom I had lived for a year when I was in college. My response to my supervisor was, "I'm going to Grandpa's funeral. Dock my pay if you need to."

I have sensed growth in my own emotional intelligence as it has evolved during the last five decades, and that has helped me do the administrative work that has come my way in my career. That is, I have increasingly thought about "self-awareness, self-regulation, motivation, empathy, and social skills" (Mental Health America). For example, early in my career, if someone expressed anger toward me, I sometimes responded in kind. Along the way, though, I learned that responding to anger with anger was almost always counterproductive—it did not produce any positive results. I learned to be more aware of what I was thinking and feeling at the moment and what kind of response would lead to the results that were needed.

Lesson Ten: Effective leaders have a sense of humor and know how to laugh at themselves.

Humor and laughter have many benefits. The Mayo Clinic, for example, notes that in the short run laughter simulates many of the body's organs, reduces stress, and relieves tension. In the long run, laughter enhances the immune system, reduces pain, helps deal with difficult situations, and improves one's mood. Because of these benefits, Mayo suggests, "Find a way to laugh about your own situations.... It does your body good" (Mayo Clinic 2023). The US Department of Veterans Affairs (2024) also notes these and many other ways that humor and laughter affect our well-being.

My favorite example of laughing at yourself occurred during the semi-final game of the NCAA's women's Final Four game between Texas and South Carolina on Friday, April 4, 2025. Bree Hall, South Carolina's star player, turned to run down the court and fell on her behind. When she got up, she laughed heartily at herself, and her coach, Dawn Staley, joined in laughing with her. Hall's response to falling down reassured everyone that she was not injured; it also was a moment of wonderful comic relief in an intensely competitive game.

When I learned to laugh at myself, especially in front of students and colleagues, I saw the ways that it affected my working relationships with them. When others have laughed with me, it has helped them feel more comfortable around me; they have told me that. For example, I have to work very hard to remember names. When the COVID-19 pandemic hit in 2020, one of the benefits of teaching via Zoom in the spring of that year was that all the students' names were right there in front of me. I was overjoyed. However, that fall, faculty were back in the classroom, and students could choose whether to be in the classroom or on Zoom. By spring 2021, students were all back in the classroom, but everyone wore a mask. For several years, my method for learning students' names had been to make their roster photos into flash cards with their names on the backs of the photos. I would carry the photos in my pocket and review them many times each day until I had learned all the names. However, when everyone was wearing masks, the photos did not match the faces that I saw in the classroom. My solution was to use a felt-tipped pen to draw masks on every photo. It worked! When I shared this with my students and with colleagues, I laughed at myself for needing to use the flash cards and to draw masks on them, and everyone laughed with me because they understood how hard I was working to learn their names.

Lesson Eleven: Effective leaders know when to say, "I'm sorry. I made a mistake."

Last time I checked, all humans make mistakes. When we make a mistake, others in our organization know that we made a mistake. When we don't acknowledge the mistake, they will infer that we were either unaware that we made the mistake or that we are hoping that no one noticed. Which is better for one's ethos—being perceived as being clueless or being perceived as dishonest? That's a tough call. However, when we acknowledge that we made a mistake, our ethos benefits. People see us as self-aware, as honest, as human. If it is a mistake that negatively affects others, we of course need to make it right. We also need to apologize and let others know what we have learned from the experience. Kendra Cherry notes that "[e]veryone makes mistakes, and looking at them with humor can make them easier to cope with" (Cherry 2022).

At the beginning of each of the hundreds of writing workshops I facilitate, I quickly make a seating chart with the first names of participants so that I can use their first names during the session. For the people who have been participating in my workshops regularly for as long as fifteen years, I know their names. However, for people who started participating only a few months ago in monthly workshops, I have a very difficult time matching names with faces. That bothers me because when they greet me by name when they enter the room, I can't reciprocate. And when I make the seating chart, I sometimes need to ask them to remind me what their names are. This really bothers me at the prisons because the men and women have told me how much they appreciate being addressed by their first names. My solution is to apologize to the whole group for not remembering some of their names, and then I make a self-effacing joke about my memory. The group laughs, and we move on. They realize that I have a shortcoming, but they know that I care enough about them to work to overcome the shortcoming.

Lesson Twelve: Effective leaders strive to make people feel valued, supported, respected, and that they belong. They foster a culture of care.

I begin by noting that effective leaders are committed to diversity, equity, and inclusion. However, I have learned that using the words *diversity, equity,* and *inclusion* to describe that commitment can be counter-productive in some settings. As evidence, I point to enacted anti-DEI legislation in states such as Florida, Texas, and Iowa (Martinez-Alvarado and Perez 2023). However, in my conversations with a range of stakeholders, people more readily embrace the idea that we should foster environments in which everyone in the organization feels welcomed, valued, supported, respected, and that they belong. This has reinforced the lesson that I learned earlier in life and in my rhetorical education: The words we choose matter.

Michael Crow, president of Arizona State University, has modeled what it means to make certain that people feel welcomed, valued, supported, respected, and that they belong. He has steadfastly led the institution by fostering a culture of care. As noted earlier in this chapter, the ASU charter is a reminder that we must stay focused on a culture of care for students and the community. At the annual LIFT (Listen, Invest, Facilitate, Teach) Summit at ASU in 2024, President Crow summed up the institution's commitment: "We are still looking for more ways to follow the golden rule in the way we run this institution. No one will be left out for any reason, because the sum of us is too important" (quoted in Faller 2024). I will add that President Crow's comments and his decades of work also demonstrate that he advocates that we follow the platinum rule—that we treat students and the community as they want to be treated.

Lesson Thirteen: Effective leaders muster the courage to do the right thing even when it is not easy.

Courage is the ability to overcome fear to take action. It entails being able to face situations that we perceive to be harmful or dangerous. When Aristotle reflects on courage in *Nicomachean Ethics,* he notes some of what we fear in life: "disgrace, poverty, disease, friendlessess, death" (Aristotle 1973, 1115a, 10–14), and he explains why those fears are not insurmountable and why we need to consider them in light of a higher purpose. I learned to overcome the fear of death when I was in eighth grade. In January of 1963, our dairy barn burned to the ground. As soon as we realized that the fire could not be extinguished, we flew into action to get the cattle out of the burning building. We opened all the stanchions and the exterior barn doors so that the cows could get out. However, in the confusion of all that was happening so quickly, there wasn't time to ask my dad whether all the calf pens had been opened. Without hesitation, I ran into the burning barn to make certain that the calves could get out. While I was doing that, the barn filled with smoke so dense that I could not see my own hands in front of me. Fortunately, I knew the barn so well that I was able to feel my way along the walls to get to an exterior door. Along the way, though, that journey was challenging because cows kept running into me as they were escaping. I almost did not make it out of the building. After that incident, I felt more confident that I could overcome other kinds of fears.

People in leadership positions sometimes need to make decisions in situations that seem difficult to navigate. For example, there are situations in which a colleague's actions are harmful to others in the organization. Title IX violations fall into this category. When dealing with a Title IX case, institutional policies usually determine what happens in situations when there is a Title IX violation. Therefore, the supervisor of the person who engages in the violation doesn't determine the outcome of the case. However, the supervisor participates in the case in one way or another. For example, the supervisor may be required to sign a letter terminating employment.

In other cases, there may not be a legal requirement to terminate employment, but the supervisor understands how a colleague's words and actions are harmful to others in the organization. In those cases, it can be difficult to muster the courage to do what is in the best interest of the organization and other people in the organization. In a case where a colleague needs to leave the organization, the stress level rises, and the easier way out may be to ignore the individual's harmful behavior. However, ignoring the behavior will result in ongoing harm to others in the organization.

Leading up to the moment that a colleague's employment is terminated, the supervisor can feel considerable stress and even the fear that "I'm ruining this person's career." The moment when a supervisor informs a colleague that employment is ending can be very difficult. However, in the days and weeks after the supervisor has informed the colleague, the stress and fear give way to a sense of "I've done the right thing for the organization and others in the organization." And even though personnel actions need to remain confidential, others in the organization will notice the absence of the person who has caused harm. That realization will do much for morale in the organization, and enhanced morale will benefit the organization in many ways. In cases that I addressed, the harm was usually caused by some form of harassment.

In other situations, finding courage can be even more difficult—e.g., challenging the ideas of someone higher in the organizational chart. The same principle applies, though: do what will benefit the organization and others in the organization.

Lesson Fourteen: Effective leaders foster resilience in themselves and in others.

Resilience is "the process of adapting well in the face of adversity, trauma, tragedy, threats or even significant sources of stress" (American Psychological Association 2012/2020). Because I have had cancer twice and because cancer has taken the lives of so many loved ones in my life, I feel that I have a responsibility to encourage others to get recommended cancer screenings. However, I also use my experience with cancer to reflect on my own resilience and to help others think about the ways that they can find/develop the resilience that they need.

When I was diagnosed with prostate cancer in 2014, I had surgery and then moved on with my life. When I was diagnosed with mouth cancer in 2017, I thought, "I've been down this road before. No big deal." However, I quickly learned that where the cancer is in your body makes a big difference, and I have frequently laughed at myself for being so naïve. In 2017, I had two surgeries, six chemo treatments, and thirty-two radiation treatments. I lost more than forty pounds. There were days when I thought that I would not see the next day. There were also days when I did not want to see the next day. I would not wish my experience on anyone else, but I don't regret that I had to go through it because I learned much about my body, about medicine, and especially about resilience.

After I had recovered from the two surgeries, the radiation and chemo treatments began. In preparation for the thirty-two radiation treatments, the clinic staff made a plastic mesh mask that fit the shape of my head. They did that by heating the mask and stretching it to fit my face and head tightly. Because some patients feel claustrophobic when the mask is bolted down to the table, the clinic's staff asked whether I wanted to be sedated. I declined the offer, but I realized that I needed to do something to distract myself from focusing on having my head being bolted to the table. I decided to close my eyes and then name all fifty states, all the provinces of Canada, and as many European countries as needed to get through the treatments. It worked—probably because I'm so easily distracted.

The after-effects of my chemo treatments were challenging. For example, after my first treatment, I had nonstop hiccups for seven days, and for about eight weeks during and immediately after the treatments, almost all foods and beverages tasted awful, which meant that I lost more than forty pounds, which is not necessarily a bad thing. If it hadn't been for scrambled eggs and Boost, more pounds would have flown away.

Although the after-effects of chemo were unpleasant, the chemo treatment sessions were relatively easy, albeit time-consuming—several hours for each one. I read during those treatments, but I also realized that I could engage with the other chemo-treatment patients in the room—sometimes more than twenty. My favorite form of engagement was humor, and I relished the opportunity to get patients and healthcare workers to laugh. I enjoyed that opportunity so much that I looked forward to driving to the clinic each week for chemo treatments and each day for radiation treatments. Focusing on the welfare of other patients and healthcare workers shifted my attention away from myself. That did much to activate my resilience.

When I talk to others about my resilience during that challenging time, I acknowledge that what worked for me may not work for them. But when I tell the story, others chime in with stories about their own ways of being resilient. Sharing our own stories of resilience when life is challenging helps others realize that they too can get through tough periods of life.

Lesson Fifteen: Effective leaders understand the importance of relationship-building.

Early in my career, I showed up for meetings five minutes before the start time so that I wouldn't miss any of the discussion. However, I noticed that others were already there chatting with people in the room. It dawned on me that I was missing an opportunity to engage personally with other people in the room, so I began to show up fifteen minutes before meeting start times, and there were people already engaged in conversation. This was especially the case when, as vice provost of one of Arizona State University's campuses, I attended many off-campus meetings with business, educational, and government leaders—sometimes several dozen each month. So I began showing up at least thirty minutes early for those meetings. By doing so, I had many opportunities to develop working relationships and friendships with a wide range of community leaders—mayors, city council members, college presidents, school superintendents, business owners in the Phoenix area. As it turns out, I also had many opportunities in those pre-meeting conversations to explain to individuals how my university was serving students and the community. Among other things, some of those conversations were with parents of high school students who were contemplating which college to attend; in some cases those conversations resulted in recruiting students to attend my university. Those conversations were easy because I simply had to be interested in the person I was talking with.

Lesson Sixteen: Effective leaders are willing to take risks.

Early in life, I was relatively risk-averse—except for those times when my brothers and I, in our pre-teen years, floated down the Rush River near our farm in western Wisconsin each spring when the melting snow flooded the river and broke the ice into small chunks. Dressed in winter clothes, we would certainly have drowned if we had fallen off those small sheets of ice—something that our horrified parents made clear when we told them years later about what we had done as children.

Decades later, I learned how and why to take strategic risks—one of the lessons that I learned most vividly as a faculty member at Arizona State University for nearly three decades. ASU has embraced innovation wholeheartedly for more than two decades to better serve students and the public. Because of this commitment to innovation for the public good, ASU has been ranked the most innovative university in the country for nine consecutive years, beginning in 2015 (ASU News). ASU's commitment to innovation is fostered by President Michael Crow's view of risk. I have frequently heard him say that we should try new ways of serving students and the public, and if something doesn't work, we should try something else.

The most salient lessons that I learned about risk-taking came from my experience with online courses and programs. In the late 1990s, when I directed the writing program at Arizona State University, I worked with some graduate teaching associates who were eager to learn about the ways that digital technologies could enhance learning. I supported their requests to offer sections of writing courses in classrooms equipped with a computer for every student in the room. The undergraduate students in those sections seemed to enjoy and benefit from the experience. That was a small risk that paid off.

In 2004, I was asked to move from ASU's Tempe campus to develop new courses and programs at ASU's Polytechnic campus, located on an abandoned Air Force base, Williams Field. During my first summer, faculty across a range of fields in the humanities, social sciences, and the arts offered course sections that enrolled a few hundred students. When I asked students about summer enrollments, I learned that many of them went home for the summer, and a fair number of them enrolled in summer courses at colleges near their homes. When I asked them whether they would enroll in online courses in the summer, many said that they would. As a result, I encouraged faculty to offer online summer courses, and many did. As a result, approximately sixteen hundred students enrolled—about a seven hundred percent increase over the prior summer. Not everyone was happy about what I had done that summer, but soon after that, units in other colleges started offering online course sections in the summer and then during the fall and spring semesters.

Based on what I had learned from offering summer courses, I encouraged faculty to work with me to offer online degree programs—some of the earliest online degrees at ASU. When we launched our first online program in the college, enrollment grew relatively quickly. When I talked with students in the program, they emphasized a common theme: "I work full time; my children keep me busy; and I'm engaged in my community. My only option for earning a degree is an asynchronous online program because it provides the flexible schedule that I need. I couldn't attend synchronous on-campus classes even if I lived a block from campus." Those conversations made me realize that we must offer options that serve the needs of people who have been left behind by higher education. For some students in-person classes meet their needs; for others that option doesn't work.

In 2011, once I had become more comfortable with taking risks, I accepted an invitation from the administrator whose office supports the online programs offered by ASU's colleges— what is now named EdPlus. I was invited to work with other ASU faculty in my field to develop a low-risk first-year writing course that students could take as part of a suite of courses for Global Freshman Academy (now called Earned Admissions), an earned-admission program for students who don't automatically qualify for admission. The work was challenging, and some external critics voiced their skepticism. However, once again the risk paid off. Students who have been successful in the GFA courses have subsequently been successful after being admitted to college.

Coda

I opened this chapter with an excerpt from Doris Kearns Goodwin's book, *The Leadership Journey: How Four Kids Became President* because it effectively captures the gist of what leadership is all about. My heart sang as I watched a C-SPAN2 interview with Goodwin conducted by CNN anchor Bianna Golodryga in 2024. She talked about her book, written for students in the middle grades, focusing on the childhood experiences of Abraham Lincoln, Theodore Roosevelt, Franklin Delano Roosevelt, and Lyndon Johnson—with an emphasis on the qualities that they exhibited early and life and that shaped the way that they served in office later in life: "Some of the most important qualities you may have been born with or you can develop are humility, empathy, resilience, self-awareness, self-reflection, the ability to communicate, and the willingness to take a risk because the ambition for the greater good has become more important for you than the ambition for yourself" (Goodwin 2024, 5). I was especially excited during the interview when Goodwin noted that empathy is the most important of the qualities. My wish is that every young person in the country will read Goodwin's book so that they can see themselves as leaders every day of their lives and that they will continue to learn from and reflect on their experiences.

References

American Psychological Association. 2012/2020. "Building Your Resilience." *American Psychological Association.* https://www.apa.org/topics/resilience/building-your-resilience.

Aristotle. 1973. *Nicomachean Ethics.* Edited by Richard McKean. Introduction to Aristotle, 2nd ed. University of Chicago Press.

Aristotle. 1932. *The Rhetoric of Aristotle.* Translated by Lane Cooper. Appleton-Century-Crofts.

Arizona State University. n.d. "Charter." Accessed January 21, 2025. https://www.asu.edu/about/charter-mission.

ASU News. 2023. "ASU Ranked No. 1 in Innovation for 9th Straight Year." September 17. https://news.asu.edu/20230917-university-news-asu-no-1-innovation-nine-years-us-new world-report.

Cherry, Kendra. 2022. "The Benefits of Making Fun of Yourself." Verywellmind, May 20. https://www.verywellmind.com/the-benefits-of-making-fun-of-yourself-5271389.

Chervinsky, Lindsay M. n.d. "Abraham Lincoln's Cabinet." The White House Historical. *Association.* Accessed November 1, 2024. https://www.whitehousehistory.org/abraham-lincolns-cabinet.

Cole, Matthew Lawrence, John D. Cox, and Jacqueline Stavos. 2016. "Building Collaboration in Teams through Emotional Intelligence: Mediation by SOAR (Strengths, Opportunities, Aspirations, and Results." *Journal of Management and Organization* 25 (4).

Dewey, John. 1933. *How We Think: A Restatement of the Relation of Reflective Thinking to the Educative Process.* DC Heath.

Faller, Mary Beth. 2024. "Annual LIFT Summit Highlights How Support for Black Students is Embedded at ASU." *ASU News*, September 5. https://news.asu.edu/20240905-sun-devil-community-annual-lift-summit-highlights-how-support-black-students-embedded-asu?utm_campaign=ASU_News_News+9-6-24.

Gergen, Kenneth. 1991. *The Saturated Self: Dilemmas of Identity in Contemporary Life.* Basic Books.

Goodwin, Doris Kearns. 2024. *The Leadership Journey: How Four Kids Became President.* Simon and Schuster.

Goodwin, Doris Kearns. 2024. "The Leadership Journey." Interviewed by Bianna Golodryga. *American History TV*. C-SPAN2, September 3 Temple Emanu-El Streiker Center, New York City. https://www.c-span.org/video/?538074-1/the-leadership-journey.

Goodwin, Doris Kearns. 2005. *Team of Rivals: The Political Genius of Abraham Lincoln*. Simon and Schuster.

Greater Good Science Center. n.d. University of California, Berkeley. Accessed November 1, 2024. https://ggsc.berkeley.edu/.

Guzman, Monica. 2022. *I Never Thought of It That Way: How to Have Fearlessly Curious Conversations in Dangerously Divided Times*. BenBella Books.

Heller, Marielle, dir. 2019. *A Beautiful Day in the Neighborhood*. Film. Sony Pictures.

Martinez-Alvarez, Sayda, and Sandra Perez. 2023. "A Map of Anti-DEI Efforts on College Campuses Across the U.S." *The Education Trust*, November 15. https://edtrust.org/resource/a-map-of-anti-dei-efforts-on-college-campuses-across-the-us/.

Mayo Clinic Staff. 2023. "Stress Management." September 22. https://www.mayoclinic.org/healthy-lifestyle/stress-management/in-depth/stress-relief/art-20044456.

Mental Health America. n.d. "What is Emotional Intelligence and How Does It Apply to the Workplace?" Accessed November 5, 2024. https://mhanational.org/what-emotional-intelligence-and-how-does-it-apply-workplace.

Nye, Bill. 2014. "Commencement Address." *University of Massachusetts Lowell*, May 19. YouTube video, 1:00:02. https://www.youtube.com/watch?v=wzwX-qu5fRA.

Rollnick, Stephen. n.d. "Praise vs. Affirmation." *Player Development Project* (blog). Accessed May 14, 2025. https://playerdevelopmentproject.com/praise-vs-affirmation/.

US Bureau of Labor Statistics. 2024. "Earnings and Unemployment Rates by Educational Attainment." Accessed January 21, 2025. https://www.bls.gov/careeroutlook/2024/data-on-display/education-pays.htm.

US Department of Veterans Affairs. 2024. "The Healing Benefits of Humor and Laughter." May 1. Accessed January 21, 2025. https://www.va.gov/WHOLEHEALTHLIBRARY/tools/healing-benefits-humor-laughter.asp.

Whitehead, Tony L. 2005. "Basic Classical Ethnographic Research Methods: Secondary Data Analysis, Fieldwork, Observation/Participant Observation, and Informal and Semistructured Interviewing." *Ethnographically Informed Community and Cultural Assessment Research Systems (EICCARS) Working Paper Series*. July 17. https://www.depts.ttu.edu/education/ourpeople/Faculty/additional_pages/duemer/epsy_5382_class_materials/2019/Basic-Classical-Ethnographic-Research-Methods-Whitehead-2005.pdf.

Wilkerson, Isabel. 2023. *Caste: The Origins of Our Discontents*. Random House.

Worthington, Jr., Everett, Don E. Davis, and Joshua N. Hook, J., eds. 2017. *Handbook of Humility: Theory, Research, and Applications*. Routledge.

Yancey, Kathleen Blake. 1998. *Reflection in the Writing Classroom*. Utah State University Press.

PART 2

Theorizing Practice, Practicing Theory

A simple search engine query will reveal how common it is to talk about "the theory and practice of leadership." There are many books with a variation of that title. Less common, but we think crucial, is discussion of the relationship between theory and practice.

Too often, these two terms are presented as, or assumed to be, a hierarchical dualism: theory is first, then practice; theory is tidy, practice is messy; theory is pure, practice is compromised. Consider the familiar critique: "In theory, it's great, but in practice, it won't work." Theory is put on a higher plane, above the mishigas of real life.

We invite you to consider a more productive way to understand the relationship between theory and practice: not as opposing and mutually exclusive terms, but as related and dynamically interacting activities. To theorize without any attention to practice is merely to daydream; to practice without any attention to theory is to shoot in the dark. And to think of practice as only a pale shadow of an ideal theory is to underestimate the power of theorizing practice and practicing theory.

The chapters in part 2 demonstrate that power. Like their counterparts in part 1, the authors learn from their experiences through reflective practice. They also engage in extended engagement with one or more central principles that have shaped their leadership journeys. As you'll see, these principles are not just "theories," in the sense described above, and they aren't merely *put into practice.* But nor are they simply "practices"—things the authors do to approximate a theory. They are theorized practices—or, if you like, practiced theories. Principles, in other words, are the tie that binds theories and practices together.

In the Course Overview, we previewed our pragmatic (Deweyan) view of principles as "ideas to think with." Principles are statements of beliefs, ethics, ideals, values, and identities that give focus and force to our actions. At the same time, they function as guides, not blueprints or dogmas. We use the metaphor of the North Star. When you think of the North Star, you might imagine a single point, fixed in time and space. That's why it's useful as a navigational aid—it stands still while other things move around it. But of course, the real North Star, Polaris, does not stand still: it is constantly in motion, as are you when you view it. You're both hurtling through space. And yet, if you keep your eye on the North Star, you can indeed orient yourself. It's the same with principles: neither they nor you are fixed in time and space, but they can help you make sense of where you are and where you want to go.

An unfortunate result of the theory/practice dualism is that principles get treated as expressions of theory that must be applied in practice. In this kind of linear, top-down thinking, theory gets translated into practice by way of principles. We think of it differently—pragmatically, you might say. We see a three-way relationship among principles, theories, and practices:

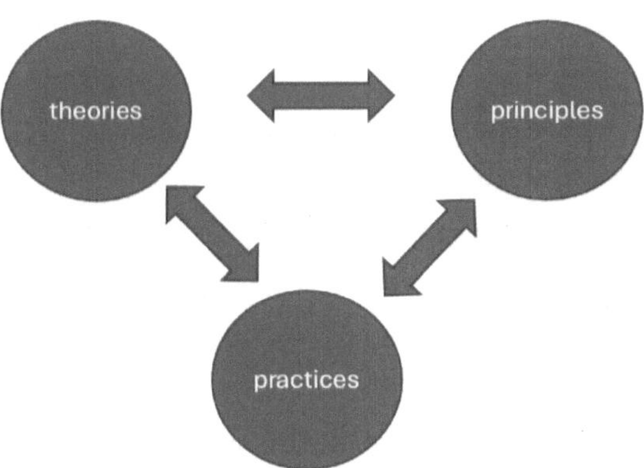

Figure 2.1. Theories, practices, and principles, shown as three interconnected circles with two-directional arrows.

As the bidirectional arrows suggest, the relationships are reciprocal and non-hierarchical. Practices inform our theories and our principles even as they are informed by them.

Or they *can*, at any rate—if we are critically reflective. Education/language theorists Cherryholmes (1988) and Pennycook (1997) have made a crucial distinction between "vulgar pragmatism" and "critical pragmatism." The former is basically what the caricature says pragmatism is: a preoccupation with functional efficiency, an unreflective acceptance of the way things are, a focus on optimizing what already exists. Critical pragmatism, by contrast, questions existing conventions, standards, expectations, and structures, along with one's own investments, behaviors, and decisions. For us, the *critical* part of critical pragmatism is the reminder to always ask: What is at stake for whom? Whose interests are served and whose are not? Whose voices are heard and whose are not? How can we work toward more just and equitable conditions, opportunities, and outcomes?

Critical pragmatism speaks to us as leaders for the same reasons it speaks to us as teachers:

- It recognizes, and draws critical attention to, inequitable institutional realities—without insisting they be overcome before any meaningful action can be taken *or* treating them as inevitable or immutable.
- It calls for a clear-eyed recognition of what is possible—while allowing us to hold on to our ideals.
- It helps us avoid dogmatism and rigidity—while preserving our integrity.
- It keeps us open to new learning—while grounding us in what we know and believe.

As you engage with the chapters in this section, we ask that you keep the dynamic relationship between theories, practices, and principles in mind. We also invite you, as we did in part 1, to pay attention to "the how"—in this case, how the contributors have learned to work within and against hierarchical and inequitable systems to promote diversity, inclusion, belonging, and justice. Specifically, consider:

- *How they navigate tensions between their personal, cultural, and institutional identities.* For example, Jonathan Alexander works to make sense of tensions between his queerness and upholding institutional norms. Sheila Carter-Tod chronicles her struggle for a sense of institutional belonging well into her leadership career.
- *How they craft leadership roles and activities that don't neatly align with institutional positions.* For example, Elizabeth Wardle explicitly crafts "in between" roles from which she can "broker" institutional change. Carmen Kynard, while refusing to accept institutional leadership positions beyond the program level, finds ways to lead—or, as she has it, to organize—and to sponsor student leadership (organizing) outside of, and sometimes in defiance of, institutionally defined (and thus heavily circumscribed) structures and processes.
- *How they keep their eyes on their North Stars, through thick and thin.* For example, Jonikka Charlton remains focused on "success for all students, especially those like Duncan" (her son, who doesn't fit easily into existing institutional systems) throughout her long leadership career. Candace de León-Zepeda holds fast to centering marginalized identities and creating *communidad* in these politically polarized times.
- *How they evaluate leadership opportunities in light of all of the above.* For example, Sheila Tod-Carter, despite seeing few people who looked like her in leadership roles and feeling like an "imposter," and even stepping away from leadership for a time, nonetheless chooses to lead again after letting go of unproductive conceptions of "expertise" and coming to "a greater understanding of agency-based social justice" work. Carmen Kynard, by contrast, lives her principles by *refusing* administrative positions in white supremacist institutions and choosing instead to lead, in her institutions and in the profession, on "fugitive learning."

While our contributors share broad commitments to social justice, *how* they pursue them differs, depending on the individual and their context. Even when they share principles, in other words, they theorize practice and practice theory differently. Notice this as you engage with the chapters; they repay careful reading.

References

Cherryholmes, Cleo. 1988. *Power and Criticism: Poststructural Investigations in Education.* Teachers College Press.

Pennycook, Alastair. 1997. "Vulgar Pragmatism, Critical Pragmatism, and EAP." *English for Specific Purposes* 6 (4): 253–69.

CHAPTER 10

Learning at the Boundaries

Feminist Invitational Rhetoric and Sensemaking toward Deep Change

Elizabeth Wardle, *Miami University*

Leadership in most institutions of higher education is understood as "positional leadership," i.e., leadership vested in the most senior personnel. These leaders have titles, staff, hiring and firing authority, and budgets. Yet most of these positional leaders have little if any training in leadership or leading change (Collins 2014, Solbrekke and Sugrue 2020). Absent systematic training and reflection on leadership, most have "implicit leadership theories" which they rarely if ever explicitly name (even to themselves). This can be a challenge for institutions, especially ones facing an urgent need to change, because the implicit leadership theories of positional leaders "create a force field in which… employees and students are obliged to play the game" (Solbrekke and Sugre 2020, 19). In other words, implicit and unexamined leadership theories create cultures in higher education. For example, higher education increasingly embodies "instrumentalist entrepreneurialism that privileges competitiveness, internationalisation, and rankings" (18). Because these cultures are surrounded by invisible theories, meaningful, innovative, and inclusive change can be challenging. If leaders do not examine their own approaches to leadership, then they can easily fall into leading change that aligns with the dominant culture of higher education that does not align with their personal values or with the academic values they seek to enact. With diminishing public funding and increasing skepticism about the value of higher education from parents and taxpayers (Flannery 2022; Jones 2024), it has been an increasing challenge for American academic leaders to enact practices that serve the public good in equitable and inclusive ways (Larabee 2017).

Rank-and-file faculty and staff can easily imagine that only positional leaders (those with titles and invested with the power to require certain actions) can make real change in their institutions. If educators do not feel agency to make change, it can be easy to be disheartened, especially if the change efforts initiated by positional leaders seem misaligned with values of equity and learning for the public good (providing an affordable and meaningful education for all students). This is particularly true in cases where top-down decisions do not include the voices and ideas of those doing the daily, on-the-ground-work of teaching and supporting students. And it can be easy to despair if the same methods for change are employed again and again with little to show for it, except hours spent in fruitless committee meetings and millions of dollars spent on external consultants (Kim 2023; Usher 2022).

I have spent all but three years of my career as a *non-positional leader*, which I define here as a person charged with some programmatic responsibilities, but who is not included in the hierarchies and org charts of institutions. For three years I was also a department chair, working with the powers of hiring, firing, and budget control. But that has been the exception. As a career-long writing program administrator (WPA), I have always been tasked with developing faculty, graduate students, and curricula, and sometimes also been charged with managing (often small and always fluctuating) budgets, and hiring and evaluating faculty, adjuncts, and graduate students, sometimes at the last minute and often for unlivable wages. In these roles, I have always had close and usually positive relationships with positional leaders (department chairs, deans, and assistant provosts, especially), but have not had their tools of power by which to seek to make change. This frustrated me early in my career, when the positional leaders I reported to would task me with major change responsibilities, seeming to believe I could simply tell my colleagues to do something—produce more credit hours, attract more diverse students, save money, teach differently—and the goal would magically be achieved. However, over time, I have come to appreciate the special nature of non-positional leadership and to explicitly begin to reflect on and intentionally shape my own leadership theory.

I have come to see the opportunity that such a non-positional leadership role allows, recognizing that this positionality presents openings to serve as a boundary broker between people in a variety of communities of practice—people who help make connections across group and community boundaries. In addition, I have come to understand that this in-between role also enables me to take advantage of a number of "levers" for change that positional leaders simply don't have (see Kezar 2018, 92). And I believe that what I have learned is also helpful for positional leaders who may struggle to guide their institutions through turbulent waters. In this chapter, I outline the framework I have been learning.

Leadership as Brokering Among Communities of Practice

Change can be hard for many reasons. One of them is that meaningful change requires working across communities of practice. Communities of practice "share cultural practices reflecting their collective learning" and members are engaged in a "joint enterprise," interacting around established norms, drawing on a shared repertoire of resources (Wenger 2000, 229). The boundaries between communities of practice can easily "create divisions" and serve as "a source of separation, fragmentation, disconnection, and misunderstanding" (233). We need only consider the disconnect between various campus communities of practice to see this division in action: positional leaders in high-ranking administrative positions such as presidents, provosts, and vice presidents are often disconnected from faculty; faculty themselves are aligned in various communities of practices with great differences: tenured faculty with job security and voting rights are in quite different communities of practice from per-credit-hour adjunct faculty; tenured faculty in the sciences or professional schools are in quite different communities of practice from tenured faculty in humanities, and so on.

Such divisions and disconnections often get in the way of meaningful efforts to lead needed change. It is easy for any leader to simply engage with people in their own communities of practice when facing hard decisions and attempting to imagine new paths forward. Looking inward, however, limits the opportunity for leading change. Wenger points out that a great deal of learning can happen at the boundaries of communities of practice. However, certain conditions must be created for this kind of learning to happen (2000, 234). Those conditions must be "intentionally promoted" by "people who act as 'brokers' between communities, artifacts (things, tools, terms, representations, etc.) that serve as what Star and Griesemer (1989) call 'boundary objects,' and a variety of forms of interactions among people from different communities of practice" (234–5).

As a non-positional leader navigating between the goals and mandates and culture of the positional leaders to whom I have reported and the many other communities of practice with which I have worked as a writing program administrator (WPA), I have frequently found myself presented with the opportunity to engage intentionally as a boundary broker. As a writing program administrator, I have always been a colleague of the faculty and staff I lead. My office has never been in an administrative building. I have always taught in the same programs as the faculty and graduate students I have led. When I led the writing program in the second largest university in the country, I knew by name every person who taught our writing classes. I could not ignore their (sometimes tenuous) material conditions, which affected their ability to engage in the academic work (and change projects) we were doing together. These teachers included part-time faculty (teaching introductory writing classes at multiple institutions for very little pay and low pay with no benefits), full-time but temporary faculty seeking to find their way into permanent positions, graduate students from a variety of English fields often teaching for the first time, and tenured faculty. I knew a lot about their varied (and often unrecognized) expertise, as writing teachers come from all sorts of backgrounds. In my current position, I lead a writing across the curriculum program. This entails extensive faculty development work supporting teachers across disciplines. In this role, I engage with people across even more boundaries, getting to know faculty and graduate teaching assistants from every discipline across campus and engaging with them across time as they seek to innovate their teaching, courses, and programs.

Engaging as a boundary broker with people across communities of practice for the purposes of making change together has meant bringing to conscious awareness my own implicit leadership theories, and learning to adjust my own behavior in order to build boundary processes to create bridges that actually connected practices across boundaries and made new knowledge. In other words, it was simply never possible to effect any kind of meaningful change at my last institution by calling a few committee meetings of the writing faculty and *telling them* to design a new first-year writing curriculum, or create a major, or figure out how to attract more students to the major we just designed. It has been even less possible in my current role to tell faculty from across the university that it is their responsibility to teach writing and that they should integrate writing into their courses. *Telling* does not result in changed ideas, and it doesn't result in change of any kind from a non-positional leader in a role supporting faculty development. This is especially true when change requires work across the boundaries of communities of practice. Wenger argues that meaningful work across boundaries requires "something to interact about … open engagement with real differences as well as common ground… commitment to suspend judgment in order to see the competence of a community in its terms," and ways to "translate between repertoires so that experience and competence actually interact" (233).

Who teaches us to create and lead such boundary-crossing change environments and efforts, however? I had no program administration training in graduate school, and the leadership seminar I participated in when I became a department chair primarily focused on management, not leadership (learning to read budget spreadsheets and abide by the accreditation guidelines for hiring, for example). When I enrolled in a leadership program for women and minorities, I received guidance about clothing and jewelry ("wearing flats instead of heels will ruin your career!" is an actual piece of advice given to me there) but no guidance in leadership or change theory. So, like most academic leaders, I was faced with the need to learn on my own.

My learning experience has primarily been one of trial and error and then finding theoretical and research frames (usually after the fact) that help explain why the methods did or did not work and provide some guidance for rethinking going forward. I am still in this process of learning, but here I will share a few of the frames and principles I have started to explicitly formulate over time, with examples. Perhaps these are useful to both positional and non-positional leaders.

Intentionally Design Opportunities for Deep Change and Sensemaking

Change theorists tell us that there are multiple levels of change. First-order change (changes to processes and policies) are usually fairly simple (or at least, not conceptually hard, even if structures don't make them easy to accomplish). But most of the important changes we want and need in higher education, given the major challenges we face, are second-order or deep changes (Kezar 2018). Deep change entails change to "values, assumptions, structure, processes, and culture" (85). One thing I have learned about leadership is that most of what is hard, interesting, and worthwhile in my experience is about deep change: helping faculty change their *ideas about writing*, for example, is the kind of precursor to the deep change that results in meaningful changes in curriculum, teaching, and assessment. Deep change cannot be mandated, since it entails conceptual and cultural change, which cannot be forced.

Because deep change cannot be mandated, leaders need a method for helping groups of people engage in the conceptual and cultural work that is necessary. Deep change requires sensemaking, which is both "an activity and a process" (Weick 1995) and entails both cognition and action (Gioia et al. 1994; Reinhardt and Gioia 2021). Sensemaking is a meaning-construction process that is repeated, ongoing, and inclusive (Kezar 2018). By its nature, then, sensemaking for deep change requires an approach to leadership that is not typical of higher education. It requires, as Wenger's boundary-crossing scholarship suggests, creating intentional conditions and opportunities for stakeholders to engage in conceptual shifts, learning from one another and imagining new possibilities together. The typical structures of higher education don't entail this kind of sensemaking. Committee meetings, department meetings, senate meetings, executive councils, advisory boards, and strategic planning efforts rarely entail inviting people from a variety of communities of practice to engage in sensemaking together.

I have learned to adapt this idea of sensemaking for deep change and add some additional components necessary for success: inviting *groups* of people to work *across time* and *engage scholarship* and theory as they *actively brainstorm and apply* what they are learning (Glotfelter et al. 2022; Wardle 2019). This kind of sensemaking structure requires careful design but not rigid oversight. This is an important distinction: as a leader, I need to design activities and opportunities that help people connect and actively ideate together, but I cannot and should not determine the destination and outcome for them in advance. This latter point is essential to the sensemaking principles I have been learning and enacting. All too frequently, committees and groups are brought together not to come up with ideas that will be received in good faith by positional leaders, but to come to the way of thinking already pre-determined by the positional leader. It is frightening, I am sure, for positional leaders to design sensemaking experiences where the outcome is not known, but such opportunities are essential if we genuinely want new learning and new possibilities to emerge, to see boundaries as opportunities, and to value and rely on the ideas of experts from varied communities of practice. In other words, deep change can't happen without methods that allow for surprises and innovations from unexpected sources.

In designing these kinds of opportunities, I have drawn heavily on learning theories (Lovett et al. 2023), the threshold concepts framework (Meyer and Land 2005), and design thinking (Grabill, Gretter, and Skogsberg 2022). For example, since 2017, I have led a program at my current institution that brings together teams from multiple programs and departments, who engage together weekly for a semester or daily for two weeks in the summer (see Glotfelter et al. 2022). The program is carefully structured so that each week participants read theory and scholarship and then actively apply it to the challenges in their programs. This application is truly *active*: they brainstorm on giant Post Its, keep journals and logs, collect and analyze data together, etc. (Some of this activity is described in Adler-Kassner and Wardle 2022).

The key to this work is that the *teams decide what problems they want to solve and what their outcomes and deliverables will be*. As a result, they often enroll in the program to redesign a course or assignment but end up completely redesigning multiple courses or entire programs, imagining new forms of assessment, or creating new opportunities for other faculty in their programs to engage in sensemaking. I have recently revised the structure as part of a Lumina-funded Sensemaking for Success Seminar (Chapin 2024), and started including an evolving Change Plan (adapted from my colleagues Alex Arreguin and Stacy Wilson at Mesa Community College) that teams adjust regularly as they learn more together about the problem they want to solve, who their stakeholders are, and what the primary and secondary research suggests.

Design thinking activities have come to play a greater and greater role in this work, as faculty engage in various activities such as "gathering empathy" (asking students, parents, staff, and others about their feedback on the problem and ideas), asking multiple "how might we" questions to clarify the goals and problems, and writing theories of change for their problem ("X would happen if Y occurred," see BeautifulTrouble.org. The Playbook also has resources to develop your theory of change.) (I am grateful to my Miami University colleague from arts entrepreneurship, Todd Stuart, and Karen Tilstra from Creativity Effect for helping me understand this approach).

I have learned to carefully craft such sensemaking opportunities by making sure that participants are guided to actively read, think, communicate, and brainstorm across boundaries—but to carefully limit my own role as a boundary broker who helps leverage their expertise but does not tell them what solution I might want or have in mind (and because I now work with faculty from so many disciplines with which I have little familiarity, I usually could not insert my own goals for them even if I wanted to—a helpful piece of this sensemaking method). The results have been transformational for many people, departments, and programs at Miami University and beyond (see Glotfelter et al. 2022), but the method I am learning is far from perfected. Every group with whom I engage teaches me something new about how to create sensemaking structures that might be more effective next time.

A Feminist Invitation to Sensemaking Efforts

Often, when I tell people about these sensemaking efforts, they ask how I "get" people to agree to participate in them, and why people would agree to spend so much time on efforts that rarely result in publication. I admit that at first, I wasn't really sure (free snacks? good jokes? none of this seemed plausible), but over time I have started to understand and intentionally design invitations and experiences that are appealing to faculty.

We live in a culture of mandates, in what Tyler Branson (2022) and Patrick McGuinn (2006) have described as a policy regime of required accountability, where the economic and cultural forces tend toward forceful telling and requiring institutions to prove compliance with what are often proxy measures (O'Neil 2016) for the things we care about. The constant decrease in funding for higher education in the United States and the push to do more with less creates a culture where anxious and sometimes desperate American higher ed leaders try to force through changes without first engaging in building consensus and identifying shared values. Moreover, we live in a broader culture right now where many people from all corners of the ideological spectrum are certain their views are correct and often try to shame or intimidate others into adopting them. None of this makes it easy for leaders to design engaged sensemaking opportunities or for potential participants to be willing to engage in good faith. We've all spent hours of our lives on committees and task forces where our work had no demonstrable impact, and it's hard to convince people who have had that experience to continue to participate.

Yet at my current institution, nearly 200 faculty members since 2017 have voluntarily participated in a semester-long sensemaking opportunity. Forty-eight of them also voluntarily participated in a three-day change retreat. Another forty-eight faculty from across Ohio, where my current institution is located, recently spent eight days of their summer in Oxford, Ohio, engaged in sensemaking efforts—with no compensation. Hundreds of faculty on my campus participate in our various development efforts each semester, including semester-long faculty learning communities. Why do they do it?

With the help of some of my current and formal doctoral students (Caitlin Martin, Mandy Angela Glotfelter, Mandy Olejnik, Rena Perez), I have come to see the invitation we have been extending through a lens shaped by feminist rhetorical theory. Rhetoric scholars Sonja Foss and Cindy Griffin describe what they term feminist invitational rhetoric, wherein leaders extend "an offering, an opening, or an availability, and not an insistence" (1993, 16). The role of a leader who engages in this kind of work harkens back to the spirit of 1970s feminism, described by Sally Miller Gearhart as creating "an atmosphere in which growth and change take place" (Gearhart 1979, 198). The programming we have been offering invites but does not demand participation; I regularly beg positional leaders never to make participation mandatory. I believe that it would be challenging for participants to trust that their ideas and solutions would be heard and valued if people forced them to participate in a program they did not choose.

The sensemaking event is also carefully designed by me and others as co-facilitators, but also co-constructed: the participants choose what problems they want to solve and how to apply what they are reading and learning to their contexts. They are treated as experts with agency; sometimes they read and discuss theory and scholarship that they reject. Sometimes they have differing views from others in the seminar. Gearhart describes the necessity, in a feminist invitational approach, of "co-creation of an atmosphere in which people…if and only if they have the internal basis for change, may change themselves" (1979, 198). Scholarship and activities are offered as "an opening" for changemaking, but participants are understood and engaged as scholars with free will who are respected. They "may *choose* to hear or choose to learn"—or choose not to (Gearhart 1979, 198 and 200, emphasis added). Many of them comment on this in their anonymous surveys about our programs, noting that they are "treated like adults" with autonomy who are respected for their disciplinary differences.

When conceptual change (around writing, learning, teaching, educational systems) occurs—and it does quite frequently—it is a result of a new process of discovery and questioning. Foss and Griffin (1995) tell us that in the traditional rhetorical model, change "is defined as a shift in the audience in the direction requested by the rhetor, who then has gained some measure of power and control over the audience" (6). But the invitational model does not see change like this as its purpose; *if* change occurs, it is "a result of new understanding and insights gained in the exchange of ideas" and because "diverse positions" can be compared in a "process of discovery and questioning" (6).

This kind of work requires safety and trust. Traditional change processes are often "accompanied by feelings of inadequacy, insecurity, pain, humiliation, guilt, embarrassment or angry submission on the part of the [participants] as rhetors [speakers, writers] communicate the superiority of their positions and the deficiencies of those of the [participants]" (6). In a feminist invitational approach to sensemaking, the leaders recognize the value of participants' "thinking and understanding" (6), even at the expense of speedy consensus. While the experience might sometimes still be painful, that pain comes from the "wrenching loose of ideas" (6), not coercion or humiliation. Communicating respect for others with gratitude is a central part of the process (6). During the COVID-19 pandemic, the center I direct began offering a variety of safe sensemaking spaces for faculty and staff and invited them to a six-week seminar on redesigning courses for justice and inclusion. During one of those virtual meeting sessions, participants drew and labeled maps of campus and indicated where they felt valued and safe. One participant held her map up to the camera and said, "I just learned the only place I feel safe on this campus is in this center. Even virtually." I was shocked—and humbled into a recognition of the necessity of inviting people somewhere safe if we are to ask them to do hard change work together.

It is difficult to imagine what higher education would look like if we approached problems as opportunities for sensemaking for deep change from a feminist invitational perspective. Early in my career I scoffed at the idea that affect, emotion, and other non-intellectual concerns should be part of the planning and implementation for any effort. But I learned, often the hard way, that trust, safety, respect, and choice were central not only to participation but also to whether any implemented idea would stick.

When I wanted to change the curriculum for a large first-year writing program (Wardle 2013), there was no possibility of just *telling* people to do it. Moreover, the people who needed to do it were among the least valued, least paid people at the institution. More than a few of them told me that their former tenured colleagues in English had worked with them for a decade or more and never spoken to them or made eye contact; at department meetings, they had been told to sit around the edges of the room instead of at the table. I learned how to make change *with* my colleagues, which resulted in a different and more robust curriculum than I would have imagined on my own. The curricular change process had to entail respect and creating trust as part of a continued effort to engage people *as though they had expertise and would be heard*. There was no reason for them to believe any words I might have said about the work; the only persuasive rhetoric was inclusive action and invitation across time. I asked for volunteers interested in teaching a pilot curriculum and truly meant that *volunteers* were welcome and no one was forced; some of the first volunteers were adjunct (part-time) faculty teaching at multiple institutions without degrees in the field of writing studies. I invited all of the faculty to participate in assessing student work and compare outcomes for the different curricula so that they could judge differences for themselves. I asked the pilot teachers to lead reading groups with their colleagues where I was not present, so that they could engage as equals around new ideas. This method took several years, but when the curriculum was officially revised using the ideas of all of those who had participated in the sensemaking process, almost everyone had bought in. I left that institution a number of years ago, but the curriculum continues (and continues to evolve) because everyone was involved in making change, and because the people who deliver it created it together.

There is a lot I could have done better. I was, essentially, making it up as I went, and I could have had a lot more humility about that fact. It was not until very recently that I even had the framework for understanding how I was trying to engage in that change effort—which is, of course, why we need training in leadership theories and methods.

Conclusion

At this moment of existential crisis for higher education, higher education leaders need to be able to make their leadership theories explicit and embrace an approach to leading change that does more inviting and less insisting, including people at the problem-solving table who are often excluded, and getting beyond committees and strategic plans to design meaningful sensemaking opportunities. Choosing to embrace feminist invitational sensemaking to work at the boundaries of communities of practice requires putting aside the typical modes of behavior expected of positional leaders and instead recognizing that there is much to be gained from engaging in a carefully scaffolded process without predetermined conclusions.

References

Adler-Kassner and Wardle. 2022. *Writing Expertise: A Research-Based Approach to Writing and Learning Across Disciplines*. WAC Clearinghouse. https://wac.colostate.edu/books/practice/expertise/.

Branson, Tyler. 2022. *Policy Regimes: College Writing and Public Education Policy in the United States*. Southern Illinois University Press.

Chapin, Josh. 2024. "Howe Center's Sensemaking for Student Success Program Receives Lumina Grant." https://miamioh.edu/news/2024/03/howe-centers-sensemaking-for-student-success-program-receives-lumina-grant.html.

Collins, James P. 2014. "Leadership and Change in Twenty-First Century Higher Education." *BioScience* 64 (7): 561–62.

Flannery, Mary Ellen. 2022. "State Funding for Higher Education Still Lagging." *NEA Today*. https://www.nea.org/nea-today/all-news-articles/state-funding-higher-education-still-lagging.

Foss, Sonja, and Cindy Griffin. 1993. "Beyond Persuasion: A Proposal for Invitational Rhetoric." Unpublished manuscript. Presented at Speech Communication Association Convention, Miami, Florida.

Foss, Sonja, and Cindy Griffin. 1995. "Beyond Persuasion: A Proposal for Invitational Rhetoric." *Communication Monographs* 62 (1): 2–18.

Gearhart, Sally Miller. 1979. "The Womanization of Rhetoric." *Women's Studies International Quarterly* 2 (2): 195–201.

Gioia, Dennis A., James B. Thomas, Shawn M. Clark, and Kumar Chittipeddi. 1994. "Symbolism and Strategic Change in Academia: The Dynamics of Sensemaking and Influence." *Organization Science* 5 (3): 363–383.

Glotfelter, Angela, Caitlin Martin, Mandy Olejnik, Ann Updike and Elizabeth Wardle. 2022. *Changing Conceptions, Changing Practices: Innovating Teaching Across Disciplines*. Utah State University Press.

Grabill, Jeffrey, Sarah Gretter, and Erik Skogsberg. 2022. *Design for Change in Higher Education*. Johns Hopkins University Press.

Jones, Jeffrey. 2024. "U.S. Confidence in Higher Education Now Closely Divided." Gallup, July 8. https://news.gallup.com/poll/646880/confidence-higher-education-closely-divided.aspx.

Kezar, Adriana. 2018. *How Colleges Change: Understanding, Leading, and Enacting Change*. 2nd ed. Routledge.

Kim, Joshua. 2023. "Universities, Consultants, and 'The Big Con.'" *Inside Higher Ed*, April 24. https://www.insidehighered.com/opinion/blogs/learning-innovation/2023/04/24/universities-consultants-and-big-con.

Larabee, David. 2017. *A Perfect Mess: The Unlikely Ascendency of American Higher Education*. University of Chicago Press.

Lovett, Marsha, Michael Bridges, Michele DiPietro, Susan Ambrose, and Marie Norman. 2023. *How Learning Works: Eight Research-Based Principles for Smart Teaching.* Wiley.

Meyer, Jan and Ray Land. 2005. "Threshold Concepts and Troublesome Knowledge: Epistemological Considerations and a Conceptual Framework for Teaching and Learning." *Higher Education* 49, 373–388.

McGuinn, Patrick. 2006. "Swing Issues and Policy Regimes: Federal Education Policy and the Politics of Policy Change." *Journal of Policy History* 18 (2): 205–240.

O'Neil, Cathy. 2016. *Weapons of Math Destruction: How Big Data Increases Inequality and Threatens Democracy.* Crown.

Reinhardt, Alexandra and Dennis Gioia. 2021. "Upside-Down Organizational Change: Sensemaking, Sensegiving, and the New Generation." In *The Oxford Handbook of Organizational Change and Innovation,* 2nd ed., edited by Marshall Scott Poole and Andrew H. Van de Ven. Oxford University Press.

Solbrekke, Tone Dyrdal, and Ciaran Sugrue. 2020. *Leading Higher Education as and For Public Good: Rekindling Education as Praxis.* Jossey-Bass.

Star, Susan Leigh, and James R. Griesemer. 1989. "Institutional Ecology, 'Translations' and Boundary Objects: Amateurs and Professionals in Berkeley's Museum of Vertebrate Zoology, 1907–39." *Social Studies of Science* 19 (3): 387–420. https://doi.org/10.1177/030631289019003001.

Usher, Alex. 2022. "How Big Consulting Thinks About Higher Education. Higher Education Strategy Associates." *Higher Education Strategy Associates.* https://higheredstrategy.com/how-big-consulting-thinks-about-higher-education/.

Wardle, Elizabeth. 2013. "Intractable Writing Program Problems, *Kairos*, and Writing about Writing: A Profile of the University of Central Florida's First-Year Composition Program." *Composition Forum* 27. https://compositionforum.com/issue/27/ucf.php.

Wardle, Elizabeth. 2019. "Using a Threshold Concepts Framework to Facilitate an Expertise-Based WAC Model for Faculty Development." In *(Re) Considering What We Know: Learning Thresholds in Writing, Composition, Rhetoric, and Literacy,* edited by Linda Adler-Kassner and Elizabeth Wardle. Utah State University Press.

Wenger, E. 2000. "Communities of Practice and Social Learning Systems." *Organization* 7 (2): 225–246.

Weick, Karl.1995. *Sensemaking in Organizations*. Sage Publications.

CHAPTER 11

Fugitive Learnings

An Endarkened Feminist Inquiry into Administrative Refusals and Creative Escapes

Carmen Kynard, *Texas Christian University*

This inquiry takes its inspiration from Cynthia Dillard's (2000) now 25-year-old treatise, "The Substance of Things Hoped for, the Evidence of Things Not Seen: Examining an Endarkened Feminist Epistemology in Educational Research and Leadership." Dillard's article has propelled a wide range of theory-building and other-world-making. Her work reframed and re-theorized leadership from the lived experiences and narratives of Black women and Black feminists. She flowed from a long trajectory of feminists of color who have rejected western, patriarchal norms of knowledge-making that require folx of color to disconnect from their own lived experiences and thereby ignore their most crucial site of theorizing and learning (Hurtado 1996). Dillard, like the Black feminists before her, calls for a transgression of accepted content, language registers, discursive styles, and disciplinary conventions and further defines this kind of educational praxis and scholarship as *endarkened* (Hurtado 1998). Thus, simplistic debates about quantitative versus qualitative methods, social justice pedagogies versus traditionalist paradigms, or digital literacies versus analog learning belong to false binaries that evade the necessary work of really interrogating the philosophical origins and methods of Black and Brown educational oppressions (Dumas 2016, Sandoval 2000). Endarkened feminist epistemology is thereby not merely another "difference" to be celebrated or placed in a sea of every other paradigm. It must unlearn traditionalist schooling and point towards something else.

I offer here an "endarkened" Black feminist inquiry into the deep failures of administrative structures and processes in addressing racial harm in American universities (McClish-Boyd and Bhattacharya 2021). This very personal-as-political narrative writing is a process that unravels my own fugitive learnings, which means I must ask: What alternative models of living, thriving, and imagining in the academy are truly available to me? (Okello 2024). As a shorthand for fugitivity, I am referencing notions of creative escape or hideaway from white supremacist structures—both literally and metaphorically—in the specific histories of Black life and aesthetics traced back to enslavement. These legacies of fugitivity remain viable as a way of life in the American university, which my endarkened narrative will attempt to uncover and recover. I would even argue that endarkened narrative writing itself is fugitive. "Endarkened" purposely counters the academy's white, bourgeois prosaic forms that date back to the European Enlightenment, most simply defined as the intellectual movement of western Europe's seventeenth and eighteenth centuries that defined the notions of humanity—kept sacrosanct today by the academy's founding disciplines and departments—during the exact time of racial enslavement and Indigenous removal. This notion of "endarkened" is an especially critical overture, because it seeks to stand on the outside of the Enlightenment's liberal humanist precondition of antiblackness (Malaklou 2021). Our disciplines and language registers are deeply rooted in antiblack origins and this shows up in the ways we cast our words about Black folx in American research and scholarship. In contrast, Black feminist "endarkened" writing is a living thing that sees, thinks, breathes, and speaks back to its multiple oppressions, all while breaking Enlightenment habits, European canons, folx's feelings, and closed white circuits. It is form, methodology, theory, and radical practice.

In this chapter, I situate myself as a race-radical Black feminist who interrogates larger university contexts from the spaces of what I will define as fugitive learning (Harney and Moten 2013; Kelley 2016; Givens 2021; Yang 2017). From my vantage point, I have continually witnessed an American academy that runs as a poorly-managed big business, holds no one accountable (especially those who are most privileged), promotes unlawful pedagogies and wider behaviors, anoints the most problematic perpetrators of harm, uses every layer of writing instruction to indoctrinate whiteness, denies the most horrific origins of its compromised and unethical histories, and shows up with as many nefarious coups and self-interest-driven alliances vying for power as HBO's eight-season series, *Game of Thrones*. I see the American university from what might be an altogether different lens from the typical liberalist humanist lens on the common good, life of the mind, and great books/great ideas (Kynard 2023). My narrative thus questions the possibilities and limitations of leading institutions still so fraught with and built upon legacies of oppression for BIPOC communities.

And so I travel back to the first year of college, to the place that I call my teaching home: the college composition classroom. It's where I have learned and unlearned everything about the violence of the western academy.

"On the Crime Side, the New York Times Side"[2]: When White Supremacist Curriculum Criminalizes Minoritized Students and Protects White Interests

In one auspicious year in a first-year writing classroom in the heart of New York City, the most populous city in the United States, a group of students came to talk with me during office hours. I assumed their concerns would be related to the course, but instead they wanted to discuss issues about a different class and professor. I was still relatively new to the college, so I had no real context or background information on who they were describing. Brown and Black students often seek my

2 Lyrics from the song "C.R.E.A.M." by Wu Tang Clan.

advice on ways to navigate the university, especially when it comes to writing, but these conversations far surpass what we often limitedly call mentoring. Instead, students and I are engaging in a way of co-learning and challenging the absurd and harmful processes of white supremacist schooling.

The students who visited me that day were interested in issues of justice and drug addiction in Brown and Black communities. They were enrolled in a course that examined these politics as well as policy and rehabilitation practices that support folx experiencing addiction. One particular assignment got them real twisted: an interview with a "crackhead," the pejorative and ableist term used to describe someone who is addicted to crack cocaine (a highly addictive drug that is produced by dissolving powdered cocaine, boiling it until a solid, drying it, and then breaking it off into chunks/rocks). This term, "crackhead," has been intentionally wielded against poor communities of color since the 1980s Ronald Reagan administration, when industries left the US's largest cities populated by mostly Black and Brown communities. More impoverished than before, these communities turned to underground drug economies, which then led to their being targeted as national enemies in the US War on Drugs (Alexander 2010; Hinton 2016). When these students asked the professor what made him assume they had such ready access to centers of crack-cocaine addiction, he simply told them to take a subway train up to the Bronx, the poorest borough of New York City, and interview "crackheads out in the streets." The students were incensed and initiated a lengthy conversation about the dangers of getting "shanked" (i.e., stabbed) for the kind of thing he was asking them to do with folx they didn't know. None of these students were familiar with IRB/human subjects requirements or qualitative research ethics, but they seemingly cared more for such issues than the actual professor who was "trained" in these practices and yet presented "crackheads" and the "Bronx streets" as a free-for-all playground for university data extraction. It was not lost on the students, either, that the professor located drug addiction solely in poor, Black and Brown communities and not in the wealthy white suburbs of nearby New

Jersey, Connecticut, Long Island, or Manhattan. At the time, those white enclaves were experiencing catastrophic loss and devastation in relation to the methamphetamine and opioid drug crises (and before that, large powder-cocaine consumption, the drug of choice for wealthy whites that was never similarly criminalized) (Jalal et al. 2018, Kim, Morgan, and Nyhan 2020). No, the professor only targeted the Bronx.

I was livid. I fully expected that students would campaign against this professor, his assignment, and his whole vibe. Instead, the students contended that this professor was very privileged at the school and in his discipline, and that it wasn't safe or wise for them to complain to the administration. Given this tangle of misfortunes, these students had a special request for me: given my age (which is always the beginning of a truly humbling conversation with young people), what were the best 1980s and 1990s movies that featured "crackheads"? Their plan was to use quotations from such movies in their papers for the required interview aspect of the assignment, make sure no two students used the same words, and simply submit this work to the professor. They insisted he would not know the difference. We sat in my office and looked up multiple movies on my computer for quite some time, mostly because I just couldn't stop laughing (maybe even laughing to keep from crying). There may have even been a moment (I plead the Fifth here) where the students were provided with a full-bodied demonstration of Samuel L. Jackson's iconic "Gator Dance" from Spike Lee's movie *Jungle Fever*.

They all passed the assignment.

I found these students' counternarratives quite radical in exactly the ways that Aja Martinez (2020) describes the impact of counterstories: narratives based on the "experiential knowledge" and "lived reality" of BIPOC in white institutions produce their own unique rhetorical and theoretical exigency. Their professor asked for problematic, racist stereotypes and they gave them to him—and no one got "shanked" in the process. However, no one learned anything transformative or even accurate about race, urban struggles, antiblackness, mental health, and addiction from his lower-division writing-intensive class. Instead, they had first-row seats to the saliency of racism in preventing wellness for BIPOC even in the professional spaces where their wellness was purportedly the focus.

This story is absolutely absurd, but white supremacy is never logical, veiled, or intelligible. The sheer lunacy of the event is matched in kind by the unwavering conviction of the majority of faculty and administration that they were providing students with a progressive, rigorous, and justice-based college education and not a set of curricular and instructional ideologies rooted solely in white supremacy.

It is neither a subtle or covert racism that insists the Bronx is the haven of crack addiction in the 2010s. The Bronx has historically had the highest unemployment and poverty rates in all of New York state and, in some years, in all the United States. Today, it is still New York state's most impoverished and unemployed county with young people of color feeling the biggest impact post-COVID-19 (Sequeira 2022). Thus, the exploitation and neglect that the Bronx has continually faced was mirrored in the curriculum that these young people of color received in college. Fewer than a dozen faculty (most of whom were BIPOC) that I personally talked with agreed with me that this curriculum was racist and especially harmful to students of color. Even fewer folx were willing to admit that this specific, beloved white male faculty member sponsored racist methods and content. True to form, I ran my mouth everywhere and anywhere: at the holiday parties, at the committee meetings, at the lunches, at the mailboxes, at the dining hall. If there was an opening, I took it. More often than not, I received a "whitesplained" story of the importance of this professor and this curriculum to the college.

I would go so far as to say that a sympathetic reader/listener to my story here arrives at a critique of this curricular event because they are traveling via my endarkened feminist learnings. If you were traveling instead via the learnings of the university, if you were just another majoritarian professor at this college, you would likely disagree with my analysis of the curriculum since most of folx who I spoke with and reported to certainly did not share my alarm or outrage. As a poor, Black child of the 1980s, I know from lived reality that the nation did not care about the crises of addiction and poverty facing Brown and Black masses in this post-Civil Rights era and responded with brutal policies and racist backlash that deliberately criminalized us more: Black women were targeted as unfit "crackmothers" delivering only "crackbabies"; Black men were targeted by what would become the beginning of the mass prison industrial complex (Davis 2003; Roberts 2000). I can never forget the specific historical context of Reagan's War on Drugs since I lived it and know it well. Contemporary white users of methamphetamine and opioid drugs have never been similarly targeted; instead, treatment, empathy, medical research, and rehabilitation have been a national priority. The curriculum that my students received further criminalized them and protected these kinds of white interests.

"You Might Win Some But You Just Lost One"[3]: When the White Supremacist University Ignores Racial Harm and Black Feminist Outcry

My indictment of the university's ethos of ignoring racist curricular harm is not exaggerated. The fact of the matter is this: had one of those students actually been hurt because a professor required them to go out and interview random "crackheads" on the street, we would have all been implicated. Quite frankly, if I were on the streets and saw some college kids taking notes on my neighborhood as a "crackhead" haven, and then trying to interview the folx beside me as part of their assignment, it wouldn't go well for them or their professor. I ain't saying I would "shank" them, but I would certainly want to. As far as I was concerned, it was only a matter of time before something bad went down. And the university, including me, would be liable.

Those students had expressed collective outrage in their classrooms about that assignment. They even spoke with many older students at the college who described similar issues and who had made more formal complaints in previous semesters. And most importantly, they came and talked with a university professor—me—about their concerns. I ain't

3 Lyrics from the song "Lost Ones" by Lauryn Hill.

no fool. I know a compliance issue when I see and hear one, and I ain't never getting hauled into court because I co-signed or ignored some white supremacist mess. Never happened. Never will. In these instances, I always "report up" according to the university hierarchy established by higher education attorneys and keep good "receipts" of my reportage. Those particular college leaders and administrators, all up and down the ladder, were informed of the risks of this curriculum and the kind of support I provided to students in their revision of the assignment (after all, I co-signed what the university handbook would call "intellectual dishonesty"). None seemed concerned; none acted on our behalf. I do not know for sure how my reporting was handled, only that the course and the "crackhead" interview assignment continued business as usual during my time at the college.

University compliance culture in the United States is certainly rooted in corporate logics, but it is sometimes all that marginalized communities have as even a small modicum of protection in hostile environments. Folx at universities don't always imagine themselves beholden to compliance regulations, though, because they consider the university a second home and second family (versus a job), which, of course, can represent all of the attending problematic and dysfunctional white family metaphors (with Brown and Black bodies as the usual domestic laborers). The "compliance university," to borrow from Jonathan Alger (2012), is as regulated at local, state, and federal levels as any other entity when it comes to discrimination, health, safety, privacy, or conflict of interest. You don't get to just do whatever you want, and if you discriminate, cause harm, and transgress boundaries all willy-nilly, that only lasts until you get caught.

There has never been a semester where I have not "reported up" a serious violation of compliance, and this instance of the required "crackhead" interview was no exception. I am often stunned that even when I frame something as explicitly "a compliance issue that I feel required to report" (my students know I do this), most administrators have understood my points of discussion as merely collegial or friendly banter, despite the fact that I have never considered any of these interlocutors friends.

As just one more grounding example, in another context and in a whole other place, I once met with an administrator about a serious issue. I had kept a lawyer on retainer for two years under that state's statute of limitations about a departmental incident from which I might need protection. I literally met with the administrator using the script that my white male legal counsel gave me, to which the administrator simply responded: "I can see you are emotional about this." Imagine the white privilege and delusional comfort that it takes to think a Black woman's required, legalistic meeting is just an emotional outcry. This was also a context in which the administrator always told the offending party the details of any compliance breach that I reported. I guess I was supposed to feel bad or worried when those faculty would then try and retaliate by rolling their eyes at me and/or isolating me. Despite multiple compliance violations on the one hand and retaliatory behaviors on the other, the space incessantly celebrated itself as antiracist, DEI-focused, friendly, and collegial. It's like the "upside-down world" in the TV show *Stranger Things*.

In this same institution, BIPOC and Queer graduate students often described microaggressions to me, but the instances they described often seemed more like macroaggressions than routine or casual slights. White graduate students routinely confused Black graduate students with one another, even though they were the minority, and even when they were wearing nametags; interrogated Black women's clothing and makeup choices; quizzed BIPOC students on their academic credentials; told Black students which topics of study were appropriate for only Black undergraduate students versus for everyone; and called Queer and BIPOC students an "echo chamber" in race-centered classes. While an individual instance might constitute a microaggression, when you stack these up, you have a macro-discriminatory pattern. However, teacher-talk, social media, and contemporary scholarship in US schools often labels such transgressions as microaggression, a gross appropriation from the 1970s research and purpose of Black psychiatrist, Chester Pierce (1970).

These BIPOC and/or Queer graduate students in this program were experiencing themselves as the targets of ethical misconduct in the workplace, infractions that Pierce believed required different responses from therapists than what was theorized in the research at the time, but not an ignoring of reporting requirements. When I have raised these issues in faculty meetings, some faculty simply insisted that "it's not everybody," as if that could ever be justification. Racist patterns perpetrated by white graduate students were ignored even though these students were teaching first-year writing classroom like the one I describe above, and would go on to teach such classes as new college faculty very soon. Universities that allow hostile behaviors towards marginalized communities, behaviors that even corporate compliance culture in an anti-DEI backlash rejects, and then deliberately isolate Black women who are performing mundane, required reporting are not spaces that will ever offer Black people a basic, humanizing or equity-based education.

I have taught in American universities for more than twenty-five years now as adjunct, instructor, assistant professor, associate professor, and now professor at all of the following: Black college, Minority-Serving Institution, Hispanic-Serving Institution, Predominantly White Institution; urban and suburban; private and public; wannabe "R1" (university with the highest level of research), social-climbing R2 (university with a high level of research), down-and-out comprehensive (university that offers two-year associate's degrees and four-year bachelor's degrees), and white-canon-loving liberal arts institution. Every institution where I have worked has met the minimum legal requirements that would be required for me to show and prove a pattern of racist discrimination in a court of law, not only in terms of my own personal treatment, but in terms of the wider culture that flourishes in personnel meetings and administrative interactions. I avoid legalistic court processes because they come with gag orders that would mean, for instance, that the specific learnings I am uncovering in this endarkened feminist narrative could never happen so publicly. The energy, however, that it takes to avoid the people and situations that scream "lawsuit over here—come get a hot, fresh one" is exhausting.

"My Folks Gon Keep It Solid"[4]: When Fugitive Learning Interrupts and Rewrites the Logics of Oppressive Institutions

As fate would have it, when I left the university where students were assigned "interviews with crackheads," that college faced a lawsuit from recent alumni that was widely published across national news outlets alleging multiple counts of sexual misconduct and drug use on campus and off-campus.

I didn't know any of these students who illuminated this harm in the lawsuit. But guess who was right smack dab in the middle of it? Yup, the same professor who had assigned that "crackhead" essay. Like I said, it's always just a matter of time. In the years that I was a tenured faculty member at this university, that professor was paid almost a million dollars more than me, based on my math after learning his salary as reported in national newspapers. My students and I were not surprised by the lawsuit nor the university's choice on where and with whom they had so calculatingly laid their monetary value and scholarly respect, even though it cost them dearly. All you can do is shake your head and move on.

Though my endarkened narrative inquiry sets out to deeply investigate a specific moment, my telling this story argues for the non-singularity of a singular event. Sometimes it feels like each college where I have worked has been the same place: *HotMessUniversity.edu.* When I left the university where students were assigned "interviews with crackheads," I penned a letter to the president about all the goings-on. Many BIPOC faculty embraced the letter; meanwhile, a white administrator in the provost's office, a long-standing faculty member at the college and close friend and supporter of the white supremacist professor who my students so deftly counteracted, publicly dismissed my comments. According to her, the contents of my letter simply represent the kinds

4 Lyrics from the song "Yeah, Glo!" by GloRilla.

of things that I always complain about: "Carmen always does this." One might wonder why someone appointed to the provost's office is not concerned by a racist curriculum that racially stratifies the city's residents and potentially causes physical harm off-campus. I could tell multiple stories such as this about multiple universities—all harboring the same resentments when I reveal their dirty laundry as if it is my job to simply bleach and whitewash all that. University faculty and administration will go to extreme lengths to ignore and thereby maintain toxic positivity alongside oppression.

My desire for a fugitive space and pedagogy in the academy means that I also reject hierarchical forms of leadership and instead take my cue from the history of Black feminist activists, from Ella Baker to Mariame Kaba, who have always called themselves community organizers. They organize. They do not lead. There is a distinction that they are making in relation to Black communities and praxis. I'm not dismissive of the importance of university leadership and don't support the almost automatic assumption and suspicion from many leftist corners that administrators all work for the dark side of the enterprise; institutions are just never that simple. The administration of American universities, however, is a tight system of vertical and still-too-patriarchal rankings and titles where complicated flow charts present who the leaders are, who answers to whom, what you are and are not responsible for, and where everyone rests on a bottom-up chain of command. As of today, I have turned down every university's request and every national "head-hunter's" call to join administration. For me, the most transformative work happens in the classroom and not in the department or institution. That's where the organizing happens. Organizing, perhaps a more specific kind of leadership, involves sitting in the pockets where the most radical challenge is possible. For me, that will always be the classroom, though this is never safe or easy work. As a Black feminist scholar and writing teacher, I think of the transformative possibilities of classrooms as a kind of fugitive learning, as Black studies scholars have defined it.

The prolific Black studies theorist Fred Moten argues that fugitivity involves Black people's refusal to accept unjust standards imposed from an oppressive elsewhere. He calls fugitivity a kind of desire and spirit that is always dreaming of escape and transgression even when not achievable. Fugitivity embraces living on the outer edges, plays with what is considered improper, and does not compromise with racist regimes by rendering them as inevitable (Moten 2003). Jarvis Givens (2012) further situates fugitivity as the analytic that best represents the politics of Black teaching and learning and the metanarrative of Black educational history. The very act of humanizing learning for Black masses is always already fugitive given the historical racism of anti-literacy laws in slavery and Jim Crow, more than a century of segregated schooling, government-sanctioned defunding schemes, and carceral systems of punishment for Black learners.

The notion of fugitivity is, of course, rooted in the specific history of fugitive slaves who pursued physical and psychic forms of flight: running away from plantations, deeply respecting the underground railroad and North Star as markers of freedom, hiding in the trunk of a tree or garrison, attending "night school," worshipping via alternative religious practices like the Abakua, living in maroon societies, and embracing African foodways and culinary practices (Roberts 2015). Black studies practitioners talk of fugitive learning today as a continuing practice of subterfuge against white supremacy in everyday life that connects Black ancestral understandings of chattel slavery to an ongoing praxis towards Black freedom. In this way, fugitivity is not simply a metaphor for resistance, because it roots Black freedom in the historical refusal to accept social death under racial capitalism (Best and Hartman 2005). I think especially about the work of Black feminists like Tina Campt (2017) who point out that fugitivity and refusal are intertwined. In her work on Black aesthetics, especially photography, Campt reminds us that a radical visual archive by the African diaspora sits right alongside deliberate state, global, and daily violence that intends solely to count, catalog, categorize, surveil, and degrade Black subjects; these most dispossessed makers design new possibility in the constraints of everyday life, even when attempts at self-expression cannot be fully realized (Campt 2017). Fugitive success is not experienced as a wholesale annihilation of longstanding regimes, but in cleverly and joyfully thwarting them from moment to moment.

My own desire for escape from the deep pit of white supremacy means that I work very hard to protect my thinking, aesthetic, languaging, and sense of worth from the academy's everyday norms and logics. I am trained in the discipline of rhetoric and composition studies where I often feel subjected to seemingly endless notions of writing and pedagogy as something that can be wholly decontextualized from the racist sociopolitics of the college, local area, and world. Far too many still imagine that a class where students are focused on Black Freedom and antiracism is less than or antithetical to "real" skills development in literacy instruction. Reading and writing with/as/because of/for Black freedom is, in fact, a higher force of learning and pedagogy. Trying to convince hostile groups of this fact is futile and gets in the way of the spirit and intellect that it takes to actually do that kind of teaching. So I stay fugitive.

The students who revised the "crackhead interview" assignment deployed sophisticated literacies and analyses and represent quintessential models of fugitive learning. They read that professor for filth, to his face, all up in his classroom: they openly questioned his conflations between addiction and their communities; they challenged his idea that he had a carte blanche right to the stories of everyday people walking the streets of the Bronx; they objected to his callous disregard for their safety and inability to see them as worthy of care. When the professor did not validate their critiques, they went underground and did background research on him and the politics of the university. Instead of interviewing Bronx natives about crack cocaine, they interviewed more senior Brown and Black students at the college about *the professor*. Talk about turning the ships around! They read me, too. We hadn't been together very long in the semester when they came to see me, but they seemed to know that they could talk to me about things. In fact, when they told me the professor said, "Just go to the Bronx," my automatic angry and loud response was along the lines of:

"No, *TF* he did not." I only remember my outburst because they laughed at me, like they already knew I was gonna get vexed and not support his racism under the ruse of collegiality and its code of silence at that university. The students' plan to just quote from movies, perform the racist stereotypes the professor liked, and then exit the course unscathed was, of course, also brilliant.

But that's not all.

Those students expected a certain kind of reading and writing in college about justice, race, and drug addiction. That expectation was already fugitive. They were not raised in Reagan's 1980s war on Black and Brown communities, but they are the heirs of that struggle, literally the children of those of us who survived. Their desire and insistence that their college learning be used towards deliberate interventions in historical racist systems challenge the neoliberalist glossings of many college mission statements about "responsible global citizens" while ignoring oppressive in-house and local systems. When the students were denied the radical, antiracist curriculum and writing assignments that they desired, they simply pursued that content and politics in the work they did in my writing class.

Like many students before them, they created pamphlets and informational packets for community centers, friends, and family about programs, grants, and events that support those seeking rehabilitation and/or new life afterwards. Some students wrote more traditional literature reviews about histories of race, addiction, and criminalization—not for the purpose of writing a schoolish paper, but for the purpose of having ready-made facts and infographics. As young people like to say today: "If you stay ready, you don't have to get ready." Other students worked on websites and materials for community organizations that focused on a range of wellness issues for Black and Brown peoples. One young woman focused on the targeting of Black and Brown folx by the Bronx's inequitable bail system and was paid as a full-time staff member at a local advocacy center by the end of the semester. For this student, learning about the pronounced racial disparities for BIPOC who are detained for pretrial court hearings ignited her interests in community organizing. Students studied and wrote all these things in their first year of college in a writing class that I themed "Digital Rhetorics/Digital Justice." The idea of the class was really simple: students would curate and join the digital spaces and events that represented the justice issues most pressing for them. I trusted them to fill in all the blanks. And they did.

Fugitive learning is therefore a praxis where college students design immediate interventions in the everyday oppression their communities face; it also recognizes, unravels, and rewrites racist logics exploiting the most marginalized communities. It transforms relationships to communities such that BIPOC leadership is not individual but relational. Historically, US colleges have understood BIPOC students as young people who will go back into their communities as "race leaders": speak as/for people of color, quell the masses, and offer bourgeois services. This definition of leadership, however, is not the same as a radical solidarity with and understanding of the lives of racially subordinated groups. Fugitive learning directs a differing affect, direction, and purpose for leadership for both students and teachers.

In a moment such as this one where any college class related to BIPOC, race, gender, and sexuality is closely surveilled and demonized, administrative leaders who link college education to large-scale justice initiatives face a heightened level of public (and trustees') scrutiny and punishment, perhaps more so than classroom teachers. Administration is a public-facing practice at the local, state, and/or national levels, so there's just not as much hiding or charged invisibility that is required for fugitive practices. University presidents function more and more like CEOs of large national brands—or as *the brand itself*—who are always in the national spotlight. Administrators tied to provosts' and deans' offices are often local/city/state leaders as much as campus leaders. It seems less and less likely that any upper-level administrator can be a radical champion of educational justice and not get fired. At their very best, they hold the dogs back and off of the rest of us, a task that is also not easy. Teaching, on the other hand, is classroom-facing and student-community-facing and so fugitive possibility is endless. There is more flexibility to de-focus the myopic lens of white supremacy's microscope.

By the time the "crackhead"-interview-assigning professor was facing a lawsuit and possible dismissal from the university, most of the students in my class had graduated and were long gone from the university. I always suspected, however, that we were experiencing the hauntings of their brave defiance, alternative registers, reworkings of oppressive educational requirements, and dreams of different futures—not just at the college, but in the city at large. Their fugitive learning was not just about a refusal to accept racist knowledge and unfair systems in fanciful and creative ways, though it did that well. Fugitive learning is also a redesign, based on endarkened political needs and experiences, towards freedom and escape. This group of students quite literally transformed their writing classroom into an alternative universe in the midst of institutional racism and the complete disregard for the dignity of their communities. Fugitive learning doesn't just provide a critique, but also access to new possibilities for what we can do in our time at universities.

References

Alexander, Michelle. 2010. "The War on Drugs and the New Jim Crow." *Race, Poverty & the Environment.* 17 (1): 75–77.

Alger, Jonathan. 2012. "Higher Education Law and Policy 2.1—The Rise of the Compliance University." *The Center for Excellence in Higher Education Law and Policy Stetson University College of Law*, February 20. https://www.jmu.edu/audit/_files/compliance/compliance-resources/the-compliance-university.pdf.

Best, Stephen and Saidiya Hartman. 2005. "Fugitive Justice." *Representations* 92 (1): 1–15.

Campt, Tina. 2017. *Listening to Images*. Duke University Press.

Davis, Angela. 2003. *Are Prisons Obsolete?* Seven Stories Press.

Dillard, Cynthia. 2000. "The Substance of Things Hoped for, the Evidence of Things Not Seen: Examining an Endarkened Feminist Epistemology in Educational Research and Leadership." *International Journal of Qualitative Studies in Education* 13 (6): 661-681.

Dumas, Michael J. 2016. "Against the Dark: Antiblackness in Education Policy and Discourse." *Theory Into Practice* 55 (1): 11–19.

Givens, Jarvis. 2021. *Fugitive Pedagogy: Carter G. Woodson and the Art of Black Teaching*. Harvard University Press.

Gumbs, Alexis Pauline. 2014. "Nobody Mean More: Black Feminist Pedagogy and Solidarity." In *The Imperial University: Academic Repression and Scholarly Dissent*, edited by Piya Chatterjee and Sunaina Maira. University of Minnesota Press.

Harney, Stefano and Fred Moten. 2013. *The Undercommons: Fugitive Planning and Black Study*. Minor Compositions.

Hinton, Elizabeth. 2016. *From the War on Poverty to the War on Crime: The Making of Mass Incarceration in America*. Harvard University Press.

Hurtado, Aida. 1996. "Strategic Suspensions: Feminists of Color Theorize the Production of Knowledge." In *Knowledge, Difference and Power: Essays Inspired by Women's Ways of Knowing*, edited by Nancy Goldberger, Jill Tarule, Blythe Clinchy, and Mary Field Belenky. Basic Books.

Hurtado, Aida. 1998. "Sitios y Lenguas: Chicanas Theorize Feminism." *Hypatia* 13(2): 134–159.

Jalal, Hawre, Jeanine M. Buchanich, Mark S. Roberts, Lauren C. Balmert, Kun Zhang, Donald S. Burke. 2018. "Changing Dynamics of the Drug Overdose Epidemic in the United States from 1979 through 2016." *Science* 361.

Kelley, Robin. 2016. "Black Study, Black Struggle." *Boston Review*. March 1. bostonreview.net/forum/robin-kelley-black-struggle-campus-protest/.

Kim, Jin Woo, Evan Morgan, and Brendan Nyhan. 2020. "Treatment versus Punishment: Understanding Racial Inequalities in Drug Policy." *Journal of Health Politics, Policy and Law* 45 (2): 177–209.

Kynard, Carmen. 2023. "'Oh No She Did NOT Bring Her Ass Up in Here with That!' Racial Memory, Radical Reparative Justice, and Black Feminist Pedagogical Futures." *College English* 85 (4): 318–345.

Lorde, Audre. 1984. *Sister Outsider*. The Crossing Press.

Malaklou, M. Shadee. 2021. "Reaching Backwards in Time: The Feltness of Unfreedom in an Antiblack World." *Theory & Event* 24 (2): 598–604. https://dx.doi.org/10.1353/tae.2021.0029.

Martinez, Aja. 2020. *Counterstory: The Rhetoric and Writing of Critical Race Theory*. National Council of Teachers of English.

McClish-Boyd, Keondria and Kakali Bhattacharya. 2021. "Endarkened Narrative Inquiry: A Methodological Framework Constructed through Improvisations." *International Journal of Qualitative Studies in Education* 34 (6): 534–548.

Mogadime, Dolana. 2021. "Living at the Margins: Black Feminist Pedagogy as Transformative Praxis During the 1980s–1990s and Epistemic Exclusion in the 21st Century—Where Do We Go Now?" *Journal of Contemporary Issues in Education* 16 (2). https://doi.org/10.20355/jcie29442.

Moten, Fred and Stefano Harney. 2004. "The University and the Undercommons: SEVEN THESES." *Social Text* 22 (2): 101–115. https://muse.jhu.edu/article/55785.

Moten, Fred. 2003. *In the Break: The Aesthetics of the Black Radical Tradition*. University of Minnesota Press.

Okello, Wilson Kwamogi. 2024. "Unspeakable Joy: Anti-Black Constraint, Loopholes of Retreat, and the Practice of Black Joy." *Urban Education* 0 (0). https://doi.org/10.1177/00420859241227956.

Pierce, Chester. 1970. "Offensive Mechanisms." In *The Black Seventies: An Extending Horizon Book*, edited by Chester Pierce C. and F. B. Barbour. Porter Sargent Publisher.

Roberts, Dorothy. 2000. *Killing the Black Body*. Vintage Books.

Roberts, Neil. 2015. *Freedom as Marronage*. University of Chicago Press.

Royster, Jacqueline Jones. 2000. *Traces of a Stream: Literacy and Social Change Among African American Women*. University of Pittsburgh Press.

Sandoval, Chela. 2000. *Methodology of the Oppressed*. University of Minnesota Press.

Seid, Brianna. 2024. "The Facts on Bail Reform in New York: How Pretrial Detention and Release Works Now." *Brennan Center for Justice*, March 13. brennancenter.org/our-work/research-reports/facts-bail-reform-new-york-how-pretrial-detention-and-release-works-now.

Sequeira, Bobby. 2022. "With the Highest Unemployment, Poverty in the State, What's on the Horizon for Bronx Job Seekers?" *Bronx Times*, December 28. Accessed January 17, 2025. bxtimes.com/with-the-highest-unemployment-poverty-rates-state/.

Yang, K. Wayne. 2017. *A Third University Is Possible*. University of Minnesota Press.

CHAPTER 12

Language and Identity Politics in Leadership

Cultivating *Comunidad*

Candace de León-Zepeda, *Our Lady of the Lake University*

In an era of intense political polarization, US higher education institutions have become arenas where language, identity politics, and leadership collide—spaces that I, as a Chicana academic leader, navigate daily. The resurgence of white nationalism, a driving force behind Donald J. Trump's presidency and his 2024 bid for reelection, has emboldened public expressions of white national pride, bringing deeply personal issues of identity and belonging to the forefront of my work. As public accusations of universities promoting a liberal agenda and "woke culture" saturate public discourse, the surge of this rhetoric challenges not only the foundational values of higher education but also my personal commitment to fostering inclusive academic communities.

During Trump's first presidency, divisive slogans like "Build the Wall!" and "Make America Great Again" didn't just increase tensions on campuses nationwide—they brought those tensions directly into my office. Located in San Antonio, in the heart of South Texas and near the US-Mexico border, our campus is also federally recognized as the birthplace of the Hispanic Serving Institution (HSI) designation. With more than 76 percent of our student population identifying as Latino/a or Hispanic, I frequently witnessed students voicing their fears and discomfort, calling for leadership intervention when peers wore MAGA hats. Their pain was palpable, and it mirrored my own struggles with the rise of nationalist language that sought to diminish our worth. Yet, I also had to grapple with right-leaning students and faculty who embraced Trump's language, believing it to defend traditional conservative values and national pride. In these moments, I felt torn between my responsibilities as a leader, tasked with maintaining an objective stance guided by internal policies, and my own convictions as a Chicana feminist, who understood too well the damage such rhetoric can inflict on marginalized communities.

Trump's inflammatory characterizations and generalizations of immigrants as "rapists" and "blood-thirsty criminals" ignited not just campus-wide debates but internal conflicts within me. As a second-generation Mexican American whose grandparents migrated to the US and whose parents labored as migrant workers, these cruel depictions stood in stark contrast to the lived experiences of my own family and community. I reflected on the dignity, resilience, and sacrifice my grandparents embodied in their journey to this country, and how my parents, shaped by the hardships of migrant work, instilled in me the values of hard work and community. Their story is one of perseverance and contribution, making Trump's dehumanizing rhetoric not only offensive but also deeply personal. This tension—between public discourse and my personal truth—exacerbated conflicts over topics of race, identity, and belonging, both within my institution and within myself.

The overarching theme of anti-other that is veiled in extreme rightwing rhetoric also includes public attacks on LGTBQ+ people, women's healthcare access, and public education. These topics have left college and university leaders with decisions of how to respond (or not) to hateful rhetoric and the state of national policies that impact their students, employees, or communities. With the threat of "new white nationalism" with the aim of "reduc[ing] the number and narrow[ing] the demographic of people included in the construction of Americanness" (Gavin 2023), *how we learn how to lead* in higher education has never been more critical. It is my purpose to offer a deeply personal and insightful exploration of how I navigate these dynamics, grounded in my lived experiences as a Chicana feminist, cultural rhetorician, and the sole Dean at a small, faith-based university grappling with the dual crises of enrollment declines and budget cuts.

Transitioning from a faculty role to an administrative position amid a deeply politically divided country has required me to navigate the complex linguistic and cultural terrains of academia, where norms of communication and the politics of identity are often shaped by historical power structures. To explain, I am acutely aware of my otherness and marginalization in the following ways: as an academic dean who identifies myself publicly as Chicana and feminist; as one of 4 percent of full-time faculty who are labeled as "Hispanic females" teaching in degree-granting postsecondary institutions (National Center for Education Statistics 2024); as a woman of color who makes up less than 1.5 percent of identified academic deans in the nation (Silbert, Punty, and Ghoniem 2022, 12); as an unapologetic caregiver to my three school-age children; and as a first-generation college graduate from a low-income family background.

Without question, these facets of my identity profoundly shape how I approach and respond to issues of diversity, equity, inclusion, gender and sexual identity, and racial justice. Central to my leadership philosophy is a commitment to fostering inclusive and impactful community engagement—what I refer to as cultivating *comunidad*. This authentic leadership approach is not merely about creating a sense of belonging; it is about actively challenging and disrupting the traditional narratives and practices that have long marginalized voices like mine.

This practice involves acting on a commitment to fostering inclusive and impactful community engagement with my team of department chairs and school directors while embracing a pedagogy of disruption—one that catalyzes transformative shifts in both perspective and imagination, which I later introduce as shapeshifter leadership. Through the lens of Chicana feminist theories, particularly Gloria Anzaldúa's concepts of "*mestiza consciousness*" (Anzaldúa 1987, 100), "a theory in the flesh" (Moraga and Anzaldúa 1981, 23), and the "Coyolxauhqui imperative," (Anzaldúa 2015, 50), I share ways I learned how to lead and cultivate community during periods of political discord and public tensions. (In

Aztec mythology, Coyolxauhqui is the moon goddess and daughter of Coatlicue. Her brother Huitzilopochtli, the god of the sun and war, butchered and decapitated her for planning to kill her mother. Her myth was commemorated on a large stone disk which was excavated at the base of the Templo Mayor, Tenochtitlan, and dates back to c. 1473.)

Coming to Consciousness: *la Gloria*

For over twenty years, I have been deeply drawn to the transformative theories and creative scholarship of Gloria Anzaldúa. To me, she is not just a scholar but *la Gloria*, a guiding presence, almost like a close friend, who has challenged me to unlearn and relearn ways of being and thinking about myself, my community, my language, and my education. She holds a special place in my academic journey as the first Chicana scholar I was introduced to in a college classroom. This moment came during a graduate seminar, a pivotal experience that not only shaped my intellectual path but also underscored the glaring absence of curriculum or authors reflecting my lived experiences and the realities of my community. That absence was both troubling and a powerful reminder of the urgent need for representation in academic spaces. Through her essays and creative scholarship, Gloria gave voice to Latinxs and borderland communities, while also centering those marginalized within their own communities, including women and queer identities.

Early on in my education, Anzaldúa taught me to shift consciousness toward a decolonial framework that was transformative, inclusive, visionary, and unapologetic. Gloria boldly called out how spaces either foster or deny the visibility of one's gender, race, culture, or class. I was captivated by her vision and theoretical framework of "*conocimiento*" (Anzaldúa 2002, 540), or consciousness, a profound process of transformation that offers the possibility of a more just and equitable world. *Conocimiento* is an iterative journey, a deliberate act of deconstructing and reconstructing oneself, others, and the social world in ways that transcend normative hierarchies and dualistic ways of thinking and being. As I transitioned from faculty to administrator, I found that

Gloria's theoretical concepts were not only relevant but also invaluable in the practice of leadership. To me, her work offers a blueprint for navigating and transforming institutional systems while centering equity, inclusivity, and collective growth.

Navigating Identity and Language in Academia

Navigating identity in academia is a multifaceted challenge, particularly for those who occupy marginalized or intersectional identities. Even as a tenured professor, I fully understand that language is still often the first battleground where identity is contested. For many, like myself, this journey begins long before entering the ivory towers of higher education—it is rooted in the lived experiences of our communities, our families, and our cultural heritage. In my experience, the struggle with language began in my early education, where the dominance of English and the suppression of Spanish were clear indicators of the power dynamics at play. My parents, both products of a segregated education system in South Texas, instilled in me an awareness of the social location of schools as unwelcoming spaces for people of color. Their experiences of being punished for speaking Spanish in school and being discouraged from pursuing higher education were reflections of broader systemic efforts to erase cultural identities and enforce assimilation.

The process of navigating language in academia is not merely about linguistic competence; it is about negotiating the value of one's cultural and linguistic heritage in spaces that often devalue or dismiss it. This negotiation is deeply tied to identity formation. Gloria Anzaldúa's theoretical concept of *mestiza consciousness* is particularly relevant here. Anzaldúa explains that this consciousness is the struggle of living in a constant state of flex, shifting between borders, cultural codes, languages, rituals, and identities (Anzaldúa 1987, 78–81). For Anzaldúa, a *mestiza consciousness* embraces multiplicity and celebrates dualistic ways of thinking and collective consciousness. It is a consciousness that deconstructs patriarchy and colonialism and reclaims spirituality and feminist archetypes, while voicing the experience of living in marginalized spaces. For marginalized individuals, this consciousness is not just an intellectual exercise but a lived reality. Gloria's ideas focused on language and identity form the foundation of my leadership approach, as I will demonstrate in the following section of this chapter.

Language and Identity

The practice of cultivating *comunidad*, grounded in the framework of *mestiza consciousness* (Anzaldúa 1987, 100), recognizes that language is inseparable from identity. In my leadership, I approach communication with my team of eleven department chairs and school directors through a lens of authenticity that acknowledges and embraces the multiplicity of both my identity and theirs. (The team includes two men, one of whom identifies as African-American and first-generation American) and nine women, three of whom identify as Latinas, and three as first-generation Americans.) This approach manifests in various ways, including but not limited to the following two examples.

Consistent and Authentic Communication

Each week, I send out a Monday email that weaves together personal reflections with professional updates for the week ahead. One example of this occurred when I was late to a meeting because my toddler, captivated by a butterfly, kept my attention. That week, my email included the following message:

> *Dear friends, at times, the universe sends us messages to slow down and invite the beauty of nature into our day. I was late to a meeting this morning. "It's dancing, mama!" My daughter pulled at my arm to take notice of a beautiful monarch that seemed to float around us as if dancing. "Come see, come see it dance!" I placed my work bag down, grabbed her small hand, and took time to notice the beauty of the butterfly and my daughter's wonder. With the help of a toddler, I slowed down. I share this experience to encourage you to take notice this week of the beauty that surrounds you. We need these moments to*

refuel and encourage us to take notice. Sending love and light for a week where you can capture beauty in nature.

Personal messages like this foster vulnerability, create connection, and invite my team into my life as a mom with school-age kids. This practice of sharing personal insights and reflections has created a culture where authenticity is encouraged, and both my team and I are able to show up as our full, multifaceted selves.

Individual Chats Shaped by Language

I hold bi-monthly thirty-minute sessions with each chair and school director, either in person or remotely. To maximize the value of these meetings, I have found great success by anchoring each conversation around three consistent themes, using reflective questions: (1) Joyful—What is currently bringing you joy, personally or professionally? (2) Messy—What challenges or complexities are you navigating, in your personal or professional life? (3) Mindful—What should I be mindful of as we move forward, in both your personal and professional worlds? These topics create space for meaningful conversation that acknowledge the full scope of their experiences, both within and beyond higher education. I also encourage my colleagues to reflect on and write about these themes beforehand, which helps track their epistemological growth and reveals how their knowledge is either nurtured or constrained in academic spaces. This approach has been overwhelmingly well-received, allowing my team to celebrate personal growth and professional wins (e.g., new publications, grandbabies, grant ideas, or completing their first 5k run) while also addressing "messy" concerns (e.g., faculty conflicts, promotion and tenure challenges). Additionally, it invites them to share matters I should be mindful of before our next meeting (e.g., health, financial, or relationship issues). This structure fosters trust, transparency, and holistic support within our leadership team.

This approach fosters community with others, celebrates diversity of experience, and rejects traditional binaries between supervisor and direct report. Including diverse voices and perspectives in meaningful ways is not a matter of political correctness but a recognition of the value of multiplicity in knowledge production. My leadership approach centers on first understanding the individual—their unique knowledge base, lived experiences, and the influences that shape their identity.

This leadership approach is influenced by Anzaldúa's scholarship, which I learned challenges the notion that there is one correct way to be or to know. She advocates for a pluralistic approach that acknowledges the legitimacy of different ways of knowing, including those rooted in lived experiences, cultural practices, and community wisdom. Her introduction of "a theory in the flesh" (Moraga and Anzaldúa 1981, 23) is another framework I have adopted when cultivating *comunidad* in leadership. This framework transgresses boundaries of genre, method, or content as any theory should also recognize collective experiences of those othered (Hurtado 2003, 215). Namely, a "theory in the flesh" supports a Chicana feminist saying that the personal is political, a frequent assertion of feminist scholarship that draws attention to Mexican-Americans living in the borderlands. In the next section I provide ways I adopt this theory by using everyday life experiences, thereby drawing attention to the bodily space of the learner (to include their homes and communities).

A Theory in the Flesh

The practice of cultivating *comunidad*, grounded in the framework of "a theory in the flesh," recognizes that lived experiences have rich meaning and theory should emanate from what we live and breathe. This framework also posits that knowledge is partial in relation to the spiritual, which includes the emotional. How I embrace this concept while building community can be seen in the following examples:

Testimonio: A Unique Qualitative Tool

Although I recognize making data-informed decisions, when I need richer insight into the experiences of my team, I practice the tool of *testimonio* when collecting information. *Telling to Live: Latina Feminist Testimonios* defines *testimonio* as complex genre that has multiple uses to include storytelling, narratives (i.e., witness narratives, confessional narratives, autobiographical narratives), ethnographic work and life histories (Latina Feminist Group 2001, 17–19). *Testimonio* emphasizes how knowledge is produced through experiential epistemologies credited to the cultural and social marginalized communities. Unlike traditional surveys or feedback, *testimonio* delves deeper, inviting participants to engage with reflective questions that draw on memory in meaningful ways. For instance, at retreats I have invited my team to enter the space as dynamic storytellers. *Testimonio* guided reflection is mirrored in the following examples: (1) Locate a personal photo or picture that represents what initially drew you to the vocation of teaching. How has this memory evolved over time, particularly in your experience teaching at a Hispanic Serving Institution? (2) Reflect on the resources that were most helpful to you as a student in higher education. What additional resources or support would have enhanced your journey? Focus on two to three words that come to mind when reflecting on your experience. (3) Draw a culturally competent classroom using words, images, symbols, etc.

Centering the Spirit

A truly just society nurtures the holistic journey of individuals, honoring the development of the whole person—mind, body, and spirit. This means recognizing the importance of not only intellectual growth but also emotional, intuitive, and spiritual well-being. While secular frameworks often prioritize logic and reason, a holistic approach emphasizes the balance and harmony between intellectualism and intuition, and teaching and learning. It acknowledges that education is not just about acquiring knowledge but about fostering deeper connections to self, others, and the world around us.

How I adopt this practice is not difficult, as I take full advantage of our faith-based mission. At each meeting, chairs and school directors take turns centering our meeting in either prayer, a practice of mindfulness, meditation, or guided reflection. I encourage each leader to also draw in connections to local or national news that are meaningful to them and find connections to our mission and our call to action to be servant leaders. My team has used these opportunities to express their advocacy or call to action in, to name a few, the following events: the mass school shooting on May 24, 2022, at Robb Elementary in Uvalde, Texas, where nineteen students and two teachers lost their lives, and seventeen others were injured; Russia's invasion of Ukraine; the call for a ceasefire in Palestine; and natural disasters—hurricanes, tornadoes, wildfires, etc.

These two examples highlight how I cultivate holistic support and opportunities, drawing on the interconnections of mind, body, spirit, and lived experiences. Anzaldúa's scholarship taught me to view such interconnections as an ongoing, dynamic process with her theory, a "Coyolxauhqui imperative" (Anzaldúa 2015, 50). For Anzaldúa, the *imperative* of Coyolxauhqui—the vital importance—lies in the understanding that with every act of deconstruction comes an opportunity for reconstruction, and with this process comes fragmentation and imperfection. This framework, symbolized through Aztec mythology, offers a visual metaphor for the continuous, lifelong process of learning and unlearning. Anzaldúa reclaims this ancient symbol to represent the cyclical nature of growth and transformation which has profoundly shaped my approach to leadership. I strive to lead as an authentic agent of change, recognizing that identity is never static but constantly evolving and refiguring our identity like Coyolxauhqui. Cultivating *comunidad* embraces not only the journey of growth and healing but also the recognition of our brokenness, where the true evolution of identity takes place.

The "Coyolxauhqui imperative"

By viewing my colleagues as engaged in their own journeys of self-reconstitution, I approach academic spaces with a deep commitment to validating and uplifting their diverse identities an experience, especially those from marginalized backgrounds This perspective not only fosters a culture of inclusivity but also cultivates a deeper, more empathetic engagement with the diverse community I am honored to lead.

Holistic Performance Review

An example of how I adopt the framework of the *Coyolxauhqui* imperative can best be represented in my version of holistic performance review. Traditional annual evaluations often focus on basic performance metrics and future goals, but I find it far more impactful to encourage my team to reflect on their inner growth to learn. Instead of simply reviewing job performance, I ask them to consider how they've evolved personally and professionally throughout the year, urging them to reflect on their own journeys of learning and transformation. Assessment aligned within this framework takes the following form: What have you learned about yourself (i.e., community member, scholar, faculty member, and campus leader) this year that brings you joy or pride? What burdens or learned behaviors are weighing on your spirit or leadership that you wish to release or unlearn?

This example shows mestiza leadership in action with the ultimate goal of fostering deeper, more intentional conversations about holistic development of the mind, body, soul, and experience. When chairs and school directors recognize my commitment to nurturing both their personal and professional growth, we cultivate a shared sense of comunidad—growing together not just as colleagues, but as individuals on a collective journey. This approach to leadership demands adaptability and fluidity, particularly for those of us from marginalized backgrounds, and is best described as shapeshifter leadership. I borrow Zaytoun's (2022) broader concept of "shapeshifter" in *Shapeshifting Subjects: Gloria Anzaldúa's Naguala and Border Arte* to define a style of leadership that is not a fixed role but a dynamic, multifaceted process that requires us to continuously shift between identities and responsibilities, while actively transforming the very structures we inhabit.

Leadership as a Shapeshifter

The concept of leadership within the context of higher education is often narrowly defined, focusing on hierarchical structures, administrative efficiency, and institutional prestige. I find Anzaldúa's study of *la naguala,* or shapeshifter, meaningful in my administrative role as it best describes my fluid identity as a Chicana and Dean, but Zaytoun's broader concept of a "shapeshifter" captures the reality of my leadership style. My leadership ambition is to empower chairs and school directors "toward interconnection, creativity, hope, and loving transformation" (Zaytoun 2022, xv). I adopt Zaytoun's position that Anzaldúa's scholarship "reminds us that we can change shape, that we have a 'dreaming body' one that, if we are paying attention, feels as real as flesh and bones" (Zaytoun 2022, xiii-xiv). The shapeshifter is an outsider (Zaytoun 2015, 70) who "encourages a change in how experiences of subjectivity and identities are created" in an effort "that will facilitate more harmony, personally and collectively, and more potential for coalitional work across differences" (Zaytoun 2015, 74). Due to the existing disparities of representation among women of color in leadership roles in higher ed, I accept my otherness as an outsider and draw on my distinctiveness to provide an alternate leadership style. I am drawn to the philosophical concept of shapeshifting and that spaces can be transformative, leading one to shift consciousness.

Strategies I adopt as a shapeshifter that other marginalized university leaders might find useful include some of the following examples:

Navigating Roles to Empower Diverse Perspectives

It is fair to assert that in most universities and colleges, leadership transitions and preparation for department chairs are often lacking in structure and support. From the first day of my appointment, I announced the need for our university to develop a successor model for all leadership positions, including my own, and I would be developing an emerging leadership plan. During meetings I host, instead of simply leading from the front, I shift between facilitator, listener, and peer contributor roles. I actively encourage team members to take on leadership positions temporarily by assigning them to lead specific discussions or projects. This approach fosters collaboration, and you can model adaptability by shifting between authoritative and supportive roles, depending on the needs of the conversation. This example shows fluidity in leadership styles and allows chairs and school directors to see themselves in various roles, encouraging them to explore their potential as leaders.

Encouraging Interconnections and Creativity

When approaching a new project or challenge, instead of dictating a solution, I encourage chairs and school directors to sign up for projects that are meaningful to them, such as defining a program head's duties and responsibilities, defining service, defining wellness, providing mentoring support, and completing course release activity reports. In those spaces, smaller teams brainstorm and contribute innovative ideas for a solution. I often encourage teams to consider unconventional solutions that might work, which opens the space for creative thinking. This example shows how I shift from a directive leadership role to one that empowers creative freedom and collective input, creating a space where diverse voices can shape solutions.

Leveraging Outsider Perspectives to Challenge Norms

I frequently bring in diverse speakers who address topics related to inclusion, diversity, equity, and access. I do so to encourage chairs and school directors to think critically about representation and inclusivity in their work as campus leaders. This example embraces the outsider experience and encourages my team to reflect on their own identities and how they can inform inclusive, boundary breaking work as campus leaders.

Facilitating Coalition Building Across Differences

Every bi-monthly meeting I organize for chairs and school directors includes guests from across the university including vice presidents, student affairs, graduate admissions, and student retention staff. The goal is for us to identify synergies between our programs or divisions. A question I frequently ask is, "How we can leverage strengths to create something more successful together?" This strategy promotes coalition building and unity in diversity. It also encourages adaptability, inclusivity, and a dynamic approach to problem solving and personal growth.

—

Shapeshifting is a powerful metaphor for the kind of leadership that is necessary in today's academic environment. A shapeshifter is someone who can move fluidly between different identities and roles, who can adapt to changing circumstances, and who can challenge and reconfigure established norms and practices. This ability to shapeshift is not about deception or inauthenticity, but about the strategic use of one's positionality to effect change.

To explain, as a Chicana feminist, I am acutely aware of how my identity positions me within the institution. I am often the only person of color in leadership meetings, and one of the few women, which places me in a unique and sometimes isolating position. However, rather than seeing this as a limitation, I view it as an opportunity to bring new perspectives to the table and to advocate for policies and practices that support diversity and inclusion.

Shapeshifter leadership also means being able to navigate the tension between institutional expectations and personal values. There have been times when my own institution prioritized goals or initiatives that did not align with my commitment to social justice and equity. For instance, like many other small, faith-based institutions, we are grappling with budgetary constraints driven by low enrollment. In response, executive leadership is exploring difficult options, including program closures and faculty layoffs. A shapeshifter approach to leadership is acutely aware of audience and language. Rather than publicly criticizing decisions from leaders who are disconnected from faculty, I propose strategic compromises and finding creative ways to integrate social justice principles in decision-making. I proposed the need to reframe our liberal arts core courses into a university College which will serve as a port of entry for all incoming freshmen and potentially reallocate faculty positions. This reimagining of our College of Arts and Sciences can help transform our liberal arts legacy in new and innovative ways. This isolated example illustrates how shapeshifter leadership is about reimagining what is possible. This involves questioning (or disrupting) existing structures and practices and envisioning new ways of organizing and leading that are more inclusive, equitable, and just. It is about leading with a vision for the future, one that prioritizes the well-being and success of all members of the academic community, particularly those who have been historically marginalized. In my experience, cultivating *comunidad* as a shapeshifter in higher education requires a personal commitment and the courage to disrupt the status quo.

Cultivating Comunidad Through Disruption

A core element of my leadership philosophy embraces what I call a *pedagogy of disruption,* not to incite division, but to courageously challenge entrenched structures and practices that sustain inequality and exclusion. My approach fosters an inclusive environment that empowers every member of our academic community to feel genuinely seen, heard, and valued. By intentionally creating spaces that welcome diverse voices and experiences, I strive to cultivate a culture where transformative learning and growth can thrive, empowering individuals to redefine their roles and contributions within our institution. This approach to teaching and leadership is rooted in the belief that authentic learning and meaningful growth emerge when we are pushed out of our comfort zones to engage with new ideas and diverse perspectives. This praxis is exemplified in the following ways:

Staff Connections

Faculty often overlook the valuable insights and broad institutional perspective that staff members bring, from administrative personnel to housekeeping and groundskeeping teams. I actively encourage chairs and school directors to forge intentional, respectful connections across all staff roles, recognizing these relationships deepen our collective understanding of the university's dynamic and foster a more cohesive, inclusive academic community.

Pláticas y Comida (Talks and Food)

I encourage chairs and school directors to share meals together with their faculty as frequently as possible. This act disrupts the typical formal dynamics and creates an opportunity for genuine connection. Gathering around food allows for natural, open conversation, breaking down hierarchical barriers and fostering a sense of camaraderie. This simple act also encourages faculty to engage with one another on a personal level, building trust and mutual understanding that enhances collaboration.

Frequent Student Forums

Disruption also involves challenging the traditional power dynamics that often exist in the classroom and in the broader academic community. I request that chairs and school directors create spaces where students and faculty can engage in open and honest dialogue, where they can share their experiences and perspectives without fear of judgment or retribution. A pedagogy of disruption means recognizing and valuing the knowledge and expertise that students bring to the table and finding ways to incorporate their voices into the decision-making processes of the institution.

Language of Inclusion

The language of academia is often rigid, steeped in tradition, and reflective of dominant cultural narratives that marginalize diverse voices and perspectives. To cultivate truly inclusive academic communities, I ask chairs and school directors to critically examine and actively reshape the language used in their departments and programs. I advocate for frequent decolonization of academic language that demands that students conform to modes of expression that may feel unnatural or disconnected from their lived experiences and cultural identities.

—

As a Chicana feminist scholar, I have often faced pressures to conform my voice to dominant academic norms. In early drafts of this manuscript, I was struck by how frequently the editors flagged moments where I had unconsciously distanced myself through formal academic language. Decades of past trauma, publishers dismissing my work as "non-academic," serve as a powerful reminder of how the language of academia can operate as a gatekeeping tool, marginalizing those who do not fit the narrow mold of the ideal scholar. This experience highlights the subtle yet pervasive ways in which academic discourse excludes voices that challenge its conventions, making it crucial to resist these pressures in my writing and scholarship. The editors' encouragement to embrace my most authentic voice has been profoundly liberating, affirming a core principle of my pedagogy of disruption—that decolonizing language is not about rejecting academic discourse but about expanding the horizons of expression and knowledge creation. This approach is committed to crafting spaces where multiple languages, dialects, and registers are not only welcomed but valued, allowing diverse cultural and intellectual traditions to coexist meaningfully. This means recognizing that there is no single "correct" way to speak, write, or think, but rather a rich tapestry of linguistic and cultural practices that can contribute to the collective work of learning and scholarship. In practice, this requires a deliberate and sustained effort to challenge the linguistic norms of academia. For example, I ask chairs and school directors to discuss with faculty in their departments the ways they could recognize and value diverse linguistic expressions or provide resources and support for multilingual students. By promoting linguistic inclusivity, we can begin to dismantle the barriers that prevent marginalized voices from fully participating in the academic community. Other examples include:

Curriculum Assessments

I often advocate for departmental programs and curricula to include more diverse voices and perspectives. This has also included rethinking the ways courses are structured and taught. I ask for all faculty to reconsider traditional lecture-based models and incorporate more collaborative and experiential learning opportunities, where students can engage with the material in ways that are meaningful and relevant to their own lives and experiences.

IDEA (Inclusion, Diversity, Equity, and Access) Council

At the institutional level, cultivating *comunidad* through disruption involves a call to action for policies and practices to adopt language rooted in diversity, equity, and inclusion. At my university, I led a strategic planning team to advocate to our former university president the adoption of an IDEA Council. The Council included faculty, staff, and student members and focused on ways to change our institutional culture, where exclusion and marginalization are deeply entrenched. Some of the earlier projects included implementing mentorship programs for first-generation students, developing initiatives to support the recruitment and retention of faculty of color, and advocating for changes to admissions policies that take into account the diverse backgrounds and experiences of applicants. This example shows why it is important to build alliances with like-minded colleagues, students, and administrators who can help to amplify efforts to decolonize language and promote inclusion. It also involves engaging in ongoing dialogue and reflection, being open to feedback, and continually refining our approaches to ensure that they are effective and aligned with our goals.

—

In summary, one of the most important aspects of this work is the recognition that disruption is an ongoing process. It is not something that can be accomplished through a single initiative or policy change but requires sustained effort and commitment over time. It involves continually questioning and challenging the status quo and being willing to take risks and make sacrifices in the pursuit of a more just and equitable academic community. Disruption also requires resilience. There will inevitably be resistance to change, both from within the institution and from external forces. I have faced pushback from faculty, staff, and students on various fronts, including something as foundational as my commitment to using equitable language. Yes, you read that correctly—my consistent use of equitable language. In response to a recent survey after our fall convocation, one faculty member wrote, "I am tired of all this DEI language used by administrators and especially the dean. It is useless and the language excludes people like me. Let's just stay focused on serving our students and doing our job in the classroom." Another example came from a student majoring in Criminal Justice who approached me to say, "My professor is always trying to teach us about equity and justice. I just want to learn my major without this DEI stuff." A staff member once complained to me after our Center for Teaching of Excellence Director posted a lecture series rooted in DEI, "Candace, this stuff is useless and doesn't serve me in my day-to-day job. Can't we just learn how to use Microsoft?"

These are just a few examples, and each response I provide is tailored to the specific situation, always beginning with careful listening. I frequently turn to our university's mission: "Founded and sponsored by the Sisters of Divine Providence, Our Lady of the Lake University is a Catholic, Hispanic-serving, inclusive learning community. Through quality, innovative undergraduate and graduate education, we foster spiritual, personal, and professional growth." I also turn to our core values of Community, Integrity, Trust, and Service, which underscore our commitment to "social justice, embracing equity, access, and care of creation for the common good." They serve as guiding principles, reinforcing our shared responsibility to uphold these ideals in our work and interactions. Anonymous faculty feedback can often be valuable—it gives me insights to help chairs and school directors anticipate resistance and equip themselves with strategies to address it. Deciding how, when, or even if I choose to respond is an exercise in patience and in gauging the most effective language to use.

At my institution, we are fortunate that the entire executive leadership team of vice presidents and our university president are committed to social justice and mindful of inclusive language. Cultivating *comunidad* through disruption is about creating a sense of belonging and empowerment for all members of the academic community. It is about recognizing and valuing the diverse experiences, perspectives, and identities that people bring to the table, and finding ways to incorporate these into the fabric of the institution. It is about creating spaces where everyone can thrive, where everyone can contribute to the collective work of learning, teaching, and leading.

Conclusion: Towards a Radical Transformation of Academia

The work of cultivating *comunidad* in academia is both urgent and ongoing. It requires a radical reimagining of the ways in which we think, speak, and act within these spaces. The example strategies I've shared show that the path to creating truly inclusive academic communities is neither straightforward nor easy—it demands a deep commitment to equity, justice, and the continuous disruption of entrenched power structures. The process of navigating identity and language in academia, as discussed, is foundational to this work.

Leadership as a shapeshifter offers a powerful model for effecting change in these environments. Shapeshifter leadership is inherently flexible, adaptive, and transformative. It allows us to navigate the complexities of institutional life while maintaining a commitment to social justice. It empowers us to challenge existing structures and to imagine new possibilities for what academia can be. As leaders who are willing to disrupt the status quo, we can create spaces where diverse voices are heard, valued, and respected. Moreover, the act of cultivating *comunidad* through disruption is about more than simply challenging the status quo—it is about building a new kind of academic community, one that is rooted in principles of mutual respect, solidarity, and collective action. Disruption, in this context, is a form of care. It is a way of showing that we believe in the potential of our institutions to be better, to do better, and to serve all members of the academic community with fairness and dignity.

The language of inclusion, as we have seen, is both a tool and a goal in this work. It is through inclusive language that we can begin to break down the barriers that have historically marginalized so many voices. Inclusive language recognizes the diversity of experiences, identities, and perspectives that make up our academic communities. It challenges the idea that there is a single, correct way to be, know, or speak in academia. By embracing linguistic diversity, we open the door to new ways of thinking and learning that enrich the entire academic enterprise. Yet, none of this work can be done in isolation. The transformation of academia into a space where *comunidad* thrives requires collective effort. It demands that we build alliances across disciplines, identities, and roles within the institution. It calls on us to be both leaders and collaborators, to share our insights and to learn from others. Most importantly, it requires a shared commitment to the values of equity, justice, and inclusion—values that must be at the heart of everything we do in academia. In conclusion, the work of cultivating *comunidad* in academia is about creating a future where everyone belongs—a future where the diversity of our identities, languages, and experiences is celebrated, not marginalized. It is about transforming our institutions into spaces where every individual can thrive, where the richness of our collective humanity is reflected in the knowledge we produce, the relationships we build, and the communities we create. This is the work of a lifetime, and it is work that must begin now, with each of us taking up the mantle of leadership, disruption, and inclusion. Together, we can build an academic community that truly embodies the spirit of *comunidad*—a community where all voices are heard, all identities are respected, and all contributions are valued.

References

Anzaldúa, Gloria. 1987. *Borderlands/La Frontera: The New Mestiza*. Aunt Lute.

Anzaldúa, Gloria. 2015. *Light in the Dark/ luz en lo oscuro*. Edited by Analouise Keating. Duke University Press.

Anzaldúa, Gloria. 2002. "Now Let us Shift…the Path of Conocimiento… Inner Work, Public Acts." In *This Bridge We Call Home: Radical Visions for Transformation*. Routledge.

Gavin, Michael. 2023. "Presidents Must Speak Out Against White Nationalism." *Inside Higher Education*, January 5. https://www.insidehighered.com/advice/2023/01/06/college-presidents-must-denounce-white-nationalist-attacks-opinion.html.

Hurtado, Aida. 2003. "Theory in the Flesh: Toward an Endarkened Epistemology." *International Journal of Qualitative Studies in Education* 16 (2): 215–225.

Latina Feminist Group. 2001. *Telling to Live: Latina Feminist Testimonios.* Duke University Press.

Moraga, Cherrie, Anzaldúa, Gloria. 1981. *This Bridge Called My Back: Writings by Radical Women of Color*. Persephone Press.

National Center for Education Statistics. 2024. "Characteristics of Postsecondary Faculty." In *Condition of Education. US Department of Education, Institute of Education Sciences.* https://nces.ed.gov/programs/coe/indicator/csc.

Silbert, Andrea, Mariko Punty, and Emanuela B. Ghoniem. 2022. "The Women's Power's Gap at Elite Universities—Scaling the Ivory Tower, 2022 Study." *Eos Foundation.* https://www.womenspowergap.org/higher-education/scaling-the-ivory-tower.

Zaytoun, Karen D. 2015. "Now Let Us Shift: Tracing the Path and Posthumanist Implications of La Naguala /The Shapeshifter in the Works of Gloria Anzaldúa." *MELUS: Multi-Ethnic Literature of the United States* 40 (4): 69–88.

Zaytoun, Karen D. 2022. *Shapeshifting Subjects: Gloria Anzaldúa's Naguala and Border Arte.* University of Illinois Press.

CHAPTER 13

An Imperative for Leadership & Institutional Transformation

Going Back to Code

Jonikka Charlton, *The University of Texas Rio Grande Valley*

"Every student at The University of Texas Rio Grande Valley is someone's baby, *tío*, sister, or friend." That was the first line of a slide I shared with the 170+ staff and faculty in the student success division at my institution who gathered for our annual development day in the summer of 2024. Every year, I start this workshop by inviting us to re-ground ourselves in our shared vision, values, and commitment to a strategic, proactive, and collaborative approach to student success. That year, I felt the need even more profoundly.

My baby recently came home after his first year in college, and the night before he started the drive cross-country, we got the call his dad and I had been waiting months for. "I don't want to go to school anymore. I gave it a shot—for me and for you—and I'm done." My heart had been breaking for years, knowing this day would come, not because choosing a life that doesn't require college means he can't have a great one, but because his entire experience with school since kindergarten has shaped him into someone who believes "school" isn't for him. This is someone who will spend hours listening to podcasts with graduate students talking about their scientific research or philosophy, someone who has watched entire oeuvres of directors and actors he respects and is hungry for someone to talk to about it. But no one in a school environment ever saw those parts of him. They never knew how curious he is, how deeply he thinks, what potential for ingenious connection he has. They never saw my baby. No one ever tried to see his strengths and meet him where he was.

The educational system that engineered this outcome for Duncan and countless others in most American schools was broken. The sometimes written, sometimes unwritten set of rules and principles governing how people should behave in an organization—its code—was shaping macro- and micro-educational systems all around me (and him) and needed to be fundamentally rethought. I learned through this experience that even good people, well-meaning faculty and staff, often *do not know how* to do this work well. It's my leadership imperative to change that.

An analogy I find helpful in thinking about how we could begin to change the code of higher education comes from computer science. In very simple terms, people write code using programming languages to get computers to carry out a particular action. That code governs every choice and action within the system. Over time, it is common for programmers to revisit code that was previously written to reflect on what worked as expected and what didn't, to get better at problem-solving, and to learn new techniques or ways to avoid future mistakes. As programmers add to the original base code over years, it can become unwieldy or even break, requiring that they go back to the base code and begin again. This analogy is not a perfect one, of course; higher education systems are far more complex than any computer code. And trying to understand what the base code of higher education is/should be in order to re-engineer it is, of course, an incredibly difficult thing to do because of the long history of higher education and the complex tangle of intellectual, social, political, and economic forces that have shaped its context for hundreds of years. However, the idea of needing to revisit the code that governs higher education as a system, to try to untangle why certain rules and governing principles have come to be the way they are and to think about whether that code still works for today's purposes or might be productively re-written, seems valuable in the context of higher education. I have seen the system fail far too many people I care about, both in my own home and in my classrooms. For me, then, starting from scratch in our thinking about what we want our students to learn and how we can create the most optimal learning conditions by focusing on *who* we're doing this work for and *why* is what it means to me to "go back to code" in a higher education context, something desperately needed to ensure our institutions deliver on a promise to make education truly accessible to all.

If I was asked to describe myself in only a handful of words, I would say I'm hyper-reflective and self-aware, a person who is resolutely metacognitive. Yet, trying to articulate how I learned to lead has been unusually challenging for me. I have been engaged in leadership—successfully so—for most of my adult life. Being a higher education leader simply feels natural to me after twenty-five years; trying to understand such a fundamental part of who I am is incredibly difficult. In fact, I almost gave up trying to make sense of it, thinking that I would just put this "extra" sensemaking opportunity aside and dive back into the day-to-day job of administration. The trouble with abandoning this effort to understand how I learned to lead is that, for me, the most important part of the work I do every day is continuing to learn *and to teach others* how to lead for the success of *all* students, especially those like Duncan. I am driven by the desire to inspire others to commit first to changing ourselves and our practices so that we are ready for the students we have, to ensure no one else's baby goes unseen and abandons the life-changing experience of higher education.

Leading for this kind of student success requires grounding our relationships with others and the activities in which we engage in a particular set of values and beliefs about students, about teaching and learning, about ourselves and the roles of our institutions. I've spent most of my professional life designing and delivering professional development for faculty and staff, but the most impactful versions of that work I've ever done have not been focused on specific teaching strategies or student success platform capabilities. The most powerful accelerator of professional growth and learning I've ever utilized for teachers and student success practitioners has been reflection, specifically dedicating the time to reflect on moments in our lives when learning has and hasn't worked best for us; when we have experienced (or haven't experienced) a sense of belonging, motivation, or engagement; and what factors enabled (or disabled) those experiences. The point is not simply to blindly replicate those conditions for students; what worked for us may not work for the students we serve today. It can be humbling to realize how little we *intentionally* design learning environments in higher education thinking about the *people* for whom we're doing it and how that knowledge might lead us to do things fundamentally differently: to create a new code for higher education to govern more just behaviors and actions.

Culturally speaking, higher education is not very good at going back to code. Centuries of tradition; allegiance to our academic disciplines, often at the expense of student needs; and rigid governance structures that accumulate and contribute to very slow change in how we operate (see Rosenberg 2023 for an extended critique of the current model; see Pikus and Penphrase 2024 for a nuanced discussion). Yet, taking it back to code is one of my strengths and has led directly to my success and longevity as a higher education leader. This chapter reflects the best sense I can make (for now) of how I came to internalize a very particular set of values and ways of thinking and acting that have led me to find continued success (and stand out) as a leader in higher education. The lessons I share below, the ones that so fundamentally shaped my worldview about education and leadership, were borne of relationships—with my kids, my students, my mentors, and colleagues—that showed me repeatedly why we have an imperative to keep "going back to code."

Learn to Meet Students Them Where They Are

To my surprise, these words my first mentor said to me thirty years ago were echoed in a late-night phone conversation with my older son, Ian, just a few months ago. Teaching a part-time gig as a percussion director at a local high school for the first time, he's struggling to understand how you can teach a whole class of students at once when he fundamentally believes that each one needs something different from him. “I don’t know, but it just seems like you have to meet them where they are,” he tossed off casually. It stopped me in my tracks and brought me back to my first time as a teacher in a regional, public institution in Northeast Texas that serves a lot of students who are the first in their family to go to college and who come from mostly rural areas. While Ian wears the label of teacher uneasily and still isn’t sure he wants to own it, clearly growing up in the house with me and my husband, who learned to teach and lead alongside me, has taught him a thing or two about fundamental conditions for learning and leading. His code is solid.

One Student at a Time

I learned this one in the first job I had in higher education, working as a tutor in the writing center at the institution where I was earning my master’s degree. As a tutor, I saw all sorts of students, and they all had one thing in common: they didn’t want to be there. They’d been classified as “not college ready” (despite being admitted to the university) based on their performance on a single state-mandated college readiness exam measuring their proficiency in “basic” reading, writing, and math. I worked with them one-on-one, sometimes in small groups. Many were embarrassed, ashamed, or angry at the “remedial” label they’d been given. Others adopted that label as if it were a well-worn, comfy sweater. For years, these students had been told in a variety of explicit and implicit ways that they couldn’t write, that they weren’t good readers, that they were not college material. Sitting side-by-side with a student like that, drawing attention to ideas and insights from their writing that genuinely interested me, and watching their belief in themselves and their intelligence and self-worth grow because of my belief in them—this shaped my purpose as a future leader on a very personal level. Taking the time to see each student and to learn their unique needs, strengths, and assets was critical to my success as a teacher and is fundamental to my leadership vision and values.

Look for the Good

My first teaching mentor, Donna Dunbar-Odom, taught me the value of meeting students where they are and to look for the good, to build on their assets. Thirty years ago, sitting around a large square table, surrounded by other graduate students who had just been assigned their first college class to teach, she told us about our students, "Don't look for what they *can't* do; look for what they can." She encouraged—and expected—us to look for that kernel of a brilliant idea in students' work and take the responsibility for figuring out how to get them to keep building on it. As a writing teacher, that meant looking at a student's text not just as a static piece of writing that does or doesn't meet certain conventions, but as an opening to engage with the person who wrote it. It's an opportunity to learn more about what they think and what they might want to do with what they're writing. This approach has influenced everything I do as a leader. It's why/how I'm still doing it thirty years after Donna first showed me how—by paying attention to the assets and needs of one student at a time. Tia Brown McNair and her coauthors call for this kind of change in *Becoming a Student-Ready College: A New Culture of Leadership for Student Success:* "[W]e want to create…a paradigm shift, from focusing more on what students lack to focusing more on what we can do, as educators, to create stronger, higher-quality educational environments that promote full inclusion and continuous improvement" (McNair et al. 2022, xiv, emphasis added). It is this emphasis on what our responsibility as institutions and institutional leaders is that drives my work today.

Don't Just Watch as Students Struggle; Do Something

I knew from my first experiences teaching (and had it reaffirmed at every institution I've been at since) that it is baked into academic culture that higher education is a meritocracy, that students who work hard will succeed, and those who can't hack it will be (appropriately) weeded out. I walked by other faculty's classrooms on the first day of class and heard faculty (some from less privileged backgrounds themselves) telling students that only half of them would finish the semester since their standards were so "rigorous." Many who see education as meritocracy believe that distributions of grades along a bell curve are not only expected, but just—that it's "unfair to other students" to make accommodations for a single student who wasn't able to finish a test because their unreliable internet connection went down mid-way through the exam. This view of education places the entire burden of success on the student, absolving faculty and academic leaders from any responsibility to acknowledge—and *act* on the knowledge—that many of our students do not come to us on a level playing field. But we cannot expect that all students have had the same rigorous preparation for college or that they all fit the mold of the "traditional" 18–24-year-old student with no significant family obligations and the ability to treat college as a full-time job. Most of my experience in higher education has been at institutions with clear missions to serve their local communities, to contribute to the social and economic mobility of their students and, by extension, their families. This reality reinforces the lesson that the students we serve are going to have different needs, driven by a wholly different set of life circumstances than we may have experienced ourselves, and we have to actively do something when we see they have needs that are not being met.

My work with those labeled "remedial" students at my first institution showed me that my values were not aligned with those of many of my colleagues who genuinely believed that only the most "worthy" (read *privileged*) should survive college and graduate with a degree. The students I first taught, and the experience of my son Duncan, so different in background and privilege from those I tutored in my early twenties, yet all so utterly failed by their educational systems—all of these showed me that I must work to spread different values, to construct different kinds of programs and systems that would help a more diverse group of students like them grow and flourish. These experiences inculcated and later reinforced in me the lesson that it is my responsibility as a higher education leader to drive the kind of institutional changes that would create the conditions for learning in which every student can succeed, not just those who came to us already primed to thrive in a meritocracy.

Learn to Meet Faculty and Institutional Leaders Where They Are, Too

Just as we must create institutions governed by a code of meeting students where they are, I also learned in my first faculty leadership role that I had to meet *faculty and other institutional leaders* where they are, as well. I currently serve as the Senior Vice Provost for Student Success and Academic Affairs at a large Hispanic-serving institution, with a distributed set of campuses in the heart of the Rio Grande Valley, but I began my faculty leadership journey as the administrator in charge of our first-year writing program at an earlier iteration of the same university (formerly known as UTPA, the University of Texas Pan American). As our institution grew and I began to move from department-level leadership positions to institution-level ones, the scope and complexity of my work grew rapidly, and early lessons about how to lead for/through significant change as a writing program administrator served me well later in a senior leadership role when the state legislature decided to turn UTPA into a new institution (The University of Texas Rio Grande Valley, UTRGV) with a medical school and distributed campuses across a three-county region on the southern border with Mexico. When Ronald Heifetz and Marty Linsky write about how to be successful leading through significant change in *Leadership on the Line: Staying Alive Through the Dangers of Change*, their words echo what I came to learn through first-hand experience:

> For transformative change to be sustainable, it not only has to take root in its own culture, but also has to successfully engage its changing environment. It must be adaptive to both internal and external realities. Therefore, leadership needs to start with listening and learning, finding out where people are, valuing what is best in what they already know, value, and do, and build from there. (Heifetz and Linksy 2017, *xiv)*

Get Out of the Way and Let Others Do the Talking

One of the most valuable things I learned in my program leadership role is that sometimes I was not the right messenger for change. Making big changes to curriculum, for instance, required understanding who I was working with, what mattered to them, and when to step out of the way and let others do the talking. A few years into leading our first-year writing program, I was trying (relatively unsuccessfully) to get our faculty excited about a new curricular approach, one whose merits had been touted in a lead article in one of our flagship journals around that time. It was a bold divergence from the more traditional approaches to teaching writing, and one of my teaching assistants, Dalel, decided to pilot it at a time when most other faculty seemed unconvinced. Sold on its value myself but recognizing that what the curriculum asked of our faculty was a radical departure from what they were used to, I knew that simply asking them to "go back to code" with me, especially knowing that they would need to change deep-rooted curricular and pedagogical beliefs and practices to do so, was not going to be successful. I needed them to see the impact of the new curriculum on our students if I wanted them to be moved to change, so I asked Dalel to bring some of her students to one of our monthly professional development workshops to share their experiences and what they had learned. I was stunned when half of her class showed up, but was less surprised to see how many faculty left that room committed to giving it a try.

Let Students Speak to the Impact of Our Choices about the Curriculum, Policies, and Pedagogical Practices on Their Lives

I learned that day that it's not always the intellectual arguments that we make as leaders that are convincing; sometimes we need to see the impact of changes on our own students to believe something new is worth trying. In fact, what Dalel's students taught me is that they and their peers can be far more powerful catalysts for change than I can be in many cases. They are, after all, the primary motivation for taking it back to code. I have used this lesson often as a leader to remind myself that I may not always be the right messenger for needed change.

Co-Design the Work, Even When You Think You Know Best

This is a lesson I learned when we first opened UTRGV, and I led the task of creating a new academic advising model for the institution. With the new institution, we had to integrate faculty and students from UTPA and the University of Texas at Brownsville. The prior institutions had diametrically opposed academic advising models (centralized staff advisors versus decentralized college/department faculty advisors). The new institution's leadership made the choice to centralize advising with professional staff, a decision that we believe ensured consistency and accuracy in advising and made the best use of institutional resources. But it seemed like one stakeholder group or another was voicing complaints about the model every time I turned around. For several years, I listened to the pain points experienced by students, staff advisors, faculty, and department/school leadership. "*Advisors don't know anything about* our *degree plans.*" "*Students are being told the wrong thing.*" With rare exceptions, none of this was true, yet deans, chairs, and faculty consistently believed every outlandish story they were told, which always led to the same thing: "*We need our own advisors in the college.*"

I couldn't understand why the misconceptions continued and found myself screaming to myself, "It's not the model that's the problem! If the people participating in the model trust and work with one another, it will work!" I had experience with both models from a variety of positions (student, faculty advisor, centralized advising leader) and knew that there were pros and cons of both and that, despite how it may have sounded listening to what everyone wanted, there was a lot of common ground among the various stakeholder groups. In my position, I was uniquely situated to hear that breadth of feedback, so, while I was incredibly frustrated by the response to the decisions we'd made, I knew that we could arrive at an implementation of the model that honored what each stakeholder wanted most: for *their* students to get the best advice possible.

To do that, we had to all participate in co-designing the strategies and approaches together. Together, we were able to ensure that the overall approach aligned with best practices in academic advising, accomplished institutional student success goals, and built in enough flexibility to meet the unique needs of each college/school. There were plenty of times when I just wanted to stop listening to all the complaints. I really did have more knowledge about how to make advising work for students than most of the people who complained about it. However, I learned that I had to take a path that led to implementation of a model that could meet our faculty, our students, and our institution where we were at the time. I did that by listening, building in what I heard to a model aligned with best practices, and co-designing it with invested faculty and students so it could be adapted to better meet each set of students' unique needs.

After all, one size does not fit all. UTRGV's student population is over 90 percent Hispanic, but that statistic masks an incredible amount of diversity. There is a similar complexity and diversity of needs, priorities, and beliefs represented in the eleven colleges and schools that make up our institution. Each one has its own culture, values, norms, and ways of operating. While I oversee our Student Success division, which drives student success priorities on the institutional level, I learned quickly from the advising redesign that one-size-does-*not*-fit-all when it comes to engaging faculty who are deeply embedded in these microcultures in student success work.

Learn to Be Adaptive

So much of my success as a higher education leader hinges on whether people I work with believe they can trust me, believe that I respect and value their contributions, and believe in the vision for and collaborative approach that I take to the work. That begins with meeting them where they are, but to parlay that into meaningful change, I had to learn how to reconcile where people are and the realities of where the institution is and where I—or more senior leaders than me—want us to be. Heifetz and Linsky note that "You need both a healthy respect for the values, competence, and history of people, as well as the changing environment, to build the capacity to respond to new challenges and take advantage of new openings" (2017, *xiv*). At my institution, I have been in a leadership position, either in my department or at the institutional level, for eighteen of the nineteen years I've been here. I've seen department chairs and deans come and go, as well as at least seven provosts and three presidents in that time. I've seen plenty of examples of good and bad leadership, and I've tried to learn from each of them, even and especially when it was painful to do so. It is almost a cliché, albeit an accurate one, that higher ed has historically moved at a snail's pace. We study and critique and plan everything to death. Meanwhile, students suffer, and the world outside our walls moves on without us.

This was a lesson I learned before the COVID-19 pandemic, when I asked one of the strongest members of my leadership team if she would take on the additional responsibility of overseeing our Academic Advising Center (AAC). The AAC had been plagued by a negative workplace climate, with many staff feeling overworked, underpaid, and undervalued, leading to burnout and resignations on a scale that threatened operations. The person I asked to step into this role had a strong record of leadership built on teamwork and collaboration, and she understood deeply how to build and assess programs. In the context she came from—tutoring and peer collaborative learning—these skills served her, her team, and our students very well. If you've ever been an advisor, especially in a centralized system where advising is central to an institutional student success strategy, you know that this unit has many different pressures from all over the organization, and you're often called upon to be all things for students. This leader went from having seven or eight direct reports in her "home" unit to leading two centers with over eighty staff in a year.

She was used to spending dozens and dozens of hours planning with her team before deciding on strategies and taking action. In this new context, however, an advisor's job is to be responsive to what students bring them in their advising appointment, never knowing exactly what complex mix of issues they might face from one hour to the next. Because there was no time during the day to do the kind of planning and discussion she was used to with her leadership team, in this new context, those meetings stretched on to the evening hours after everyone else went home. Campus partners (who operate in a culture very different from ours, one that adjusts and changes rapidly in response to changing needs) needed her to make some timely decisions about how advising would function at orientation. I remember clearly that she told me, "Jonikka, advising is like a big ship. You just can't steer it in a new direction very quickly." In my head, I thought, "We need to build a new ship."

I had and still have incredible respect for this leader, but it became clear to me that she was not able to adapt quickly enough within this new leadership context that required us to be quickly responsive. We didn't have the kind of time higher ed usually takes to study, plan, pilot, implement, assess, and repeat. Sometimes there is an urgency to help students now, and we must move faster. This moment helped solidify for me that the further I move up in leadership, the more often I'm called upon to adapt and be responsive, to move more quickly than higher ed typically does. Learning how to help others who are deeply committed to a different code begin to think differently about moving with urgency is something this moment with my advising director really drove home for me.

Learn How to Translate

All higher education leaders operate from the middle of an organization, and one of the most challenging aspects of leading from the middle is toggling between the needs, desires, understandings, assumptions, and values of those above and below you in the institution. Many of the chapters in this book address how our author-leaders dealt with the ethical choices we must make from this position in the middle. Here, I'm concerned with our work as translators of institutional context, culture, and decisions up and down the organization. For instance, when my provost or president makes certain decisions, my staff and faculty don't always understand why. They may not see how the decision fits with what they see in their day-to-day work, and it is my job to provide the larger institutional context, to understand what's missing and how to translate that decision so that it makes sense from their vantage point in the institution.

Provide Much-Needed Perspective

In my doctoral program, I gained a lot of institutional perspective that I could use for this kind of translation when I took a course with Thomas Rickert called the Rhetoric of Institutional Discourse. This course tapped into my long-standing fascination with thinking about why we do what we do in higher education. We read writers across the centuries and continents who explored the purpose of the university in their time, and we paid careful attention to the discourse that had been used to discuss and frame those purposes. In the first writing classes I taught five years prior, I, too, had asked my students to read different perspectives on the purpose of the university and the role of a liberal education and asked them to write about their own ideas about how the university fit into their own goals and worldview. Even then, I was asking my students to go back to code, and this doctoral course cemented my preoccupation with this effort. It's not just a fun exercise to try to make sense of the institutions I'm in—what the culture is, who the people are, what the policies and practices we enact say about what we value, and more. It is an imperative to continuously pay attention to what you see and hear all around you at the institution. Most of all, share what you see and think with others around you—up and down the organization's structure. These insights are important at all levels in shaping decisions.

Connect Data to the Things People Care About

I have found that faculty and staff alike can bristle at senior leaders' constant (it feels) focus on metrics and data, particularly retention and graduation rates. These things can seem very disconnected from the work that faculty and staff do on the front lines with students every day in their classrooms and offices. From my time as a faculty member, I saw many assessment "coordinators" and others develop assessment plans meant only to check a box for our accreditors. When I found myself in charge of the general education curriculum at my institution, I used that opportunity to take an institutional imperative for assessment for accreditation purposes and reframe it for faculty as an opportunity to learn something about their students that they *actually* want to know. My own early experience with assessment leaders showed me how frustrating it is to be asked to engage in bureaucratic tasks with no purpose. Since faculty regularly engage in research as inquiry into real questions of value to them, it was easy to translate this requirement into language that was not only familiar to them, but connected to their values, as well.

Humanize the Data (Especially for Senior Leaders)

Similarly, senior leaders need to understand that data and metrics need to be humanized and placed within a context in which faculty understand their role in making a difference in these lagging indicators. Aside from finances and mental health, the most important thing that impacts whether a student returns for the next year is how well they do academically in the previous one. I learned how valuable it is to humanize this data for faculty when my husband and I designed Conexión, a scaffolded professional development academy for faculty at UTRGV. At my current institution, if new first-year students fail two classes in their first term, they have only a 50 percent chance of coming back. That's a stunning statistic, one with a lasting impact on Conexión faculty who teach first-year students. We spent a whole afternoon sharing institutional data with them as we explored data and profiles of who our students are. We ended the day privately sharing each participant's course success rate trend data with them and asking them to reflect on any patterns they saw. The framework for inquiry we designed for this academy focused on teaching for student success at an institution with a 90 percent Hispanic student population is very simple. It is designed to both meet faculty where they are and ask them to meet their students where they are. We ask: (1) Which of your students are struggling? Which are doing well? (2) What do you know about why? And (3) What can *you* do (through course or project redesign, pedagogical professional development, more effective feedback and assessment strategies, use of direct student feedback, integrated academic support, etc.) to ensure all your students are successful?

I arrived at the use of this framework because I was struggling to translate why student success data should matter to faculty. One of my early leadership mentors at UTPA was a clinical psychologist who hired me into an institutional student success leadership position. I noticed that she regularly looked at data like course completion percentages and numbers of hours completed each term/year. I had never considered looking at data like that nor had I thought about the relationship between those metrics and things like retention and graduation rates or seat capacity (having enough seats to meet student demand). At our institution, students would often come back, but they hadn't always done well academically the prior semester. Clearly, our students were resilient and committed to being in school, but they dropped and/or failed enough classes that graduating in four years was out of the question. Knowing this helped me understand far better how critical the faculty role in student success is. Without her mentorship and attention to those metrics, I'm not sure I would have realized how important they were, how the data represented *my students* who may or may not have come back after they left my course. I don't think I could have conceived of a professional development academy designed to "translate" student success data for faculty had I not had a mentor who made it make sense for me. Data like course pass rates—most closely aligned to faculty's day-to-day life—matter to overall institutional metrics that senior leaders track so closely, and they are tied explicitly to the financial health of the institution and, more critically, to how well we make use of our resources to best serve students. Faculty need to be part of that conversation, and I found a way to invite them into it in language they understand.

Learn to Choose What Hills to Die On

Higher ed leadership is emotional work. It can be hard to maintain resilience, to stay grounded in your values, and to remain patient and gracious. A lot of my work, beyond building strategy and relationships, is focused on mentoring/sponsoring other student success leaders at my institution, both those who report directly to me and others in leadership positions in the colleges/schools.

I remember Donna Dunbar-Odom (the mentor mentioned earlier) telling me thirty years ago, "Choose the hill you want to die on." In my context as a new teaching assistant at the time, I thought of that advice in the context of not getting riled up if my students didn't read. As I have taken on leadership positions, it has taken on a far more important role in contributing to my leadership longevity. I get irritated fairly often and occasionally even outraged, but few things rise to the level of hills I want to die on. I think of my work as a very long game, and I want to stick around to play it.

It's (Most Often) Not about You. Move On.

Since Donna was the writing program administrator who supervised me and other teaching assistants while I was in my master's program, she was the one who mentored us through our first student complaints. "Never take more than twenty minutes of grief from a student," she said. She believed that when students were upset and complaining about their grades, "it's rarely about you." She was right—about the student complaints I had back then and about the faculty, staff, administrators, parents, and students who bring complaints to me now. I try to remind myself of that every time I have to endure a challenging emotional eruption. We're all complicated, emotional, whole human beings, and there are usually many stresses and pressures and fears weighing on all of us at any particular time. I tend to be a linguistic mimic, and a few years ago, I watched an awful lot of *New Amsterdam*, a show in which the "I'm-going-to-change-the-world" medical director of a major public hospital in New York routinely begins conversations with everyone he meets with, "How can I help?" For at least six months after that, I found myself, without thinking, asking everyone who came into my office, "How can I help?" It can be very hard to remember that it's not about you when people are determined to tell you all the ways your decisions and your institution have ruined their life or the academy as we know it. But I encourage you to carry Donna's words with you; they've helped me, and the people I've mentored, as well.

Learn to Get Right with Being Wrong

I am a perfectionist, and for most of my childhood and adolescence, I was mortified by the idea of being called out for being wrong. I did well in school, and it seemed like most of my peers were just waiting for any sign of a slip-up (I am embarrassed by the self-centeredness of such a notion, but that's how I felt). By the time I began my undergraduate degree, the pressure to always be right was wearing pretty thin. In my first-year composition class, I read Robert M. Pirsig's *Zen and the Art of Motorcycle Maintenance*, and I embraced (at least partially) the idea that grades aren't everything, that perfection was not necessary. I'm not sure all parts of my brain got that message, but somewhere along the way in my life, something shifted in my relationship with being wrong. In my first institutional leadership position, I began a common book program in which all first-year students were asked to read the same book, and we encouraged faculty across the institution to find ways to integrate the book into their curricula. The choice I lobbied for was *Being Wrong: Adventures in the Margin of Error*, by Kathryn Schulz (2010). That book was a revelation to me and immediately influenced all parts of my life, but especially how I approached my work as a higher education leader. Maybe it's because I had been struggling with how to be a good mom to kids who struggled in school settings and rebelled in ways that I couldn't relate to. Maybe I had just seen too many students over the years who felt they could never get school right, and I just wanted them to know it was okay to fail, to get things wrong.

This quote, in particular, resonates with me: "All of us outgrow some of our beliefs. All of us hatch theories in one moment only to find that we must abandon them in the next. Our tricky senses, our limited intellects, our fickle memories, the veil of emotions, the tug of allegiances, the complexity of the world around us: all of this conspires to ensure that we are wrong again and again" (Schulz 2010, 9). This is not something that seems baked into the code of higher education and academic culture—to our peril. We all get things wrong sometimes. We need to be able to speak those things, to acknowledge our mistakes, to be forgiven, and to be celebrated for and supported in trying again. When we take it back to code, we ask ourselves whom we're doing this for and why. When we meet people where they are, we may find them in the aftermath of failure(s) of their own or even of *our* making. Rather than despair, we should embrace this part of ourselves:

> Far from being a moral flaw, [being wrong] is inextricable from some of our most humane and honorable qualities: empathy, optimism, imagination, conviction, and courage. And far from being a mark of indifference or intolerance, wrongness is a vital part of how we learn and change. Thanks to error, we can revise our understanding of ourselves and amend our ideas about the world. (Schulz 2010, 5)

When I think of *how* I came to learn how to lead in higher ed, I always return to how personal this learning has been. It's something a mentor said to me. It's a value I learned directly from seeing the impact of my choice to see the brilliant ideas of a student who's been told she doesn't belong instead of seeing her comma splices. It's in seeing how a chemistry faculty member responds to realizing that he never felt like he belonged in any of his chemistry classes as a student and he's now replicating the same experience for his own students. I, you, we—all of us get it wrong all the time, but as Schulz says, it's also what makes us most human, and that's how I learned to be a leader.

References

Heifetz, Ronald, and Marty Linsky. 2017. *Leadership on the Line: Staying Alive Through the Dangers of Change*. Harvard Business Review Press.

"Improve Programming Skills: Discover Data Science." 2022. DiscoverDataScience, June 23. https://www.discoverdatascience.org/articles/how-to-improve-programming-skills/.

McNair, Tia Brown, Susan Albertine, Nicole McDonald, Thomas Major Jr, and Michelle Asha Cooper. 2022. *Becoming a Student-Ready College: A New Culture of Leadership for Student Success*. 2nd ed. Jossey-Bass.

Pikus, Noah, and Brian Penphrase. 2024. *The New Global Universities*. Princeton University Press.

Pirsig, Robert M. 1974. *Zen and the Art of Motorcycle Maintenance*. Mariner Books.

Rosenberg, Brian. 2023. *Whatever It Is, I'm Against It: Resistance to Change in Higher Education*. Harvard University Press, 2023.

Schulz, Kathryn. 2010. *Being Wrong: Adventures in the Margin of Error*. Harper Collins.

CHAPTER 14

Queering the Administrative Brew

A Possible Impossibility

Jonathan Alexander, *University of California, Irvine*

This chapter tracks my rise into administration, first through directing a composition program and then through oversight of campus-wide initiatives, including general education and student support programs. While partly accidental, my movement into administration, which has dominated two of my three decades as a higher educator, has benefited from expertise I developed in composition theory and pedagogy. What I learned from composition in terms of course design, curricular sequencing, and the assessment of student learning became extremely useful as an administrator building student support programs, curricular design, and the purpose and execution of liberal educational programming. With that said, my public identity as a queer person and scholar has laced all of my institutional involvement with a strong critical bent, one of skepticism about programs that work from normative—or normalizing—understandings of students' identities, positions, demographics, backgrounds, and potentialities. That is, what I have learned from my engagement with queer studies and queer theory seems to work against what I learned from composition. However, in practice as an administrator, I have learned much about how to balance working within educational and bureaucratic structures that attempt to provide normative pathways for what we call student "success" while trying to keep open—or "queered"—a notion of what success is. This chapter should be of interest to anyone occupying a traditionally marginalized identity position who is also considering a move into administrative work.

Becoming an Administrator: An Origin Story (of Sorts)

I don't exactly know how I got into administrative work—which strikes even me as odd because, in my thirty-plus-year career, I have easily spent over two decades administering a variety of different programs on two different university campuses. That variety extends from directing composition programs (not an atypical move for someone in my field, Writing Studies), to administering campus-wide general education programs, to coordinating campus-wide upper-division writing courses, to chairing a department, and to serving as an associate dean for undergraduate education overseeing diverse student support programs. But while administering a composition program might, as I suggest, be a *typical* opportunity (or in some cases obligation) for someone claiming Writing Studies as a disciplinary home, that does little to explain my apparent *persistence* in administering university programs. Indeed, after first directing a composition program at the University of Cincinnati just over twenty years ago, I have not stopped being an administrator and am now regularly tapped at the University of California, Irvine, for many different administrative tasks. I plan to step down from my current administrative work in three years and intend to retire five years after that, but no one—not any colleague I talk to about my plans—believes that those final five years will be free of administrative work, no matter how much I protest that they *will* be. (To be frank, I'm not always sure I believe myself; my colleagues may know more than I do.)

I suspect my story is not all that uncommon. I think that, from discussion with many different colleagues across the country, many of us find our way to administrative work, even when we didn't set out to be administrators, and then we find ourselves staying on, even if we do not imagine ourselves as following an administrative career trajectory. What I mean by that is this: despite my persistence in administrative work, I have eschewed a "track," which would typically be movement from program director to chair to dean to provost. I'll be blunt: I hated chairing and thankfully only did it for two years, and I have no interest in being a dean or anything "higher." I *did* enjoy my stint as an associate dean, which was a position primarily overseeing a variety of programs for students, and the story of my administrative career is one of such program oversight. I enjoy creating, maintaining, and assessing programs that directly serve students. I do not want to manage faculty and budgets at scale. I prefer the more hands-on administrative roles that envision and enact programs and policies that meet students' needs. So anything I say about learning to lead and becoming an administrator might best be read with that caveat in mind.

My persistence as an administrator is complicated by another factor: my queerness. What I mean by that is something a bit complicated and (another caveat) something not necessarily transferable to other queer academics. On one hand, I know that part of my persistence as an administrator has stemmed from actually enjoying the work that I do, even finding it valuable in promoting care for and investment in student learning at multiple levels and in multiple registers. As one administrative mentor once put it to me, you can get hooked on administrative work because you can see that you are actively solving problems and benefiting others, if you're doing it right, of course; in contrast, academic work, including teaching, can seem to be a study in making investments that you might never see develop into concrete returns. How often do students tell us, years later, what they've done with what we've tried to give them? (Fortunately, some do.) And how often do we know how that article we wrote and sent into the world has affected other scholars' and teachers' thinking? (Fortunately, sometimes we find out.) Administrative work often rewards with immediate satisfaction or awareness of your impact (or, conversely, your failure, to be sure). Such immediacy can be *very* satisfying.

On the other hand, though, as a *queer* administrator, I find myself often confronted with the fact that my administrative work, for all its apparent "help," is also in key ways part of a gatekeeping structure, one that is not just supporting but just as frequently assessing and making decisions about what works and what doesn't—all with the goal of creating pathways for success (a key administrative buzzword these days), and even creating at times normative trajectories for student learning based on measurable outcomes. The *queer* in me is, as I say, "confronted" by my administrative work because *my* particular queerness—which may not be everyone's understanding of queerness, admittedly—is based on a deep and abiding *questioning* of norms. That is, queerness for me manifests as a persistent desire to understand—and just as often challenge—the ways in which all of us are "normed" along certain paths and trajectories, often with the goal of achieving various kinds of "success," in relationships, in work, in developing families, in wealth accumulation, etc. Sara Ahmed, a cultural theorist and phenomenologist, describes how many "lines" or trajectories are often laid down ahead of us, guiding and directing our paths through life while also prompting how we feel about our being in the world—with good feelings often accruing mostly around following the normative path. As Ahmed puts it in *Queer Phenomenology: Orientations, Objects, Others*, "to follow a line is to become invested in that line, and also to be committed to 'where' it will take us. We do not stay apart from the lines we follow, even if we take the line as a strategy, which we hope to keep apart from our identity" (Ahmed 2006, 176).

Thinking of my administrative work in this way, I recognize that I am following certain lines, that I am indeed "invested" in creating lines that not only lead to student "success" but that value the ultimate "line" of higher education: that the pursuit of a college degree is a worthy goal, both in and of itself and for a variety of other reasons, including the supposed abilities, potentialities, and access it affords our students (if they can afford what we offer, that is). While investment in such lines might be understandable, Ahmed is keenly aware that not everyone can follow—or even *desires* to follow—such lines, such normative pathways. Extending her spatial metaphor, she recognizes that, sometimes, we are "disoriented" by the unfamiliar or taken aback by encounters along our varied paths; Ahmed argues that "disorientation is a way of describing the feelings that gather when we lose our sense of who it is that we are" (Ahmed 2006, 20). And while for some, "following certain straight lines might be lived as a pledge of allegiance on moral and political grounds to 'what' that line leads to," for others, the case might be very different: "certain lines might be followed because of a lack of resources to support a life of deviation, because of commitments they have already made, or because the experience of disorientation is simply too shattering to endure" (176).

More optimistically, Ahmed wants us to understand that our "orientation" toward certain paths may not necessarily be obligatory; in fact, she argues compellingly that "[t]he work of inhabiting space involves a dynamic renegotiation between what is familiar and unfamiliar, such that it is still possible for the world to create new impressions, depending on which way we turn, which affects are within reach" (Ahmed 2006, 7–8). That is, we are all navigating a variety of lines and paths, sometimes willingly tracing the paths laid out, and at other times more *queerly* recognizing and pursuing alternatives; sometimes we are actively creating those "new impressions" and embracing different ways of being in the world. Personally, my queerness, committed to questioning of normative paths, has been crucial to me in resisting the powerful *hetero*norms that would have had me sculpt my intimate and relational life along certain *hetero* trajectories, as opposed to my willful and dogged pursuit of queer relations, of multiple and non-normative relations that extend, exceed, and defy the monogamous coupledom touted as the only key to happiness and well-being.

But this is not a chapter about my personal queerness. It is a chapter rather about my *professional* queerness, or a chapter in which I am seeking to explore how it is that I reconcile— or live with the potential contradiction of—working administratively to implement and assess a variety of normative trajectories for students while also not living with the constant cognitive dissonance of someone who is otherwise committed to a deep questioning of such, to the creation of "new impressions," and to embracing alternative ways of being in the world.

It may be that these two dimensions of my being in the world are, in fact, *ir*reconcilable. To be sure, they are ones I have been worrying over for quite some time, nearly the length of my career. An experimental essay I wrote relatively early in my administrative career, "Queer: An Impossible Subject for Composition" (2011), coauthored with Jacqueline Rhodes, argued that queerness and composition as a field *are* in fact irreconcilable, the latter dedicated to the training of students in academically normative ways of writing that are potentially transferable to post-collegiate careers, while the former is committed to a ceaseless questioning and undermining of how norms are created, with the hope—a somewhat *utopian* hope for queer theorists like José Esteban Muñoz—of an always ongoing exploration and pushing at the boundaries of what it means to be (or to write as a) human in relation to others, humans and nonhumans alike. Jackie and I were obviously attempting to be provocative, and many have picked up this essay either to extend or dispute its provocation. But I have held firm to the fundamental *in*compatibility of queerness and traditional composition studies—the schooling of writers in established genres and modes of written communication—if not a "deal breaker," then at least as a generative tension. Indeed, I might have decided to "opt out" of administrative work altogether and instead spent my time queering the paths laid out by our institutions, helping students actively and explicitly cultivate alternatives and develop "new impressions." Even further, I might have left the academy altogether as an always already corrupt and corrupting institution that "straightens" young people out for a set of narrow and prescribed paths leading to narrow and prescribed notions of "success."

But I have not done the latter and instead coauthored another piece around the same time, this one with William P. Banks and entitled "Queer Eye for the Comp Program: Toward a Queer Critique of WPA Work" (Banks and Alexander 2009). This piece came directly out of my and Will's (separate) experiences as writing program administrators (WPAs), and as you can tell from the title, it aimed to critique, from a queerly personal and theoretical perspective, the ways in which WPA work often seems in the service of maintaining writing curriculum that both narrowly defines what writing is and does and that also serves a gatekeeping function, particularly as composition classes are some of the pivotal points through which students' eligibility to continue on in their studies are often determined. Again, as with "Impossible Subjects," the intent was to provoke, to produce what we hoped would be generative discussion, even as we recognized that our characterization of what composition administration does, and what queerness is and can be for that matter, were very broadly and somewhat stereotypically articulated. In fact, Will and I found ourselves in "Queer Eye" pivoting from pure and provocative critique to mapping out tentatively how we had both been attempting in our administrative practice to queer the "administrative consciousness." What might such a mapping look like? We suggested the following: a queer willingness to question the established status quo, to foster a deep sense of the political nature of language and language use, to cultivate a strong sense of how boundaries are created and potentially transgressed, and to develop an awareness of how promoting visibility (a cornerstone of much LGBT politicking) can assist in highlighting and valuing alternative paths and visions of "success." All of these were ways in which we were attempting to take our experiences as queer subjects and our knowledge of queer theory and actively shape an administrative practice that benefited from queer insights and ways of being.

I rehearse this work because it reminds me that one of the ways I *learned to lead* was through active critical reflection and writing about my own entrance into administration. I used the professional necessity of publishing (I've worked for the last twenty-five-plus years at research-intensive US campuses) to think about what it means to administer programs from a queer perspective. To be sure, joining administrative work with a publishing mandate doesn't seem very *queer*; after all, I was mobilizing queer critique in the maintenance of my own straight and narrow path toward merit, promotion, and success in higher education. Such are the compromises we make with ourselves, and you will find yourself, even if not queer, needing to reconcile a variety of different aspects of your identity, community affiliations, and values with the demands of administrative work. With that said, however, the editors' invitation to contribute to this volume serves as yet another opportunity for me, not only to reflect on my administrative experience as a queer person, but also—especially now, over thirty years into a career two-thirds spent as an administrator—to get back to the question with which I began this chapter: the need to account not only for having entered into but having *persisted* in doing administrative work as a very open, highly visible queer person, and one who takes their queerness very seriously as not just a personal but an ideological approach to being in the world.

Becoming a "Queer" Administrator

So how does one come to do administrative work, much less *queer* such work? You will come to administration for a variety of reasons, many of which you will only discover *after* you have taken on the tasks offered you. You might *think* of what you plan to do or even cultivate a "vision" for how you plan to "change the world" (or your little corner of it) through your administrative work, but the practice of administration—what you actually *can* do—is only revealed in the doing of it. Once I understood, through my work with Jackie and Will in writing those earlier articles, that my sense of queerness and administrative work were likely irreconcilable, I let myself discover *in the process of doing* administrative work what was possible to "queer," to push, even to question, and in some cases radically alter or reject. In accepting administrative work, I discovered that I had been "let in," as it were, and allowed to work—and play—with those in charge of creating and maintaining the structures that keep our campuses working. And while I knew I was committing myself to being one of those people who is (at least to some extent) part of the maintenance of structures, and thus part of a status quo, I strongly believed that I could use my queer insights to push at the boundaries of what was possible. All of the tentative ways in which Will and I imagined our queer selves critiquing and expanding WPA work have certainly been true to my experience, but so have other queerer possibilities that I will explore in the remainder of this chapter.

I should note before I enumerate those insights that when I say "queer insights," I'm not limiting myself to experiences of sexual orientation that have generated such insights. While it is certainly true (though not categorically necessary) that a queer sexual orientation can produce insights into the workings of normativity, it is just as true that not all LGBTQ+ people develop an attitude of "queerness"—one in which it seems not only useful but even desirable to adopt and cultivate a contrarian disposition, to question deeply normative structures and paths, and to promote capacious and alternative systems, ideas, and networks. Even more, such cultivation is hardly limited to LGBTQ+ people, and I've had many straight colleagues who are just as "queer" as can be in their orientation to work (and other areas of their lives). How does one "get to" and then decide to cultivate such queerness? Each story is different. While my queerness *has* in fact been born out of an early and seriously challenging experience of systemic homophobia, that is not the only "cause" leading to the cultivation of queerness as an *action* in the world. That action, I maintain, can originate in many life courses, but it often leads to that utopian sensibility I mentioned earlier—a utopianism arising out of a deep sense that what is given is not nearly good enough, and that what is possible must be capacious, even unexpected, plural, and rife with the possible stemming from an ability to see things aslant—to think and be queerly, in a word. And now, to the insights.

First, while recognizing that a queer approach to administrative work may not be as radical as one would like at times, there are ways to *queer* existing programs and projects, and by "queer" in this case I do not just mean making them more inclusive of and welcoming for LGBTQ+ students. Rather, I am reflecting on how I have learned in a few cases to *shift* some of the emphasis of tasks at hand so that they are functioning in not only more capacious but potentially in ways *in excess of* their original mandates—keeping in mind that one of the dimensions of queerness that makes it so fascinating is precisely its excessiveness, its willingness to consider and embrace far more than a narrow and acceptable band of possibility. When I served as campus writing director at the University of California, Irvine, I was tasked with opening up a writing center, consolidating existing and dispersed writing tutorial functions under one unit. In a way, writing centers are about as "normative" as one can get in the realm of college writing and literacy education in particular and in higher education in general. They are often centers in which students seek out (or are sent by instructors to find) opportunities to "improve" their writing—which often means making it more "standardized" and recognizable as "marketplace English." This function is often crucial for students seeking "success" in careers that rely (as so very many do) on effective, precise, and efficient forms of communication. While part of me was happy to create such a center on my campus, I also sought ways to think with my staff about not only the perceived *needs* of students to "improve" their writing but also their many and varied *desires* for writing—some of which exceed the creation of texts written in "marketplace English." That is, I wanted to think queerly *beyond* just how a writing center could foster pathways for success and also consider how our center might cultivate a love of writing for itself, even if that writing wasn't necessarily going to lead to normative notions of job readiness and career success. As such, we hosted poetry readings and even art contests, where students could express themselves in highly creative ways. We also opened our doors to student groups, encouraging them to visit the writing center to discuss *any* kind of writing project that they might have; we were thinking in particular about how student groups are often places in which students come to find their own voice and agency about a range of topics—from hobbies to political activism—and we wanted to make sure that we were serving and fostering student interests in these areas as well, areas in which the connection to job and career are perhaps tenuous or even nonexistent. In other words, we were invested in finding ways to make queerly capacious what a writing center could mean on campus far beyond "fixing" writing.

One of our most successful and innovative programs was hosting an annual Black Lives Matter writing contest, which aimed to support and promote smart and even provocative writing—ranging from the critical to the creative to even highly expressive rants and performance pieces—about race and racism on campus. This initiative came out of a couple of failed writing center visits, in which some Black students approached tutors for assistance with papers that dealt substantively with racism. These were sometimes papers in which the students allowed themselves to give voice to their frustration with racism and white supremacist systems and structures. Some of our tutors, operating with a sensibility that "good" writing presented different sides of an issue with rational calmness, counseled some of these students to "tone down" their angry comments and sentiments. The students justifiably complained, and the staff had long conversations about the importance of honestly grappling with difficult experiences and how the expression of emotion itself can be a powerful rhetorical tool. Staff had to be tutored themselves in understanding that, for some people, a calm and "rational" approach to situations that are incendiary and outraging is not only rhetorically ineffective at times but also limits and narrows what writing can do not only to facilitate expression but also to mobilize that expressivity for critical engagement with complex issues. Part of what strikes me as important about the need to intervene in staff engagement with diverse forms of student writing is the way in which we were, at the prompting of our students, actively queering our own sense of what a writing center can do and, more importantly, what kinds of writing such a center can and should be valuing. In the process, our sense of the latter expanded significantly.

Rethinking "Success" Across the University

In many ways, what I just described is not that far removed from what many writing centers do, particularly as such centers are increasingly expanding and extending the kinds of writing that they "help" students with. But what these experiences have brought home to me, extending my own sense of queerness in the world, is that students often come to us with highly varied needs, experiences, perspectives, and desires for their own education. This comment seems obvious, but it is one that we need as administrators to remind ourselves of constantly. So many of the programs that I have been a part of creating, sustaining, implementing, and revising have been focused on creating pathways through an institution, on facilitating "success" as students work toward degrees and develop employable skills.

As an associate dean for undergraduate education, for instance, I oversaw a number of "student success" programs that worked with low-income, first-gen transfer, international, formerly foster, and other groups of students for whom the institution deemed it important to set up additional resources to help them navigate a complex campus. As a former first-gen and low-income student, I was proud to help mount and maintain such programs, recognizing that I myself could have benefitted from some such when I was an undergraduate decades ago. At the same time, I *queerly* recognize that such programs, as valuable as they are, are often built (and often unconsciously so) on paternalistic positioning of students as somehow inferior; they just as often take for granted the belief that what such students want *most is* to figure out how to "belong" to the institutions serving them. Indeed, the rhetoric of "belonging" in student support services is often intense—and under-examined. The reality for many (if, admittedly, not all) of these students is that they are often bringing to campus significant ways of knowing and being in the world—ways of knowing and being they are unwilling to let go of in order to have them replaced with our institution's values and modalities. I have spoken with many first-gen and low-income students for whom securing a high-paying job or gaining admission to prestigious graduate schools—values often earmarked by institutions as worthy and important—are not their highest priority. Instead, what they often want is to build and develop skills that they can then use when returning to their home communities, helping others like them create more sustainable and enjoyable lives. If anything, some of these students are highly skeptical of the worlds we are sometimes pushing them towards, worlds of greater and greater financial success and accumulation. They frequently use their own experiences to interrogate critically the kinds of wealth disparities and prejudices that have led to many people and groups being on the short end of the economic stick. For these students, the goal is not so much to "join" the middle-classes and the aspirational pursuit of wealth but rather to return to their home communities and help create and foster alternative ways of being in the world that directly run counter to such capitalist aspirations. Moreover, for such students, the university is less a place that they want to "belong" to and more one they want to *use* to further their own particular vision of the world. Belonging, we sometimes discover, isn't an unadulterated and always desirable good or goal.

Working with such students, I realized quickly that, even as an associate dean responsible for multiple programs, I needed to queer my own understanding of student success, to enlarge my sense of what "success" means, even if such "success" run counter to some of the metrics we were using to gauge success—such as transition to recognizable careers and admission to graduate schools. Working out of my associate dean office, I spearheaded a student-led campus-wide festival for higher education in which our primary goal was to center the voices of students in helping to revision what higher education could be in the (supposedly) post-COVID-19 pandemic twenty-first century:

> This festival both celebrates our return to campus and serves as an invitation to reflect on what we learned about higher education during the pandemic, as well as what lessons we might take into the future in our post-pandemic world. Now, as we embark on the "new normal," what creative energies do we want to take with us from pandemic to post-pandemic? How will those energies continue to transform what we do, and what it means to be a "student" in the 21st century? Most importantly, how can our "new normal" in the academy proceed—from its inception—with the values of inclusive excellence? How can we turn the language of "DEI" (diversity, equality, inclusion) into transformative policies and practices that center social justice in our re-visioning of 21st century higher education? Centering the voices of students, [we] will host a week-long series of events, roundtables, workshops, speakers, viewings, and

> activities that showcase what students, staff, faculty, and community partners understand as the major innovations in higher education that are emerging now in the post-pandemic. These innovations run the gamut of what we mean when we say "higher ed"—including experiments in delivering course content, creating different forms of community at a distance, restructuring learning environments, fostering connection, and enlivening learning opportunities and relationship building. (UC Irvine, The Futures of Higher Education Festival, 2021)

The goal in mounting such a festival was to recognize that not all students want to "belong" to our campus and that many indeed have very divergent views on what higher education can mean and what it can help them do. We wanted to center *student desires* for their learning while recognizing and then actively honoring the many diverse epistemologies that our students bring to campus—epistemologies with modes of creativity and critique that we should in no way seek to replace but rather value and appreciate. If anything, what we hoped to do with this festival was create a space in which we could question our own institution's normative desires—as a reflection of capitalist culture—to inculcate within our students consumerist and capitalist notions of success and productivity.

The most radical version of this approach to higher education comes, I believe, in Stefano Harney and Fred Moten's *The Undercommons: Fugitive Planning and Black Study*, which connects colleges and universities to larger systems of indoctrination and even incarceration that manage the surveillance and control of diverse populations, particularly the systematically marginalized. According to Harney and Moten, "The university is not the opposite of the prison, since they are both involved in their way with the reduction and command of the social individual" (2013, 42). The authors advocate for what they call a "fugitive" approach to such institutions, an approach in which "one can only sneak into the university and steal what one can. To abuse its hospitality, to spite its mission, to join its refugee colony, its gypsy encampment, to be in but not of—this is the path of the subversive intellectual in the modern university" (Harney and Moten 2013, 26). In their introduction to this book, queer theorist Jack Halberstam connects Harney and Moten's radical Black thinking and praxis to queer critique, arguing that "we [should] refuse to ask for recognition and instead… take apart, dismantle, tear down the structure that, right now, limits our ability to find each other, to see beyond it and to access the places that we know lie outside its walls. We cannot say what new structures will replace the ones we live with yet, because once we have torn shit down, we will inevitably see more and see differently and feel a new sense of wanting and being and becoming" (Halberstam 2013, 6). While our Festival on the Futures of Higher Education did not actively tear down existing structures, I believe it queerly allowed students to find one another, and "see beyond" what was being offered to them and begin to envision modes of living—and making a living. Our hope was that it would allow students—and their teachers and administrators—to "see more and see differently and feel a new sense of wanting and being and becoming" (Halberstam 2013, 6).

Sustaining such work is not easy. The festival only ran for one year, but it initiated conversations that have touched many curricula, programs, and lives. To be sure, the goal of the festival was not so much to "tear shit down." Halberstam's comments, along with Harney and Moten's, remind me that part of the challenge—even the incommensurability—of being a *queer administrator* is recognizing the tension with which I began this essay: the tension between administering programs within a structure that survives on stability and the generation of "successful" through-puts (what one administrator on my campus actually calls students) versus a queer critique that is invested in ceaseless critique (tearing shit down) in order to reimagine, re-vision, rebuild. I imagine Moten and Halberstam feel this tension as well, given that they work at prestigious east coast universities.

Indeed, I think many of us have been feeling that tension recently, with 2024's student encampments protesting Israel's invasion of Gaza.

Whatever one might think of those protests politically, those encampments represented a significant calling into question of how universities are themselves part of larger national and global projects of political intervention; most explicitly, they sought to call out the involvement of higher education in varied forms of capitalist, settler colonialist, and ongoing imperialist expansion. Again, whether one agrees or not with the claims made by the protestors, the push to highlight and question higher education's entanglement with existing power structures constitutes important intellectual work; the fact that that work was being done (if not exclusively) by students and through encampments—that is, through forms that interrupted and exceeded normative modes of inquiry and education—seems to me quite queer in its way. Thinking about the encampment at UC, Irvine, I am reminded that not only did it consist of tents and spaces for meeting and conversation, but it also had a library, a collection of books of interest in explaining both the focus of the occupation as well as the importance of the strategy of occupation itself. Books on a campus may not seem much like an interruption of normative ways of "doing business" at a university, but the distribution of books outside a library, bookstore, or classroom and instead directly on a major walkway from one part of campus to another and as part of an unauthorized encampment—well, that *is* an interruption, a re-distribution of objects, namely the book, itself a metonym for knowledge production and dissemination, that signals a shift both in what knowledge is important and how that knowledge is shared. In suggesting there was something "queer" about these encampments, I do not want to align a queer approach with unquestioning support for the protesters. In fact, as a queer administrator, I found myself questioning both the student protesters and their tactics *as well as* the use of police force to disband the encampment on my campus. I will say that there were moments when passing the encampment on my campus that I simultaneously thought, on one hand, "Wow, this is so small, such a very modest kind of protest" and, on the other hand, that the word *intifada* or the phrase "from the river to the sea" made me uncomfortable. But I also reminded myself that that's the point of protest, to signal—and share—discomfort. And the point of a university campus should be to make room for divergent opinions, for holding difficult discussions, for engaging in challenging dialogues.

Toward Impossible Possibilities, or Working with Others as an Administrator

As I write that last sentence, I think back to my tutors in the writing center, those who were challenging Black writers to be less angry in tone. For sure, those tutors were very likely trying to help the writers create space for non-Black readers to engage their ideas and critiques, to join in a difficult discussion. But I might also counter by saying that our desire to create engagement and dialogue cannot always be on our terms. Divergent opinions are not always pleasantly articulated, and the registers of emotion, even unpleasant emotion, through which ideas are sometimes rendered is itself important information. The passion and force through which people offer us their thoughts and insights are at times a powerful register of their own commitment, even of the difficulties (and sometimes pain and suffering) that they themselves have encountered, the difficulties that have brought them to their ideas, their critiques, their interventions. "Toning it down" might not always do justice to the urgency of some claims.

Moreover, the larger context in which students are studying and moving into the world as citizens should give all of us serious pause. From climate catastrophe to our culture's ongoing flirtation with fascism, our students' world is on fire. We need platforms to listen to them, to engage them, to work with them on solutions to the damaged world they are inheriting. As an administrator, I hold firmly—and hopefully—to the view that the university campus is one of the last places in our culture to have such open discussions. The failure to engage our students and the move instead to enact policies that shut down discussion before every possible avenue of engagement has been tried—this is unacceptable.

With that said, I recognize that creating the rich, varied, and capacious spaces for ongoing, provocative, and probing debate is also likely an impossible challenge, and the very impossibility of it brings me back to my contention earlier in my career about queerness and the impossibility of reconciling that queerness with certain kinds of work in higher education. But my queerness is also a kind of stubbornness, an insistence, even a utopian feeling, that the impossibility of a task does not exempt us from at least attempting it. And that stubborn and weirdly utopian sense may be where my queerness as an administrator has ultimately led me; it has become the way in which I have learned to lead.

One final thought. Any administrator is prone to think about their work in the world as cultivating a kind of legacy, and it's pretty common for my administrative colleagues to consider their own legacies once they leave a position. I queerly urge you not to do this. When I stepped down as director of the university writing center that I founded on my campus, a graduate student asked me what I hoped my legacy would be. I told her that I had no sense of legacy, and that if another group of administrators had shown up the next day at the doors of the center and determined that it needed to be closed to make room for other projects, I would be absolutely fine with that. I am queerly *un*committed to my legacy, to reproducing into the future my desires, for propagating into someone else's future my sense of the world after I have left certain work behind. I have no need to reproduce myself—and I have come to think of the desire to leave a legacy behind as a kind of reproductive arrogance. We can prepare our students and others for a future, but we cannot live it for them; they will have to make their own decisions, face their own challenges, craft the worlds in which they want to live. I queerly commit to helping prepare others, as I work toward the world I want to live in *right now*—but learning to lead is as much knowing when to step aside and let others take over as anything else. And with that, I wish you the very best on your own academic and administrative journey, queer or otherwise.

References

Ahmed, Sara. 2006. *Queer Phenomenology: Orientations, Objects, Others.* Duke University Press.

Alexander, Jonathan, and Jacqueline Rhodes. 2011. "Queer: An Impossible Subject for Composition." *JAC* 31 (1/2): 177–206.

Banks, William P. and Alexander Jonathan. 2009. "Queer Eye for the Comp Program: Toward a Queer Critique of WPA Work." In *The Writing Program Interrupted: Making Space for Critical Discourse*, edited by Donna Strickland and Jeanne Gunner. Boynton/Cook Publishers.

Halberstam, Jack. 2013. "Introduction." In *The Undercommons: Fugitive Planning & Black Study*, by Stefano Harney and Fred Moten. Minor Compositions.

Harney, Stefano, and Fred Moten. 2013. *The Undercommons: Fugitive Planning and Black Study*. Minor Compositions.

Muñoz, José Esteban. 2009. *Cruising Utopia: The Then and There of Queer Futurity*. New York University Press.

UC Irvine Web Admin. 2021. "The Futures of Higher Education Festival." July 27, 2021. *UCI Division of Undergraduate Education*. https://due.uci.edu/2021/07/27/the-futures-of-higher-education-festival.

CHAPTER 15

Personal and Professional Identities, Belonging, and Change

The Process of Becoming

Sheila Carter-Tod, *University of Denver*

When I began thinking about how I would approach this chapter, I considered both the goals of the larger project and how what I may have to say might fit into these goals. In the introduction, the course is described as "intended to highlight its distinctive approach—specifically, its focus on how people learn to lead in higher education.... These leaders ... are, to be sure, experts. Their thinking is grounded in learning theory and research and in their own experiences." I made several attempts at creating a chapter that would somehow integrate my identities and experiences tracing how I, as a leader, have moved towards "expertise."

While I made multiple attempts to begin, I felt a niggling sense of inadequacy—as if I did not belong or could not be viewed as any sort of expert. It took me multiple stretches of starts, discards, and restarts to squelch my sense of self-doubt. This feeling of not belonging, or self-doubt, often called imposter syndrome (IS) or imposter phenomenon (IP), has stifled me throughout my leadership journey, as it has for many African American women in higher education, in all levels of leadership, and across all disciplines. Huecker et al. (2023) describe what I was feeling as an "essentially pathognomonic characteristic of imposter syndrome ... that occurs when individuals with IS face an assignment, obstacle, duty, or other achievement-related tasks. In those with IS, the response to this achievement-related task is generalizable into two broad categories:

over-preparation and procrastination" (Huecker et al. 2023, under "Imposter Cycle"). For me this began with an unprecedented dive into leadership and learning theory—reading and amassing large quantities of notes and ideas that I saw as essential to trying to consider and frame my leadership. Next, I moved into a prolonged stage of procrastination. I was surprised that I was so impacted by my feelings of not belonging to "a group of experts." I thought that I had moved beyond the crippling hold that feeling like an imposter had on my actions and writing, but here I was again. I finally found that it was only through writing through my fears of not belonging, that I freed up my mind to write about its impact. It may seem a bit contradictory that even while having these feelings of not belonging, I have held a host of leadership positions—from university leadership like director of composition, director of curriculum and pedagogical development, director/liaison for an $18 million university gift to professional leadership roles in the National Council of Teachers of English, College Composition and Communications, and the Council of Writing Program Administrators. When asked to accept each position, my choice to accept them was grounded in my deep desire to create and maintain greater access to educational opportunities. Before moving into my leadership journey, it is important to explain why I chose higher education as a career.

My values, my work, and my life are grounded in a clear sense of the power of language and the impact of how that knowledge (or lack of knowledge) impacts individuals and, by extension, systems. I saw brilliant people struggle with job security, housing issues because of contracts that they did not understand, and many other language-based complexities. For example, when a company decided to change procedural platforms and provided no training, my cousin, who was a data entry worker, was "let go" for inefficiencies in her data entry pace. This pacing issue was because she had to spend a great deal of time deciphering what she could of the online information that she had been given, essentially teaching herself the new platform in order to do her job. While this may be seen as one unfortunate situation, I saw many such situations occurring—from apartments lost because of overly complicated lease language to misleading language in work-based contracts.

I think that my keen understanding of language came from a deeply learned commitment to education. As early as I can remember, my parents (and those of all the children in my community) taught us that education is fundamental to success. They emphasized that understanding language and how it worked was a sign of intelligence and upward mobility. Yet, I saw very few of my near peers going on to college or university. The host of barriers that prevented them from attending post-secondary school ranged from money to academic preparedness to an understanding of how the systems of higher education work. As I grew up, I learned about so many of the obstacles that led to my community's disproportionate denied access to postsecondary education. Access to education allowed you to better understand how to interpret documents and to know what to do with them. Access to education meant the possibility of jobs that paid enough to break cycles of poverty. My love of language meant that my way of creating venues of access would be through language and literacies.

I lead with this "confessional" to illustrate that even as a later career, first-generation, African American, female professor who has been an administrator for most of my academic career, I still face the challenges of becoming. I have and am still learning to lead using my identities as assets and not deficits. I also lead with this story because I believe that with my story, I am welcoming all into my leadership process—even those who don't feel that they belong in these roles. In welcoming all, it is my goal to show that belonging, learning, and change have been integral parts of my ongoing process of becoming and being a leader.

Learning to lead is a process or a series of processes. It is often based on our personalities that we seek opportunities to lead. Additionally, schooling and/or educational processes help us develop who we are as leaders. A key part of learning to lead is reconciling who we are with what we know (about leadership). This learning process is generative, revision-based, recursive, and reflective—words frequently associated with the writing process, but equally important here. What follows is my tracing my own learning to lead process(es) through a series of stories and an exploration of theory.

Traits and Situational Leadership

There has been a long debate in leadership theory about the role of personality traits in leaders. Although currently summarily dismissed, in the mid-nineteenth century, research on leadership focused on the innate characteristics of leaders and on identifying the personality traits and other qualities of effective leaders (Benmira and Agboola 2020, 3). Popularized by Thomas Carlyle, the "Great Man" theory of leadership claimed that great leaders are born with specific innate traits that make them leaders. The "Great Man" theory later was disrupted by behavioral theories of leadership that argued that "leaders can be born or made" (Benmira and Agboola 2020, 3). While these theories have been dismissed, I can see some traces of my experience in them. Using these earlier and problematic ideas to frame my earliest experience of leadership, I would say that my earliest memories of leading were based on my personality. I was born with specific traits and shaped by environments that made me want to lead.

> *Recess time in elementary school, students would pour out of the classroom, racing towards equipment or locations to best utilize the fastest 30–45 minutes of the day. The playground was chaos. By the time we somehow got around to what we had been planning to do, most of the time had passed. Frustrated with this chaos and lack of efficiency and fueled by my need to prove my ability to beat almost everyone in short races, I organized relay races on a regular basis. We would leave the classroom for recess, and people would consult with me as to whose relay team they would be on, and which teams were racing in what order. People listened to me and did what I asked/told them—they willingly followed my lead.*

Through this story, I can't help but identify that there was something "in me" that has always propelled me to take on leadership roles. At this time, my environment was also a factor that shaped me as a leader. I was bussed to an all-white school several neighborhoods away from where I lived. My proficiency at organizing and leading during recess shaped how I navigated an environment in which I was often being judged or ignored because I was different. This elementary school experience had provided some of my first encounters with attitudes of rejection and bias focused on me specifically or my actions. Yet somehow, I believed that on that playground, my race, lower socioeconomic status, and the stigmatization of being one of the bussed kids, did not hinder my ability to lead. My speed and knowledge of the speed of others allowed me to be considered enough of an expert to lead, allowing me to create a space where I belonged. At the time, it may have been the confidence that comes with youth: my naivety of believing that "I could show them."

While I would identify personality traits as key to my earliest experiences with leadership, it was not personality traits alone that furthered my process of becoming a leader. As I describe above, my leadership journey has been a series of processes. Considering my adaptive strategies to account for the context of my environment, the theoretical framework of situational leadership serves best to describe my next memory of leading. Northhouse (2019) describes situational leadership as based on the ways in which "different situations demand different kinds of leadership… To be an effective leader requires that a person adapt his or her style to the demands of different situations… To determine what is needed in a particular situation, leaders must evaluate [their] followers" (95).

> *It was my junior year of high school, and, after witnessing what seemed to be a less than adequate treatment of our sophomore year's activities—the class officers did not plan any activities—I decided to run for class government. In this environment, my race and socioeconomic status did influence the school's sense of my consideration as a leader. Before my interests in running, only wealthy white students had held such positions. I knew that*

disrupting this hierarchy would be a challenge. What I had going for me was that I was involved in many school activities, allowing me to cross multiple school groups with ease. In the past, there had been limited knowledge of when the voting was to take place and where to vote, so I realized that my winning would need to be based on getting as many people as possible to vote from the groups that traditionally did not vote. I also knew that there were certain kinds of stickers that transcended groups, and that people liked to wear. I created stickers, buttons and flyers with my name and the office that I was running for (vice president), but instead of a slogan, I included information of where and when to vote. Having watched past elections and how various students catered to those they knew would vote for them, I knew that high school interactions of popularity, cross group relationships, and creating access to a larger group of voters were all situations that were going to be necessary to disrupt the years of "tradition" and make the changes that I wanted to see for our junior year. Winning would be situation-based and collaborative, based on needs-based decision making—finding out what students wanted and needed from their junior experience since so little had been done in our sophomore year. My strategy worked, to the dismay of those running and teachers (who had assumed the same students would win and had already planned to work with them). Based on the votes gained by my analysis of the situation, I won by a landslide.

The skills, behaviors, and practices that I used for analysis are what I would now characterize as transferable strategies from one leadership situation to another.

Unlike what I saw as leading because it was "just part of personality," my secondary and postsecondary understanding of leadership helped me to learn that a leader is not only a product of the environment from which they come, but also that leaders can disrupt or change the environments/situations in which they lead. *Listening to those who were invested* in school activities but did not feel a part of the formal school governance process, *adjusting and improving processes to ensure success,* and *spending time collaborating with all groups to brainstorm and create activities that people were interested in investing time and energy into* were skills, behaviors, and practices that I still use in all aspects of my leadership. Most recently, in my current leadership role, this has taken the form of listening sessions (both one-on-one and in small groups); adjusting days, times, and formats for faculty meetings and faculty gatherings so that they worked for a range of schedules and life situations; and collaboratively creating program initiatives based on the interests and specializations of those in the program.

When we use theoretical frameworks to explore any stories, there are aspects of each story that could be explained by multiple theories. For example, situational theory could explain the environment that made me into the playground leader as the high school situation could also be explained based on specific traits—innate and learned. In other words, much like the process(es) of becoming a leader, applying theoretical leadership models to explain stories can be recursive and easily revised by re-looking at or re-envisioning the content. While I focus my analysis here in one way, the same theoretical model with a slightly different focus on the same situations could lead to further and other insights. It is important to note that there are no "neutral" models of leadership. Each model or theory brings some things into focus and leaves others out. Additionally, the ways in which we frame leadership have implications, including overt or covert implications of who "belongs" and can or should assume or perform certain identities.

This situational leadership continued as I took on leadership roles throughout college—in social and religious groups. I continued to rely on aspects innate to my personality while also continuing to shape and be shaped by the situational environments in which I led. But I needed more. To use only what I had at hand and what I problem-solved in situations limited my ability to lead. Additionally, as I continued in higher education environments, I felt more and more like an imposter. I did not encounter other faculty who looked like me or other administrators who looked like me. The leadership models, as mentioned above, were not "neutral." I still wanted to be a leader, and I still sought leadership opportunities that allowed me to lead in ways in which I felt effective—creating environments in which I and others belonged. I was changing, personally and intellectually, and the more I learned, the more I realized how much I didn't know. In my postsecondary education, I decided that I wanted to expand my understanding of leadership academically.

In undergraduate/graduate school and in my earlier career, my becoming a leader was heavily influenced by two people through their content and example. I met the first of these two people as a graduate student in curriculum and instruction. My educational psychology course and professor taught me about learning theories, helping me to better make connections between the role of learning theory and becoming a leader. The second, a department chair I met as an early-career academic, taught me how someone who looked like me could lead and make change in authentic ways.

Learning and Leadership

Many theories of learning also parallel theories of leadership development because "[l]eadership is closely connected with the concept of change, and change, in turn, …is at the essence of the learning process" (Brown and Posner 2001). When exploring my continued process(es) of becoming a leader and leading, I can best explain and illustrate these connections with two more narratives.

> *In my educational psychology course, Dr. Bruton taught me about learning theory both through direct and indirect instruction. (The names in these narratives are pseudonyms.) After teaching us about theories of educational/learning psychology through direct instruction and through connections between and across units, we were given multiple choice tests. When he returned the tests, we were allowed to discuss why we had chosen one specific answer over another and why we considered*

our choice correct. If we had compelling content-based reasons for justifying our choice, we were given credit for that question. For example, if had chosen both behaviorism and social constructivism best fit the example that we were given, I could argue that behavior is socially constructed and thus was as suitable an answer as what he had intended for us to choose, which was constructivism.

This experience was influential in my development as a leader because it taught me about perceptions of assessment, learning, and leading. While the exam was the assessment for the unit, it was only part of our learning processes. The class period that followed the assessment was as much a part of the overall instructional environment as was the notes or case studies we reviewed in class. What he was doing through his instruction clarified the content of each educational learning theory and exemplified them. From him, I learned that educational learning theories could be combined and enacted collectively for effective instruction.

In the table below, I illustrate the connections that I make in this reflective analysis by describing what I learned about theories of learning and their connections and influences on my understanding of leadership.

Table 15.1. Learning Theories and Leadership Practices.

Learning Theory	Definition	Leadership Practices
Behaviorism	Learning is shaped by processes of behavior modifications—which often includes direct instruction and involves social learning theory.	If I am expecting someone to do something, I must make sure that my expectations are clear and provide feedback to help them shape their carrying out of those duties.

Learning Theory	Definition	Leadership Practices
Cognitivism	Learning is focused on the internal processes surrounding information and memory—which emphasize connections between past ideas and new ones.	I need to make sure that as a leader, I am clear in connecting the activities to the larger goals of the unit. I also need to provide space for discussion of how those in my unit are encountering and carrying out what I have asked them to do. And finally, I need to provide an environment that encourages transparencies in processing processes.
Humanism	Leading emphasizes the importance of personal growth, self-actualization, and whole-person development—which emphasizes the unique capabilities of each learner rather than the method or materials.	As a leader, I need to be connected enough with those I lead to understand how I can support their individual growth holistically.

Learning Theory	Definition	Leadership Practices
Constructivism	Learning builds upon previous experience and understanding—which promotes active, hands-on experimentation with interactive materials, open-ended questions which encourages students to think critically and form questions and solutions in real time.	As a leader, I must create time for and acknowledge questioning, attempts, and failures as opportunities for growth.

Theories of learning have shaped all my instructional practices and are directly connected to my continued development as a leader. But while the influence of Dr. Bruton's instruction and instructional practices played such a positive role in my understanding of leadership, it would be some time before I encountered leaders that inspired me to further consider myself a leader or leadership as a real path for my future. It may seem odd through my sequence of stories, but as I saw it, I took on leadership roles as problem-solving endeavors, while not formally seeing myself as a leader. I was in a doctoral program with leaders who were part of a concentration in leadership and was working at a university with a range of leaders. However, in both cases, their leadership styles were not anything that I wanted to replicate. They often seemed to have taken on bureaucratic, top-down, overly authoritative leadership styles that were not consistent with their personalities. For this time, and sometime after, my desire to lead was pushed back to the periphery of my vision while I focused on the immediacy of completing my PhD and finding a job in my area of study. This time of new focused energy, coupled with a lack of encounters with anyone else who looked like me, led to the strongest sense of not being good enough for or really fitting into higher education—the most intensive grounding and forging of what I earlier described as imposter syndrome/phenomenon, a term first described by Suzanne Imes and Pauline Rose Clance as an observation first among successful women and other marginalized groups (Huecker et al. 2023, n.p.).

A humanistic perspective of learning theory is one that emphasizes the importance of growth, self-actualization, and whole person development, yet that was an aspect of becoming a leader that was lost for me at this time. The models that I studied and the professors who taught me seemed to be shaped more by the theorizing of leading than by the pursuit and practice of authentically leading. The lack of visible representation of leaders of color seemed to reinforce my inadequacies for even being in higher education, let alone considering being a leader in this environment. While I was able to reject, fight against, or even try not to let what I was encountering shape my career decisions of where I did and did not belong, the institutional nature of imposter syndrome/phenomenon in higher education is much more powerful than the strength or convictions of the individual. Based on their case study research on intersectionality and imposter syndrome/phenomenon, Hewertson and Tissa (2022) further articulate the role of higher education on BIPOC scholars' feelings of not belonging when they conclude the following:

> Black women are more likely to suffer from the imposter phenomenon which affects their progress at university. Allen and Joseph (2018) explored the educational and social experiences of Black women in the academy and found that the white male perspective dominates academia. When women of colour challenge this notion, they are not seen as the typical 'scholar in training' and

> they end up having to redefine what it means to be an academic. They are in a constant fight to prove that they belong in the academy (Brunner and Peyton Caire 2000). The culture of academia can be isolating, and they are regularly battling with exclusionary practices and insensitive comments. (Hewertson and Tissa 2022, 23)

What was valued or rewarded as leadership qualities and practices seemed problematic to me. Professors were promoted by their abundance of research or by the research money they brought into the university, not by any leadership qualities they exhibited. In hindsight, I was learning about leadership by watching negative examples; I learned that I wanted to lead in opposition to what I saw as negative models, and I continued to search out what I considered positive models.

> *This perspective of higher educational leadership changed with one exceptionally positive model of leader—Professor Stone. Professor Stone had been an associate dean before taking on the role of department chair for our department of English. She was the first African American English department chair at Virginia Tech, and she was a force of nature. I was aware of her as a leader because I had interviewed her as part of one of my courses in higher education leadership while she was a dean in the college. At the time that I interviewed her, she told me that you go into administration because you have a vision for change, and/or want to accomplish something. She went on to say that once you have accomplished what you set out to do, get out—otherwise much of your work is spent on working to keep your administrative post. While she was my department chair, I watched her navigate her role within a larger institutional setting to truly forward change. She showed me what it looked like to collaboratively create a shared vision, choosing the right individuals to forward that vision and trusting them to accomplish their part with an eye to the whole. From her, I witnessed and learned lessons*

about finding ways to really listen and bring in all voices for input, and she showed me how a certain level of transparency is key to navigating relationships in multiple directions—with upper administration, with colleagues within program, and with colleagues across campus. And finally, she showed me how to consider my personal and rhetorical positionality when working with senior leaders and institutional structures. For example, she was able to secure funding for departmental inclusion initiatives by connecting them to both the university strategic plan and core curriculum requirements—illustrating how focused efforts need to be connected to larger university-based efforts and funding lines. Additionally, with an eye towards establishing the English department as research-grounded and an integral part of graduate efforts, she convened committees that were successful in developing two departmental graduate programs (an MFA and a PhD). Watching her lead, encourage, advocate for, and support individuals, committees, and initiatives illustrated that a good leader could incorporate the best of leadership theory with a clear sense of who she was and what she valued. She found a way to reconcile who she was as a person (an author, an artist, a creative writing teacher, an activist, and an advocate for women and minorities) with her leading and managing the work of a department of roughly 100 people.

While Professor Stone inspired me, she still left me with the question of how I could create a leadership style based on my own personality and values, pulling together what I had learned about leadership and who I was as an individual. This understanding moved beyond the limits of the "great person" approach to an intertwining of personality, values, situation and environment. I was not her, and outside of her example, different models of higher education leadership seemed somewhat contradictory to my values. From my experience, those who worked to further goals of equity and inclusion were undervalued.

Those who exemplified leadership in instructional or student-based realms were deemed unscholarly and were not promoted to tenure and subsequently selected for leadership roles. Leadership was given to those who were proficient researchers—publishing and bringing in grant money—but who had not developed the skills to navigate the intricacies of departmental or university operations. Except for Professor Stone, all that I had learned and valued about what it means to lead (situational analysis and needs assessment skills, communication skills, and collaborative and problem-solving skills) were not valued in the leaders being chosen.

Although I did take on administrative roles, including director of the writing program and director of curricular and pedagogical development, and was even elected to leadership roles in professional organizations of my discipline, I was steadily becoming more disillusioned with how what I was doing furthered my values and frustrated with butting up against direct and indirect questioning of my credentials or even my place in these leadership roles. By mid-career, I had stepped away from leadership/administrative roles completely. I saw no way of committing to what I valued while enacting the expectations and limitations of leaders in higher education. I struggled with how I could create opportunities for access or even develop programs and individuals with business-based models being misapplied to educational environments. As I mentioned earlier, I originally went into higher education because I believed in creating access to education for more people who looked like me. I chose my focus—linguistic equity and justice—because of the role language plays in all aspects of access and equity. Having been bussed to school for most of my childhood and then attending predominantly white institutions (PWIs) for undergraduate and graduate school, I was keenly aware of how language usage could provide or deny opportunities and how those accesses or denials shaped career and life trajectories. Becoming a Writing Studies professor was a way to help students and other scholars understand the ways in which language and social justice are directly connected. My focus on race, language, and injustices was and is guided by such language and linguistic scholars like Alim, Rickford, and Ball (2016), whose work has been critical in exploring and explaining the central role that language plays in shaping our ideas about race and vice versa; John Baugh (2018), whose research coined the phrase "linguistic profiling" based on experimental studies of housing discrimination and expanded upon those findings to promote equity in education, employment, medicine, and the law; William Labov (1972 and 1982), whose work pioneered an approach to investigating the relationship between language and society, eventually developing a field that has come to be known as "variationist sociolinguistics"; and Makoni et al. (2003), whose book recognizes and formalizes the existence of a "Black Linguistic Perspective," highlighting contributions of Black language researchers in the field of linguistics (see also Smitherman 1977, 2000). My teaching, research, and service were all acts of social justice, yet the same efforts were not easily reconciled with leadership in higher education.

In my own process(es) of becoming, I continued struggling to find ways to reconcile how my personality and values could address the systemic injustices of institutional practices within higher education, yet I am now better able to challenge some of these injustices by enacting agency-based approaches as an intersectional leader focused on addressing these injustices.

Enacted Agency-Based Leadership

> *Four years ago, I sat on a Zoom screen with 15-20 folks who lived twenty-six hours from where I was living at the time. While still not claiming expertise, I saw the potential in this place to become the leader I could imagine. In this job talk, I described myself as a relational leader (an individually centered, purposeful, approach to working with others that cultivates inclusivity, empowerment, ethical behavior, and collaboration) with a social justice focus in all that I do. I was very transparent in my articulation of who I am as a leader and what my values are. When asked what that meant, I was able to share why I had gone into higher education and Writing Studies and how*

> *I saw the discipline more broadly and this institution specifically, poised to reimagine what is possible. What had attracted me to this position was the work that the faculty/program had done related to community outreach, linguistic justice, and leading the campus in multiple equity-based initiatives.*
>
> *I was ready to enter this space at a different stage in my process than I had ever been—a more reconciled stage. I was ready to continue my learning while moving forward on a social justice-based, transformation-ally-focused model of leadership.*

I am not sure if it was navigating the challenges of COVID-19 or the social and racial unrest of the country before and after COVID-19, but I became acutely aware of changes that needed to be made and wanting to be in positions to make those changes. I wanted to lead these changes because I felt that I had the knowledge and experience to make a difference. I began to believe that social justice in higher education leadership could be possible or at least I was willing to try to reconcile these concepts. By this time, I had been in higher education for over thirty years, and I had not been in an administrative role for over six years. Having worked as the director of composition at the departmental level, diversity fellow at the college level, and the director of curricular and pedagogical development at the university level, I had a greater insight into the ways in which change comes about in higher educational environments.

As someone with imposter phenomenon, I had to learn systems of higher education from a position outside the tradition of "how things were done." I had both experience and insight to enact the change needed at this time in the history of higher education. This was a time that my insights and experiences could indeed redefine and shape the future of higher education—more than ever before. With this almost "calling" in mind, I now serve as the Executive Director of the University Writing Program at the University of Denver. In this version of myself as a leader, I brought with me the younger leader who felt the need to make some order out of the chaos. I drew upon Professor Stone's advice of having a vision for something that I wanted to change, and an ability to reconcile my understanding of teaching and learning with leading. After reading more about BIPOC leaders and watching broader ranges of how people became leaders, I developed a new and greater understanding of enacted agency-based social justice. While I could not articulate it at the time, I have subsequently found that Valarie Kaur's model of social justice has provided me with a continued foundation for articulating the enacted leadership processes that I am attempting to inhabit. In her *See No Stranger*, she has a chapter titled "reimagine" in which she says "[a]ny social harm can be traced to institutions that produce it, authorize it, or otherwise profit from it. To undo the injustice, we have to imagine new institutions—and step in to lead them" (2020, 172). My process of enacted agency-based leading is founded on reimagining what can be and building towards it.

Because I am still learning and continuing my process(es) of becoming a better leader, I can hardly say that I am an expert. Perhaps that is part of the process of being an expert. But what I have learned through observation, learning, and experience is that any leadership position presents an opportunity to further processes of becoming—navigating and negotiating personal and professional identities, figuring out how and where you belong, and seeking to enact meaningful change based on your values and the context in which you lead.

References

Alim, H. Samy, John R. Rickford, and Arnetha F. Ball, eds. 2016. *Raciolinguistics: How Language Shapes Our Ideas About Race*. Oxford University Press. https://doi.org/10.1093/acprof:oso/9780190625696.001.0001.

Baugh, John. 2018. *Linguistics in Pursuit of Justice*. Cambridge University Press. https://doi.org/10.1017/9781316597750.

Benmira, Sihame, and Moyosolu Agboola. 2021. "Evolution of Leadership Theory." *BMJ Leader* 5 (1): 3–5. https://doi.org/10.1136/leader-2020-000296.

Brown, Lillias M, and Barry Z. Posner. 2001. "Exploring the Relationship between Learning and Leadership." *Leadership & Organization Development*

Journal 22 (6): 274–280. https://scholarcommons.scu.edu/cgi/viewcontent.cgi?article=1012&context=mgmt.

Hewertson, Helen, and Faith Tissa. 2022. "Intersectional Imposter Syndrome: How Imposterism Affects Marginalised Groups." In *The Palgrave Handbook of Imposter Syndrome in Higher Education*, edited by Michelle Addison, Maddie Breeze, and Yvette Taylor. Palgrave Macmillan. https://doi.org/10.1007/978-3-030-86570-2_2.

Huecker, Martin R., Jacob Shreffler, Patrick T. McKeny, and David Davis. 2023. "Imposter Phenomenon." *StatPearls*. StatPearls Publishing. https://www.ncbi.nlm.nih.gov/books/NBK585058/.

Kaur, Valarie. 2020. *See No Stranger: A Memoir and Manifesto of Revolutionary Love*. One World.

Labov, William. 1975. *Language in the Inner-City: Studies in the Black English Vernacular*. University of Pennsylvania Press.

Labov, William. 1982. "Objectivity and Commitment in Linguistic Science: The Case of the Black English Trial in Ann Arbor." *Language in Society* 11 (2): 165–201. https://doi.org/10.1017/S0047404500009192.

Makoni, Simfree, Geneva Smitherman, Arnetha F. Ball, and Arthur K. Spears, eds. 2003. *Black Linguistics: Language, Society, and Politics in Africa and the Americas*. Routledge. https://doi.org/10.4324/9780203986615.

Northouse, Peter G. 2019. *Leadership: Theory and Practice*. 8th ed. SAGE Publications.

Smitherman, Geneva. 1977. *Talkin and Testifyin: The Language of Black America*. Houghton Mifflin.

Smitherman, Geneva. 2000. *Talkin that Talk: Language, Culture, and Education in African America*. Routledge.

CONCLUSION

Final Class

Linda Adler-Kassner, *University of California, Santa Barbara*
Chris W. Gallagher, *Northeastern University*

So here we are—our final class together. Congratulations! We hope you've enjoyed engaging with our marvelous contributors as much as we have. We've learned a lot from them, and we're thrilled to have introduced them to you.

But this is not the end of the road. For one thing, you can hear more from several of the contributors, and from us, in the videos on the Center for Engaged Learning website. More importantly, you can continue to build on and transform your learning about leading.

In closing the book, we need to invoke John Dewey one last time (we promise!). The quality of a learning experience, Dewey said, comes down to two things: *interaction* and *continuity* (1938). We hope the design of the book and the intellectual generosity of the contributors have made for rich interactions with this course. Perhaps you've also developed a community of practice around the book, in a reading group or a course. If so, keep going! Check out some of the resources and activities available in the Playbook, which you can continue to work on together.

Of course, you can also work on your Playbook on your own. It's a great way to carry forward your learning and to practice some of the tools and habits of mind you've been introduced to here. (More about the Playbook in a moment.) There are two things you can do right away. They are intended to help you retain and prepare what you've learned for future use.

First, you can *consolidate* your learning—bring it together into some recognizable whole. We know from research that how learners organize knowledge impacts their ability to call it up and build on it later. In fact, a key difference between novices and experts is that the latter are able to organize what they know and integrate new knowledge into that structure (Ambrose et al. 2010, chapter 2). This is why we forget so much of the information we encounter: that information that can't attach itself to what is already known does not enter into our long-term memories. Consolidating our learning in a way that makes sense to us makes it more likely that it'll be there, and be useful, when we need it later.

You can do consolidate your learning in different ways, but we like to use concept maps and visual representations, which can both start with the same activities:

1. Brainstorm a list of key concepts from the course. Note: *key* terms. You might start by writing down all the concepts you can remember. But then whittle them down to the 10–15 that are most meaningful or resonant to you.
2. Start to place the concepts into categories or "buckets." What connections do you see? What is the nature of the relationship between them? (Are they part of the same process? Are some of them examples or subconcepts of others? Are they thematically related? Are they in productive tension?)

Once you have your bucketed concepts, you want to find a way to represent a conceptual whole, capturing how the buckets themselves are related under a broad concept we might just call "Learning to Lead." (Feel free to use your own terms.) We have found two methods particularly helpful for this purpose:

Concept Maps (or Mindmaps)

Using some combination of shapes, colors, images, and links or arrows, map out the relationships between concepts. This could be as simple as a hierarchical chart (next page):

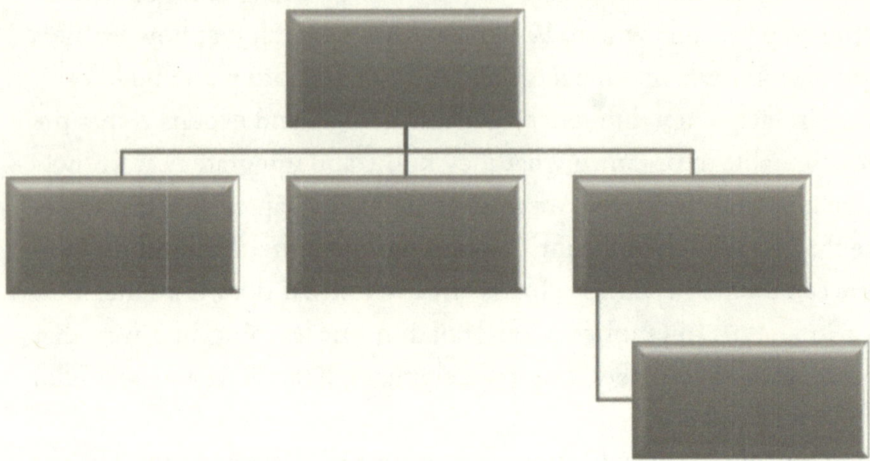

Figure F.1. Simple hierarchical chart with blank boxes.

Or something more complex, like this (the concept map and visual metaphor examples come from a recent course Chris taught on Literacy and AI):

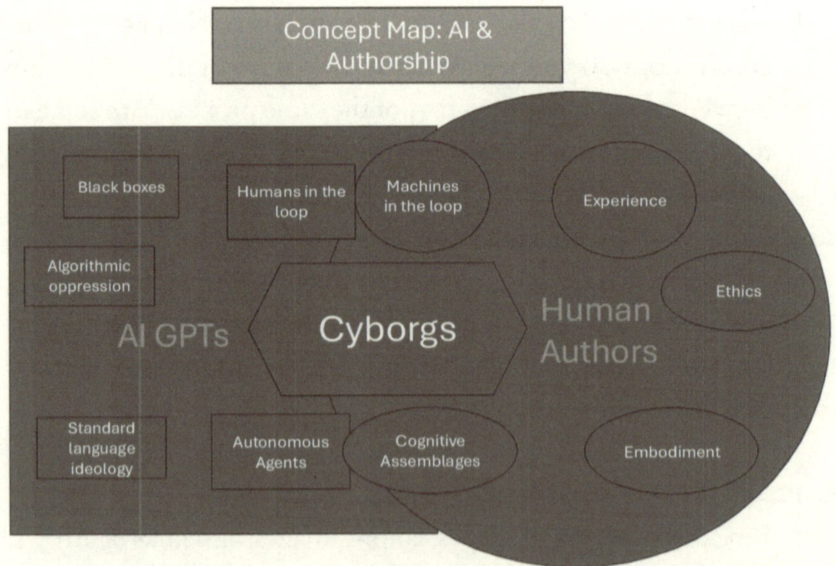

Figure F.2. Concept map of "AI and Authorship": Venn Diagram of "human authors" "and AI GPTs," with "Cyborgs" in the center.

Visual Metaphors

Create an image-based representation that captures your holistic understanding (see figure F.3). Note that this image implies *movement*. We have found that maps or images that visualize processes ("leading") are more revealing and helpful than those that represent static concepts ("leadership").

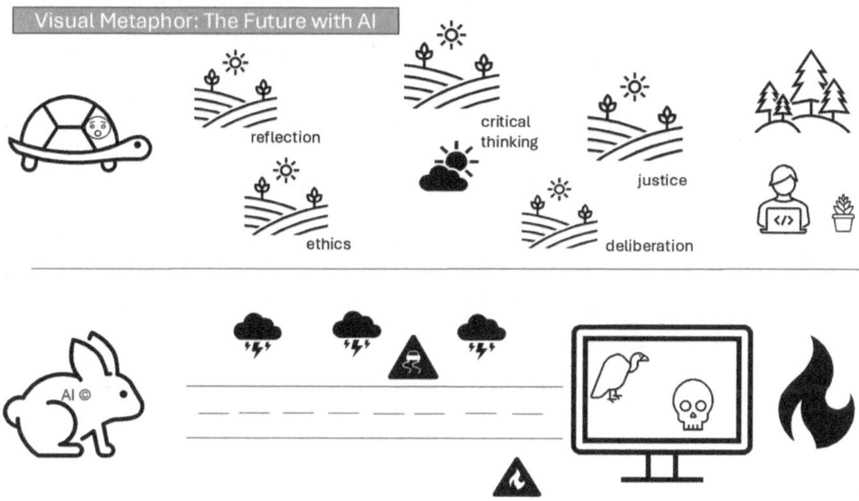

Figure F.3. Visual metaphor: "The Future with AI": Top: tortoise with stops including "reflection," "ethics," etc., leading to bright future; Bottom: hare speeding through dangers to destructive future.

Beyond consolidating your learning, you can conditionalize it—or identify the conditions under which you anticipate that it will and will not be applicable in the future. This is an important activity because learning research also tells us that in order to draw effectively on prior knowledge in a particular situation, it must be activated, sufficient, appropriate, and accurate (Ambrose et al. 2010, 14).

Whether you're already in a leadership role or aspiring to one, ask yourself: How will I retrieve what I've learned in this course to be successful in this role? Does what I've learned equip me to handle its challenges? How applicable is it to this situation? Does it hold true in this context?

Then ask yourself what you need to learn to perform to the best of your ability in this role. What do you need to know and be able to do? How can you go about learning it?

You may find these questions difficult to answer in the abstract—that's to be expected. This is where the Playbook comes in. We call it a Playbook, rather than a guide or sourcebook, because our goal is to help you map out, prepare for, and succeed in specific leadership roles and contexts that matter to you. For this reason, the Playbook is really a playbook *for* a playbook: a set of engagements designed to help you continue learning about leading, a process, we've found, that never stops. We never "arrive" as leaders. That's what makes leading so challenging—and so rewarding.

References

Ambrose, Susan A., Michael W. Bridges, Michele DePietro, Marsha C. Lovett, and Marie K. Norman. 2010. *How Learning Works: Seven Research-Based Principles for Smart Teaching.* Jossey-Bass.

Dewey, John. 1938. *Experience and Education. The Collected Works of John Dewey, 1882–1953.* (2nd Release). Electronic Edition. The Later Works of John Dewey, 1925–1953. Volume 13: 3–62.

INDEX

A

B

C

K

L

M

N

O

P

R

S

About the Editors

Linda Adler-Kassner is Associate Vice Chancellor of Teaching and Learning; Faculty Director of the Center for Innovative Teaching, Research, and Learning; and Distinguished Professor of Writing Studies at UC Santa Barbara. As a researcher, teacher, and administrator, Adler-Kassner's work focuses on studying and improving conditions for equitable and inclusive learning. She has served as a department chair, dean, and department chair. A writing teacher for more than 30 years, she has also taught courses ranging from first year composition to graduate courses in composition theory and pedagogy. Author, co-author, or co-editor of 13 books and more than 50 articles and book chapters, Adler-Kassner's scholarship has garnered multiple awards. These include *Naming What We Know: Threshold Concepts of Writing Studies* and *Writing Expertise: A Research-Based Approach to Writing and Learning Across Disciplines*, both with Elizabeth Wardle.

Chris W. Gallagher is professor of English at Northeastern University in Boston. He has published widely on teaching and assessing writing and on learning and institutional change in K-12 and higher education. He is author or co-author of five books, including *College Made Whole: Integrative Learning for a Divided World*, and many articles in writing studies and education journals. His co-written book with Kristi Girdharry and Kevin Smith, *Getting Learning Right: The Promise of Higher Education*, is forthcoming from MIT Press. Gallagher has held numerous administrative positions, including writing program director, associate dean for experiential teaching and learning, vice chancellor for global learning, vice provost for undergraduate education, and vice provost for curriculum. He teaches courses in writing and pedagogy at every level of the curriculum, from first-year writing to graduate seminars on topics such as "Writing and Community Engagement," "Literacy and AI," and "Writing, Language, and Policy."

www.ingramcontent.com/pod-product-compliance
Lightning Source LLC
LaVergne TN
LVHW041110080826
845145LV00007B/1760

* 9 7 8 1 6 4 3 1 7 5 9 3 5 *